Management Principles in Sport and Leisure Services

Neil J. Dougherty

Diane Bonanno

Rutgers University
New Brunswick, New Jersey

Burgess Publishing Company
Minneapolis, Minnesota

Consulting editor: Robert D. Clayton
Acquisitions editor: Wayne E. Schotanus
Assistant editor: Sharon B. Harrington
Development editor: Anne E. Heller
Copy editor: Laurence A. Kivens
Production: Morris Lundin, Pat Barnes
Art coordinator: Priscilla Heimann
Cover photograph: Ted Hammond, courtesy of the University of Minnesota
Cover design: Mindy Theissen
Composition: Monotrade Companies

Copyright © 1985 by Burgess Publishing Company
Printed in the United States of America

Library of Congress Cataloging in Publication Data

Dougherty, Neil J.
    Management principles in sport and leisure services.

    Includes bibliographical references and index.
    1. Sports—Organization and administration.
2. Recreation—Management.   I. Bonanno, Diane.   II. Title.
GV713.D68   1985   769′.06′9   84-15599
ISBN 0-8087-4433-X

Burgess Publishing Company
7108 Ohms Lane
Minneapolis, MN 55435

JIHGFEDCBA

DEDICATED TO

Margaret Q. Dougherty	Sam Bonanno
Margaret E. Dougherty	Jean Bonanno

Contents

11   Time Management   167

12   Summary Project   183

Appendices

Index   210

Preface

An individual often becomes an administrator because of his or her[1] performance in an area other than administration. This form of career advancement places the new administrator in the awkward position of having a great deal of knowledge and experience in the direct delivery of client services, but little understanding or skill in the manifold tasks of administration. This text, therefore, is designed to provide an overview of the fundamental principles necessary for administrative success. These principles can and should be systematically applied to all human service delivery systems. They are virtually independent of subject matter or other situation-specific variables, and in our opinion, are essential to the administration of any organization.

Examples of the application of these principles have been provided in specific situations. The reader should avoid the mistake of believing that any given principle is applicable only in a limited instance, however. The qualities of successful administration are the same regardless of whether they are applied in the area of athletics, recreation, physical education, or any other field. Further, everyone, regardless of his position within the organization, must perform some type of administrative function, with or without an official title, and must relate to other members of the administrative hierarchy. Therefore, everyone must develop skill in the application of administrative principles to fulfill most effectively his present and future professional roles.

If administration is viewed as the systematic and logical application of basic principles to the tasks an organization must complete to accomplish its mission, then these principles should lend similar structure to the development of a textbook on the subject. The chapters in this textbook therefore proceed from general administrative functions such as systems development, problem solving, and information processing to more specific functions such as facility development, financial administration, and public relations. Each chapter is preceded by a series of questions designed to help the reader process the information that follows. Chapter 12 takes the form of a summary

---

1. To avoid further awkward and artificial reference to *his or her*, we have elected to use either the male or female reference alternately throughout the text.

project in which the reader is encouraged to synthesize and integrate information from the previous chapters into the solution of a situation-specific hypothetical problem that requires a broad range of administrative skills.

We wish to extend sincere thanks to Tony A. Mobley, dean of the School of Health, Physical Education, and Recreation, Indiana University, Bloomington, for contributing Chapter 3, "Information Retrieval and Processing," and to John H. Holloway, assistant principal, Toms River North High School, Toms River, New Jersey, for contributing Chapter 8, "Computer Utilization." These chapters reflect critical elements in the success of modern-day administrators and greatly enchance the applicability of this text. We also are indebted to the Township of North Brunswick, New Jersey, for assistance in the factual development of the summary project.

What is
a systematic
approach?

What are
the elements
of a system?

Why use
a systematic
approach
to administration?

Chapter 1

Administration: A Systematic Approach

Any review of current professional literature reveals an abundance of systems. There are systems for personnel management, scheduling, financial management, teaching, and nearly every other topic. It seems, in fact, that for every isolated area of concern, someone has developed or is currently designing a systems approach.

Reduced to simple terms, a system is a group of elements all working together for a single overall objective. In administrative practice, a systems approach is a continuous process of organizing data within a selected administrative area (e.g., finance, scheduling, facility development) so that these data can be utilized in the planning, structure, evaluation, and modification of that area. Although patterned after computer techniques, the systems approach goes beyond such techniques and, as Hartley has pointed out, "subsumes an outlook, or mode of thinking, by which a particular organization may be defined, examined, evaluated, and improved."[1]

The basic elements of a systems approach are **input**, **process**, **output**, **feedback**, and **control**. The interrelationship of these elements is illustrated in the following diagram:

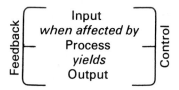

Output consists of one's desired goals or objectives. To deal with a problem or any administrative function systematically, one must first have a clear, specific idea of the

1. Harry J. Hartley, "Limitations of Systems Analysis," *Phi Delta Kappan*, May 1969, p. 516.

results that are desired. The output may be in the form of specific activities to be developed and implemented, facilities to be modified, information to be processed, behavior to be changed in the clientele, or any other reasonable area of administrative concern. The objective must be stated with sufficient clarity and detail, however, to be a productive tool in the planning and problem-solving process. Chapter 4 explains more thoroughly the process of developing objectives.

Inputs are the fiscal, human, or physical resources necessary or available to achieve the outputs. These include not only the positive elements available, but also the corollary restraints. For example, the question of what facilities are available for a proposed volleyball tournament also must be considered in light of the constraints that the identified facilities may impose in terms of the total number of games to be played per unit of time, total number of teams involved, provisions for spectators, and so forth. Another input element that is essential to effective process development and output analysis is a clear delineation of the context in which the system must operate. This would include the social and political climate of the organization, as well as the greater system of which the organization is a part.

A process is the systematic means by which inputs are used in the production of output. Essential steps in the process phase are the development and organization of the specific components of the system, as well as a plan for their ongoing management and coordination. In the case of the volleyball tournament mentioned above, during the process phase, one would need to identify the type of tournament, supervisory personnel, dates, and times involved, along with any limitations on enrollment, team size, ability groupings, fees, and costs, and the myriad other details that must be defined and controlled if success is to be achieved.

An additional element, and one that is essential to the structure and logical development of administrative thought that a systems approach requires, is an ongoing program of feedback and control. This program is sometimes referred to as a feedback loop because of the manner in which it unifies the input, process, and output elements into a continuous circuit through the ongoing feedback, control, and when necessary, modification of each element. To be of value, the feedback must be carefully planned, based on the stated objectives, and rooted in the social and political context in which the system operates. To pursue our volleyball example, if the initial proposal calls for a round robin tournament to be conducted on two successive nights, we would begin to plan for facilities, staffing, and other details accordingly. Initial reservation requests from 50 teams, however, would provide a new input that requires us to reevaluate the proposed process, as well as other controllable input such as facilities and finances and even the possible outcomes. Based on the feedback and control process, therefore, modifications can be made that affect any or all elements of the system.

Administrators are constantly working among the elements of a systems approach. While the terms may sound strange, the concept of inputs being processed to produce output is basic to any type of decision making. Unfortunately, administrators often fail to implement the continuous program of self-analysis, assessment, and control that is necessary to complete this system. The continuous systematic application of the feedback and control element most clearly differentiates the systems approach from other administrative techniques. This factor assumes even greater importance when one realizes that most administrative failures and breakdowns result from a failure to assess the variables involved in a given decision, to monitor their application, or both. Because so many of the variables in the administration of human services are changeable in nature, the feedback and control element not only must be present but also must be applied continuously.

STEPS IN IMPLEMENTATION

Although the basic elements of a systems approach remain relatively constant, the specifics of necessity must vary with the purpose of the system, the setting in which the system is applied, and the talents and interests of those who work within it. The following specific steps were designed to solve learning-related problems at the local school district level:[2]

I. Identify the problem.
II. Perform a systems analysis.
    A. Describe the system and its environment; describe current structures, functions, and roles.
    B. Describe target groups and their characteristics.
    C. Conduct a needs assessment.
    D. Identify constraints, including budgetary limitations.
III. Specify detailed goals and objectives, that is, specify intended outcomes.
IV. Outline and evaluate alternative courses of action.
V. Perform a systems synthesis.
    A. Design or redesign the relevant system, with specifications for:
        1. Inputs.
            a. Processes.
            b. Materials.
            c. Facilities and equipment.
            d. Personnel.
        2. Procedures and transactions within the system, including decision and control mechanisms.
        3. Supporting components, including information subsystems.
    B. Construct or modify system components according to the design.
    C. Begin operating the system according to the design.
    D. Conduct process evaluation.
    E. Conduct product evaluation.
    F. Assess, revise, and recycle through as many steps as necessary.

Peterson, on the other hand, used the same elements of input, process, output, and feedback loop to design the outline in Table 1.1 for therapeutic recreation service program planning.

Each of these examples contains the basic elements of a systems approach, although each has been structured to meet the needs of a specific type of situation. The

2. John L. Hayman, Jr., "The Systems Approach and Education," *The Educational Forum*, May 1975, p. 495.

Table 1.1. Outline for Planning Therapeutic Recreation Service Programs

Stages	Description
Conceptualization and Formulation	Identify issues and concerns, nature of the agency, description of clients, inventory of actual and possible resources Determine the program system, purpose, specification of objectives
Investigation	Search and compile alternative methods of reaching objectives, possible substance and process of service opportunities, possible combinations of service components
Analysis	Examine feasibility and possible consequences of alternatives Construct models for comparative and illustrative purposes
Determination	Decide on a course of action Select service components, based on available information, insight, and experience
Design	Identify purpose and objectives for each service Determine and design the actual substance and process for each service Construct criteria and evaluation schemes for each service
Operations Planning	Determine priority of program system objectives, assign rankings to each service Allocate time and resources to each service Design schedule Prepare system, train staff, purchase equipment and supplies, prepare facilities Determine assessment of performance schedule
Implementation	Put program system into operation (installation) Assess performance (evaluation)

Elliott M. Avedon, *Therapeutic Recreation Service, An Applied Behavioral Science Approach,* © 1974, pp. 137-138. Reprinted by permission of Prentice-Hall Inc., Englewood Cliffs, New Jersey.

systems shown probably would need additional modification and adaptation before they could be applied in any particular situation. Precisely this need for individual development and adaptation makes it unwise to attempt the wholesale introduction of any given system or set of systems into a particular administrative unit. A second caveat regarding the implementation of a systems approach centers on the cost element. The process is complex and time consuming and may result in increased expenditures and staff resistance. A final problem stems from the potential for the administrator to become a slave to the system. Once administrators have expended the effort and time necessary to develop and implement a system they frequently "seem to suffer from 'illusions of adequacy' in their modeling of educational systems. Elaborate analysis may be based upon poor data or questionable premises."[3] In such a circumstance, the system is doomed to failure.

Despite its flaws, a systems approach is an effective change agent. Although not equally applicable or adaptable in all situations, in many cases it does work. Further, the process of systematically analyzing and attacking administrative problems and decisions is both powerful and effective even if some particular systems are not. Using a systems approach directs one's attention to even the smallest operational component, a process that will help to eliminate the possibility of any component working in isolation from or in opposition to the remainder of the program.

This text therefore approaches the various administrative areas in a systematic manner. Although no particular system or systems are put forth as the best or only approach, the reader will notice a clear reliance on the elements of input, process, output, feedback, and control throughout. Specific implementation steps frequently are put forth, although the reader must remember that these are guides and examples, not hard and fast rules. They will need to be modified to suit the needs and capabilities of any particular administrative unit and the social context in which it is applied. In the final analysis the administrator's ability to tailor systematically the concepts learned in this or any other textbook or learning situation to the particular context in which she must operate most effectively guarantees administrative success.

3. Hartley, "Limitations of Systems Analysis," p. 516.

How does the
administrator deal
with unexpected
or recurring problems?

How do you decide
with which of
several problems
to deal first?

Are some elements
of any given
situation more
critical to
administrative
success than others?

How do you decide
which of several
alternative solutions
should be implemented?

Chapter 2

Problem Solving:
A Decision-Making Process

Administration, like life itself, in many ways involves decision-making and problem-solving processes that require action. Some individuals seem able to make decisions in a quick and effective manner; others seem to waste countless hours pursuing unproductive alternatives. Although the more successful problem solvers may be predisposed to logical, organized thought processes, anyone can learn to be a more effective decision maker. The process can be reduced to a few simple steps: defining the problem, gathering and analyzing the pertinent data, ascertaining and evaluating the potential causes, taking action.

WHAT IS YOUR PROBLEM?

A problem exists whenever performances or results fail to measure up to administrative expectations. The problem may be potential or actual, and it may result from your own actions or the actions of others. In any case, the more rapidly you are able to anticipate and recognize the problem, the less time there is for the situation to intensify and the more effectively the problem can be solved.

Obviously, not all problems are of equal importance, nor can all of them be recognized with equal ease. The key to recognition is a carefully developed set of objectives against which to measure both actual performance and the deviation of that performance from original expectations.[1]

Before an administrator can begin to solve a problem, he must be certain that he knows exactly what it is. As noted above, this calls for a precise description of the differences between expected occurrences and those that were observed. Additionally, the administrator must determine with what he is dissatisfied, and more importantly, why. Until these issues are resolved thoughtfully, the problem-solving process cannot begin.

1. See Chapter 4 for a complete explanation of the nature and importance of objectives.

This procedure may appear simple, but caution often is necessary. Many times what appears to be one problem in reality is a cluster of several problems that must be analyzed and described separately. Let us provide an example of just such a situation. The equipment room at Edwin Eden Community School was vandalized several times during a two-week period, with no indication of who caused the damage. The problem was compounded by the fact that three separate programs shared use of the room. These programs were the physicial education and athletic departments of the school, and the municipal recreation department. As might be expected, each program claimed that one or both of the other parties were responsible.

Clearly, the situation raises a number of separate issues: Who was responsible for the control and supervision of the equipment room? Who vandalized it? How? What safeguards would prevent future recurrences? Who should pay damages? How should the guilty parties be dealt with? Addressing any single issue, such as future safeguards, might provide productive solutions to that issue, but probably would do nothing to solve other, equally important issues such as the problem of cooperation and understanding among the three agencies. An effective, systematic administrator would isolate the separate problems, develop alternative solutions for each, then select the individual solutions that, when combined, offered the greatest promise for overall success.

A major step in the process of defining any problem is separating the important aspects from those that are less important. Specifically, which program components are affected by the problem and which are not? Are all components affected or not affected at certain times and under certain circumstances only? What specific differences exist between those times when the problem occurs and those times when it does not? The answers to these and similar questions allow the problem to be identified and isolated, and start the administrator on the path to an effective solution.

In the example under study, some elements have greater importance than others, at least in defining the problem: The vandalism seemed to occur during the evening hours when no program was actively in progress, in each case entrance appeared to be gained through one of two windows, and there was no clear policy regarding supervision and security of the equipment room. These elements should be regarded as more important than, say, the fact that the total damages amounted to $1235, or the question of which program should accept responsibility for the damages. The latter two elements, while useful in assessing the relative severity of the problem, offer little to its possible solution.

A problem that has been pinpointed in terms of its effects, and also the frequency and circumstances of those effects, can be evaluated much more easily with regard to its relative importance. We must consider whether the problem is worth a major expenditure of time, energy, or money. This is particularly true when, having isolated and defined a cluster of problems, we find one or two elements that are of such minor consequence that they can be ignored temporarily while the more important issues are attacked.

HOW MUCH DO YOU KNOW ABOUT YOUR PROBLEM?

Having defined the problem clearly and having decided that some form of solution is necessary, you next should embark on a process of information gathering and analysis. At this point develop an exhaustive data base concerning all relevant variables. You already will know some information from the questions you asked in defining the problem. Now, you should probe the matter more deeply, and measure each piece of infomation against all others to determine which pieces are most closely related to the problem. A data base should be developed systematically and sequentially. This is best accomplished by tracing the course of the situation from a point prior to the problem's onset through the point of its discovery. In this manner, you can identify and analyze each factor, and can avoid the large information gaps inherent in a brainstorming type of approach.

Let us return to the example of the break-in. The first break-in was reported on 15 November. As of that date, the high school football team was suffering through a particularly lackluster season, interscholastic basketball practice for men and women and recreational basketball programs for youth and adults had begun the previous week, and report cards were issued on 12 November. Any of these factors could have precipitated the vandalism. The vandals could have been frustrated with the outcome of a particular game or practice or season or with their grades. On the other hand, the vandals could have been strangers who walked in off the street. The critical questions of how the break-ins occurred and how future recurrences can be prevented still remain unanswered.

In each break-in, access apparently was gained through one of two outer windows. The windows are approximately three feet wide by four feet high and five feet above the ground. The frames are wooden and the glass is frosted and impregnated with wire mesh. The vandals appeared to have broken through the glass and central frame with the aid of a heavy instrument and then unlocked and raised the window in order to gain access to the room. The outside area in the vicinity of the windows is in the rear of the school and generally secluded from sight. There are no lights in the area and a number of large bushes further obscure the vision of passersby. The equipment room is down the hall from the gymnasium, and hence, out of the direct line of sight or hearing range of anyone who is teaching or supervising in that area. This information provides insight into the method of access as well as the factors that facilitated that access.

The personnel of the school and recreational programs are careful to keep the equipment room locked, but no uniform policy exists regarding security or maintenance. Repairs to the facility, when done at all, are usually handled on a "see who can hold out the longest" basis, and there is no organized policy of inspection or supervisory control. The equipment, however, is maintained by the individual user programs, and in general is well kept, clearly marked and labeled, and neatly stored. The marking and labeling procedures offer a reasonable explanation as to why the equipment damage was heavy, but the theft was minimal.

WHAT COULD HAVE CAUSED IT?

The determination of possible causes is really a matter of systematically sifting through the data base that you have developed in order to determine which new or uncontrolled factor caused the divergence in the planned course of events. The causes should relate directly to changes in the expected pattern of events.

A number of potential causes may be identified; however, only one will explain adequately the presence of all observed effects and the absence of those that are missing. This cause should be considered the most likely one, and it bears further testing.

The probable causes of the break-in at Edwin Eden Community School can be reduced to three major categories: program and participant variables, supervisory policies, and physical security.

The recent increase in the number of programs added to the number of persons who would be in the area of the equipment room and would have ample opportunity to break in either before or after their scheduled activities. Furthermore, the losing football season, recent report card distribution, and the general intensity of the first few weeks of basketball practice all reasonably could be expected to result in the type of frustration that, in certain people, could manifest itself in an act of vandalism. These causes, while possible, are very difficult to control or modify effectively. Also, removing these causes would not prevent future break-ins should a different set of frustrations arise or another well-attended program be implemented.

The absence of supervisory policies poses a number of problems. First, there is no clearly specified inspection procedure. Although each time a person uses the equipment room there is, in a sense, an informal inspection, the room sometimes remains isolated and unchecked for long periods of time. The lack of cooperation among the three user groups results in poor maintenance. Poorly maintained areas are more susceptible to vandalism because they give the impression that no one really cares about them. These causative factors are easily corrected, and although they do not appear to explain how access is gained, they certainly offer more insight into the when and why of the problem.

The physical security of the equipment room represents the most reasonable answer to the question of how the problem occurred. The facility, quite simply, is too easy to break into. Until the room can be made more secure, there is little hope for a total solution.

Before you accept the most likely cause as the real one, one final test should be applied. Mentally recreate the course of events leading to the problem, including the suspected cause. Does it appear that the same critical results would be produced as those specified in your problem description? Would this result be forthcoming consistently under the same circumstances? If so, you have every reason to believe that the source of the problem has been found and corrective action may now be considered.

If the previously identified critical elements in the Eden School vandalism problem are held constant, in other words, if the vandalism can continue to occur in the evening hours when no program is in progress, if access can continue to be gained through one of two specific windows that are both relatively secluded and easily accessible, and there continues to be no policy regarding the supervision and security of the equipment room, then it is highly probable that the break-ins will continue to occur. The roots of the problem have been identified.

TAKING ACTION

Basically three types of action can be taken in response to a problem. The first consists of those provisional actions that are taken at the first sign of trouble. Such actions may include: notification of the people concerned, institution of special warning procedures, or other temporary actions designed not to solve the problem, but to stall for time. Actions of this type allow the administrator to keep operations going while a permanent solution is sought.

The second type of action is designed to remove or reduce the probability of the most likely cause. This type of action is usually the most efficient and desirable; however, it is only possible after the cause has been determined.

Unfortunately, the cause of a problem cannot always be removed. Sometimes the cause cannot be determined or isolated. On other occasions, the cause may be identifiable, but irremovable. Sometimes shortcomings can be traced directly to inadequate facilities, and the cost of replacement cannot be borne. In such situations, the administrator must consider a third type of action: the development of a survival technique that will enable her to live with the problem and minimize its impact.

The process used to determine which type of action to take essentially is the same regardless of whether you are considering an interim measure, attempting to correct the problem, or trying to find a reasonable way to live with the problem. Develop alternative courses of action, compare these alternatives with unit objectives to determine the best possible choice, and then implement the chosen solution.

Provisional Actions

The director of recreation, who first discovered the vandalism at Edwin Eden Community School, took immediate provisional action. He notified the director of athletics, the physical education chairperson, and the building principal, and he directed the custodian to make whatever repairs were necessary to secure the room. The principal notified the police and drafted a memorandum to the participants in all school and recreational programs outlining the severity of the offense and the adverse effects that any further occurrences would have on all programs. The custodian immediately boarded over the damaged window and made arrangements for permanent repairs to be made at a later date. The next morning, the physical education chairperson called the elementary and junior high schools within the district and made arrangements to borrow equipment to replace those items that were damaged or stolen.

Although none of these actions offered a permanent solution, each did provide the time and equipment necessary to conduct business as usual while the problem was analyzed and long-term solutions were sought. The lone exception to this was the principal's memorandum, which was more of an emotional reaction than an intellectual one and offered little to either the long- or short-term solutions. The memorandum carried no new information or policies, and although several thousand copies were sent, all but a very few went to persons who would never dream of taking part in a serious act of vandalism. The letter was, therefore, an inefficient use of time and resources.

Alternative Solutions

Shortly after the discovery of the vandalism at Eden School, the physical education chairperson and the directors of recreation and athletics met together to discuss the problem and alternative solutions. One thing was clear immediately. Only a cooperative effort would succeed. Nothing was to be gained by blaming one another or by trying to avoid sharing in the responsibility for and implementation of some form of corrective action. The three administrators therefore began to define the problem, gather and analyze the pertinent data, and ascertain possible causes. As a result of this cooperative effort, the following alternative solutions were developed:

1. Seek a new location for the equipment room. The new room should be either above the first floor level or have no exterior windows.
2. Develop policies and guidelines regarding the daily supervision and maintenance of the equipment room as well as for the repair and replacement of broken and damaged equipment.
3. Have bars placed on the interior of the equipment room windows. (It was decided that interior bars were preferable to exterior ones because they preserve the outside appearance of the building and did not draw attention to the secure area.)
4. Cut or remove the hedges near the windows to facilitate easier visibility of the area by supervisors and passersby.
5. Install lights in the area outside the equipment room.
6. Install an alarm system in the equipment room.
7. Hire security personnel to patrol the school grounds during the evening hours.

DEALING WITH THE ALTERNATIVES

Given the objectives of the administrative unit, the problem faced, and the cause that has been determined, what solutions offer the greatest promise? How many alternative means of problem reduction or elimination are available?

Once alternative solutions have been developed, each must be compared with the established objectives to select a tentative course of action. The choice that most completely satisifes all objectives obviously is the best solution. Before accepting this, however, consideration also should be given to any possible long- or short-term disadvantages that may be associated with the decision. These adverse effects might present a compelling reason for abandoning the first choice in favor of a second one that would meet fewer of the objectives but also would carry fewer adverse effects. Which solution is most likely to give the preferred result for the least effort and cost? Which solution would most impress those who must be satisfied? Which solution would be of the greatest interest to the persons involved?

In seeking the best solution or solutions to a problem, it is often advantageous to make a list to show readily the advantages and disadvantages or adverse effects of each alternative. Table 2.1 shows the solutions developed for Eden Community School.

In assessing these alternatives, the administrators decided that more than one solution would meet the needs of the situation best. The idea of relocating the room was rejected because of the cost and difficulty of finding a suitable location. They decided that new policies were badly needed and would be developed immediately. They also agreed that by installing bars on the interior of the windows and by cutting back the outside hedges, the greatest degree of security could be provided at the least cost

Table 2.1. An Alternative Solution Analysis at Eden Community School

Solution	Advantages	Disadvantages
1. New room location	Better security More central location Larger and better organized facility	Costly Time consuming
2. Develop policies and guidelines	Outlines responsibilities Standardizes procedures Better organization and coordination	Will not necessarily reduce vandalism May restrict individual freedom of users
3. Interior bars	Prevent entry through windows Relatively inexpensive	Will not prevent window breakage
4. Cut hedges	Increase visibility outside of room Make it more difficult for anyone to break in without being observed	Outside area will be less attractive
5. Install lights	Increase visibility outside of room Make it more difficult for anyone to break in without being observed	Relatively high initial cost with constant cost for electricity
6. Install alarm system	Increase likelihood of catching anyone attempting entry	Will not reduce attempts at break-ins Relatively costly Likelihood of equipment malfunction and false alarm
7. Hire security personnel	Provide security during nonuse hours	Relatively high, continuous cost Gives oppressive appearance

and with the fewest adverse consequences. The installation of lights and an alarm system and the employment of security personnel were rejected for the present because of their expense. One or more of these additional measures might be used if the new security measures proved insufficient.

IMPLEMENTING THE DECISION

In implementing the decision, give attention to the control and monitoring of the identified disadvantages. Also, establish careful controls to guarantee that the solution is implemented as planned and thus will have the greatest likelihood of success. A specific implementation plan should be set up to include timetables, individual responsibilities, and the procedures by which all involved personnel will monitor and report their progress.

At Edwin Eden Community School, the following implementation plans were developed:

1. The school custodian was directed to trim back the hedges outside the equipment room immediately. He was asked to preserve as much of the attractive-

ness of the area as possible, and to use low plantings to replace tall ones that had to be removed.

2. The principal invited bids for the installation of window bars. Construction began immediately after the contract was negotiated.

3. The chairperson of the physical education department, the director of athletics, and the director of recreation immediately began developing policies for the use and maintenance of the equipment room. Once developed, the preliminary policies were distributed to the members of all three departments for comment, and then finalized and implemented.

4. The security of the facility was reviewed in six months to determine the effectiveness of the steps taken and the possible need for further action.

In summary, problem solving is accomplished best through the application of a systematic decision-making process. A careful examination of the situation at hand in light of program objectives and desired effects is essential to the process. Although the procedure, as outlined, may appear cumbersome and time consuming, remember that, with practice and experience, many of the separate functions can be accomplished in less time than it takes to explain them. The thoroughness and care with which the process is approached, however, distinguishes the effective decision maker from her less successful counterparts.

Can the
administrator be
an expert in
all aspects of
his unit's
operational scope?

How do you stay
abreast of the
rapidly expanding
knowledge base?

How is an
information
search initiated
and conducted?

Are there
established
resources or trained
professionals who
can provide assistance?

Chapter 3

Information Retrieval and Processing

by Tony A. Mobley

The tremendous growth and expansion of knowledge in modern society make it imperative that all professionals concentrate their attention on keeping current with developments in their professional fields, as well as with matters related to society at large. This is particularly true for the administrator or manager who is responsible for leading an organization toward the accomplishment of its stated goals and objectives. Accurate and up-to-date information is necessary if the executive is to make valid decisions and to chart an appropriate course of action. It is important to obtain the correct information quickly from the massive amount of information that is being established by the expanding knowledge base.

New information in the fields of physical education and recreation is having a dynamic impact on the character and the historical structure of these two disciplines. The knowledge of administrators in these fields quickly becomes outdated unless some systematic method is used to obtain and employ the latest information. Years of experience in a professional field can help an individual to develop wisdom, but wisdom is only valuable to the extent that it aids the application of current information to the administrative task at hand.

INFORMATION PROCESSING

During any discussion of information retrieval and application, many persons incorrectly assume that the reference is to *electronic data processing*, that is, to the use of a computer. **Data processing**—whether electronic or otherwise—and **information processing** are related activities in that the foundations of both are built on data, or facts that describe persons, places, things, or events. Specific facts indeed constitute an essential part of any data base. Facts alone, however, provide little useful *information* to the administrator until they are combined in unique ways to answer specific questions that the decision maker must ask. Data may be classified, indexed, sorted, calculated, summarized, and stored. The combination of data and decision-oriented data processing that assists the individual in selecting a course of action is information processing.[1]

A great deal of data may be obtained from the library or from the records of a school or a recreation and park agency, but this information usually must be combined (processed) and applied to be useful. For example, you may obtain information from a published research project on the most effective method for teaching a particular skill. You also may know the amount of funds available in the budget for instructional purposes in this area, as well as the number of students to be enrolled in the classes. By combining these data in different ways, you may determine the number of instructors to be employed, the schedule for facility use, and the size of each class, as well as the most effective teaching techniques.

Information retrieval is a broad term that covers many activities. Most commonly the term is used synonymously with a literature search, that is, the process of searching some collection of documents that deal with a particular subject. In this case, the concept of *documents* should be seen in the broadest sense. Any system that is designed to assist in searching the literature may be called an information retrieval system. An efficient information system should provide access to almost any document available on a particular topic. Depending on the design of the system, the output may take the form of factual data, bibliographical reference, abstracts, or in some cases, the actual text of the document that has been stored in the system.[2]

SIGNIFICANCE OF INFORMATION

The need and importance of information should be obvious, and hundreds of examples could be cited. A recent study indicates that approximately 80 percent of an administrator's time is spent in 150 to 300 "information transactions" each day.[3] Decision making must be based on accurate information that bears directly on the subject at hand. Inaccurate information or information of the wrong kind can produce only bad decisions. A person must be thoroughly familiar with both the basis and meaning of the information to be used in making a decision. If a decision on whether there are adequate funds to offer a particular recreation program is based only on the cost of the supervisor and the supplies, it may produce the wrong results, because other costs such as utilities, repair and maintenance, and security are not included.

Another important use of information relates to the evaluation and assessment of programs and services offered by the organization. What is the value of the program to the participant? Is the leader performing at a competent level? What is known about the

1. James A. Senn, *Information Systems in Management* (Belmont, Calif.: Wadsworth Publishing Co., Inc., 1978), pp. 3-6.

2. Wilfrid F. Lancaster, "The Functions of Information Retrieval Systems," *Information Retrieval Systems: Characteristics, Testing and Evaluation,* 2nd ed. (New York: John Wiley & Sons, Publishers, 1979), pp. 5-11.

3. Alvin Toffler, *The Third Wave* (New York: William Morrow and Co., Inc., 1980), p. 203.

cost-benefit ratio of the program? Is this program accomplishing the objectives of the organization? The questions are endless, but they can be answered only with good information. Evaluation and assessment must be conducted in a systematic manner, and they require a detailed plan to produce useful results.

Perhaps one of the most significant ways of generating good information is to tie the process to long-range planning. The failure to do this has been a shortcoming in the fields of physical education and recreation in the past. The planning process, however, is a major topic in itself and is handled in Chapter 4 of this text. It should be noted here that good planning is based on good information, whether drawn from historical or current sources or appropriate future projections. Because proper planning is a continuous process, it should become a part of any information retrieval system used by an organization.

TYPES OF INFORMATION

Two types of information must be processed and used on a regular basis by the administrator. The first type, **in-house information**, is developed and stored within an organization and therefore tends to be relatively easy to locate and obtain. Common examples of in-house information include data concerning personnel, budgeting, inventory, and participants. These data as topic areas are discussed at length in other sections of this text, and techniques for their storage and retrieval are covered in Chapter 8, "Computer Utilization."

Outside information, on the other hand, is usually available only from other organizations or through some combination of outside sources and hence is more difficult to monitor and obtain. As society becomes progressively more complex, legal provisions and restrictions become more numerous. The administrator therefore must have at her disposal a wide variety of legal information that would describe:

1. Legal authority and powers relative to the function of the organization
2. Taxing or bonding powers or both
3. Building and safety codes
4. Personnel certification or registration
5. Auditing requirements

A second type of outside information that is essential for administrative success is a complete listing of outside funding sources and the rules pertaining to their procurement.

The administrator also must be constantly aware of the results of pertinent research. Although a vast array of research results may pertain to physical education or recreation and leisure services, the administrator should have a method available for obtaining the latest research results that may enhance her ability to achieve the goals of her organization effectively. Common among these would include research information on the most effective teaching methods and techniques, planning information, the effectiveness of equipment, maintenance procedures, program effectiveness, and other types of information depending on the purpose, function, and scope of the organization's activities.

SOURCES OF INFORMATION

ɔ administrator must have a broad understanding not only of the range of infor-
___ ɪ available to him, but also of the sophisticated technology through which such
information can be delivered. Alvin Toffler dramatically outlines several developments
related to information technology in his book, *The Third Wave*. Basically, Toffler suggests
that the office as it is presently known, with its clerks, typists, and secretaries processing
paper information, is already a thing of the past. The need for information has completely
overloaded the system until it has become impossible to move the "mountain of paper"
that has been generated, Toffler says, and a "word quake" may result.[4] Indeed, both the
volume and the cost of paper have caused enormous problems in this regard. Technology
has produced equipment like computer terminals, optical scanners, high-speed printers,
micrographic equipment, facsimile machines, and many others to a point where the
"paperless" office may be a reality in the near future. The result will be a tremendous
increase in the speed and scope of information available at a reduced cost.

In any discussion about sources of information, one typically encounters the phrase
management information system (MIS). This generic term refers to any planned and
organized approach designed to provide managers with the information they need.
Therefore, almost everything discussed thus far in this chapter could be considered as
part of an MIS. The term, in other words, could refer to all sources of information of the
type that have been described, rather than to a specific source.

Regardless of the technique used to access them, the sources of information available
to the administrator can be viewed from both an external and internal perspective.
Internal sources could include budget records, personnel files, and long-range plans.
External sources could include national organizations and professional groups, formal
retrieval systems through libraries, and consulting firms. Many of these sources provide
quantitative, or number-oriented, information, but a total information system is likely to
produce the most complete information if it includes informal or subjective information
such as that which might come from an expert on one's staff or from a consultant, as well
as the more formal results of sophisticated research.

Many organizations provide external sources to assist the administrator. The American Society for Information Science, for example, can be of enormous value in providing
guidance to an organization.[5] Also, the Information Industry Association published
Information Sources, which is a listing of more than 100 private and governmental
sources providing information to business, industry, and other organizations.[6] A closely
related development is the growth of fee-based information services, or independent
information specialists such as free-lance librarians, information brokers, and information consultants. Approximately 300 such services are in existence.[7]

4. Toffler, *The Third Wave*, pp. 203-204.

5. Martha E. Williams, ed., *American Society for Information Science: Annual Review of Information Science and Technology* (White Plains, N.Y.: Knowledge Industry Publications, Inc., 1979), 14:5-7.

6. Faye Henderson, ed., *Information Sources 1980-81: The Membership Directory of the Information Industry Association* (Washington, D.C.: Information Industry Association, 1980), p. i.

7. Lorig Maranjian and Richard W. Boss, "Surveying a Growing Field," *Fee Based Information Services: A Study of a Growing Industry* (New York: R. R. Bowker Co., 1980), p. 1.

Several information systems relate directly to physical education and recreation. The Information and Research Utilization Center (IRUC) of the American Alliance for Health, Physical Education, Recreation, and Dance (AAHPERD) published a *Guide to Information Systems*, which is an extremely useful document to the administrator in these fields. The guide identifies and provides detailed information on more than 25 information systems that cover a wide range of topics. A listing of the names and addresses of some of these systems is provided in Table 3.1.

Table 3.1. Information Systems

Information and Research Utilization Center (IRUC)	Leisure Information Service
American Alliance for Health, Physical Education, Recreation, and Dance (AAHPERD)	729 Delaware Avenue S.W.
1900 Association Drive	Washington, DC 20024
Reston, VA 22091	Sport and Leisure Resource Centre for Special Populations
A Park and Recreation Information Service (APRISE)	Department of Recreation
National Recreation and Park Association	University of Waterloo
1601 North Kent Street	Waterloo, Ontario N2L 3G1
Arlington, VA 22209	Canada
Microform Publication	Information Centre
College of Health, Physical Education, and Recreation	The Sports Council
University of Oregon	70 Brompton Road
Eugene, OR 97403	London SW3 IEX
	England
Music Therapy Index and Abstracts (MTI/MTA)	Therapeutic Recreation Information Center (TRIC)
Division of Music	University of Oregon
Meadows School of the Arts	1597 Agate Street
Southern Methodist University	Eugene, OR 97403
Dallas, TX 75275	World Leisure and Recreation Research Documentation and Information Service Network
National Documentation Centre for Sport, Physical Education and Recreation	World Leisure and Recreation Association
The University of Birmingham	345 East 46th Street
P.O. Box 363	New York, NY 10017
Birmingham B15 2TT	
England	The National Leisure Data Archive
	Inter-Univerity Consortium for Political and Social Research
Outdoor Recreation Technical Assistance Clearinghouse	Box 1248
U.S. Department of the Interior	Ann Arbor, MI 48106
Division of Cooperative Services	
Washington, DC 20240	Sport and Recreation Index
	Sport Information Resource Centre (SIRC)
Recreation Information Management (RIM)	333 River Road
USDA - Forest Service	Ottawa, Ontario K1A 8B9
South Building	Canada
12th and Independence Ave. S.W.	
Washington, DC 20250	

Examples of some of the most commonly used sources of information for the administrator in physical education and sport or in recreation and parks are discussed below.

I. **Information Systems.** In addition to the general information systems discussed above, the reader may find three specific systems to be of great value.

   A. **ERIC.** The Educational Resources Information Center (ERIC) provides a national information system that consists primarily of unpublished materials, and is a major source of documents on education. For a nominal cost, you may obtain interpretive summaries, bibliographies, research reviews, and listings of titles and abstracts. ERIC is supported by the National Institute of Education and was designed by the U.S. Office of Education. There are several clearinghouses located primarily at universities throughout the country, and most major libraries have access to the entire ERIC file. At the present time, the information covers 16 broad areas related to education.[8]

   B. **IRUC.** AAHPERD has developed the Physical Education and Recreation for the Handicapped: Information and Research Utilization Center (IRUC), which provides abstracts, bibliographies, information packets, referrals, and other publications. As may be obvious from the title, the major thrust of IRUC is to provide information on physical education and recreation for the impaired, disabled, and handicapped. Much of the information, however, is pertinent to individuals of all levels of ability and disability.[9]

   C. **SIRC.** The *Sport and Recreation Index* is published by the Sport Information Resource Centre (SIRC), and is designed to fill the information needs of teachers, researchers, coaches, and sports practitioners. Information is provided on individual sports, recreation, sports medicine, physical education, and sports history. Newsletters, journals, monographs, theses, and conference papers are collected and indexed. The index may be accessed through computer-assisted reference services found in many university libraries.

II. **National Organizations.** Various national service and professional organizations have information retrieval capabilities that they frequently offer to their members. Ordinarily, these would not be comprehensive information retrieval systems, but would relate to special topics that are of interest to the organization. The AAHPERD sponsorship of IRUC is one example. The National Recreation and Park Association (NRPA), through its sponsorship of A Park and Recreation Information Service (APRISE), is another example. Other organizations that relate in some way to the fields of physical education and recreation can be of similar service. These might include organizations such as the National Education Association, the American Camping Association, the Society of American Foresters, National

8. Bruce W. Tuckman, *Conducting Educational Research*, 2nd ed. (New York: Harcourt Brace Jovanovich, Inc., 1978), p. 41.

9. Physical Education and Recreation for the Handicapped: Information and Research Utilization Center (IRUC), *Guide to Information Systems in Physical Education and Recreation for Impaired, Disabled and Handicapped Persons* (Reston, Va.: AAHPERD, 1983), p. 8.

Association for Physical Education in Higher Education, and other closely related organizations.

III. **Publications.** Numerous popular and professional publications provide the administrator with up-to-date information on the latest issues in the particular subject field. Good administrators will scan a large number of journals and other publications for information that is helpful to their organizations. These might range from popular news magazines to sophisticated research journals. Publications frequently used by administrators in physical education and recreation include the *Journal of Physical Education, Recreation and Dance*, and the *Research Quarterly for Exercise and Sport*, which are both published by AAHPERD; and *Parks and Recreation* and the *Journal of Leisure Research*, which are published by the NRPA. *The Chronicle of Higher Education* is a valuable information source for the individual involved with colleges and universities. A large number of other publications are related to special topics such as *Athletic Purchasing and Facilities* and the *Journal of the National Intramural and Recreational Sports Association*. The creative administrator will identify these publications and review them on a regular basis.

IV. **Internal Documents.** Documents, plans, and records maintained within the organization are an excellent source of information for the administrator. In most instances, these items are used more often than outside sources. These could include organizational long-range plans, all records of the organization's budget and financing provisions, annual reports, personnel policies, administrative manuals, and other similar information.

V. **Faculty and Staff Expertise.** A primary source of information for the administrator is located within the faculty and staff of the school, university, or recreation and parks agency. If the organization has been careful in the employment of high-quality personnel, an enormous amount of talent will be within the organization. These individuals should be used as resource persons who can provide information on a wide range of topics. Use the following techniques to get them involved:

A. Delegate the responsibility and authority for a particular task or decision directly to an appropriate staff member.

B. Appoint a staff member to serve as a consultant on a specific issue.

C. Organize a committee or task force to provide information and to make recommendations.

D. Ask individuals or groups to prepare a "staff report" on a topic.

VI. **Library Search.** In addition to the sources of information outlined above, many of which directly involve the library, the administrator or her staff also can conduct a basic library search. This would consist of using the card catalog, as well as reference publications and indexes such as the *Education Index*, the *Reader's Guide to Periodical Literature*, and many others. Government documents also represent a valuable source of information. It may be most beneficial for individuals engaged in this type of library research to work with the reference librarian as soon as more specific topics have been identified.

ORGANIZATION AND APPLICATION OF INFORMATION

As indicated earlier in this chapter, data processing and information processing may be viewed as a continuum that begins with "data," or facts, and moves toward "information." Statistical analysis, using the computer or some other method, is obviously one of the ways that data can be turned into information, although the process of combining, sorting, and summarizing data also can produce the desired results. The development of comparative indices is another example of a helpful technique.

Qualitative, subjective, or narrative materials require a very different type of organization and storage process. This information may take the form of reports, position statements, working models, and other nonquantifiable data-reporting techniques. With the new technology, however, it is now common to store this type of information electronically. The primary advantage is that it can be called forth immediately and displayed visually on a terminal in the administrator's office.

No amount of data or information stored in a data base or retrieval system is of any value unless it is organized in such a way as to respond to specific issues with which the administrator is involved. Each agency or institution must structure its own approach to information retrieval. The administrator must ask the right questions of the system in order to obtain meaningful results. One must begin by identifying the types of information that may be needed and anticipating the questions to be asked. The information system should be organized to answer these questions and provide the needed information.

Please recognize that the emphasis in this chapter has been placed on the concept that information retrieval and application must include all types of information that can help the administrator. Although they are an important part of any information system, "hard data" represent only one type of information. The effective manager must synthesize both quantitative and qualitative information to handle her responsibilities.

Information retrieval for application of that information to a specific problem is only a part of the decision-making process. The successful manager supplements available internal and external data with his personal experience and the experience of others in reaching a decision concerning a course of action for the organization. A healthy dose of intuition often is mixed into the entire process.

Research by Alter indicates that information systems are being developed and used to *support* the manager responsible for making and implementing decisions.[10] The purpose of information systems is not to *replace* the decision maker. In line with this concept, a large number of organizations are using what might be called "decision support systems" to improve their managerial effectiveness. These systems supplement and assist the administrator, who obtains various inputs to aid her in reaching a good decision.

Organizations that implement a comprehensive system sometimes become en-

10. Steven L. Alter, "How Effective Managers Use Information Systems," *Harvard Business Review* (November-December 1976): 97.

slaved by the system, rather than having the system work for them. The system is to be the servant, not the master.

At any point when the administrator faces a difficult decision, she may consider it highly desirable to have additional information. Even with the best information retrieval opportunities available, difficult decisions often are made with less than complete information; that is one of the reasons why they are difficult. The effective administrator, however, will make every effort to use whatever resources are available to obtain relevant information and apply it to the decision at hand. Speed in retrieving the information is obviously an important factor, but it is not always a primary consideration. The correct kind of information obtained from an accurate data base is essential. Once all of the relevant information has been obtained, and appropriate input has been received from faculty, staff, boards, and other responsible individuals, the administrator must assume a dynamic leadership role in moving the organization toward the accomplishment of its objectives.

AN EXAMPLE OF AN INFORMATION SEARCH

The discussion of information retrieval in this chapter has been thus far broad-based in its approach. In this section, a specific example of a "computer-assisted search" is used to outline the procedures that an administrator could follow in an information search using one of the established data bases. One of the current areas of interest and attention in recreation and parks and in physical education is high risk, high adventure programming. This topic therefore was chosen for the search.

The steps in the procedure are as follows:

Step 1. The first step is for the administrator to identify an appropriate agency or institution with the capability of conducting a computer-assisted search. In this example, the university library's main computer-assisted research system (CARS) was used.[11]

Step 2. With the assistance of the reference librarian or the person designated to conduct searches, the administrator identifies the information system or systems that are most likely to provide the best information on the selected topic.

Although the administrator in this example would not be concerned directly with such matters, some information vendors own systems that contain data bases related to specific topics. These vendors provide this service to libraries or any other organization desiring service.

Step 3. It was determined that ERIC was the most appropriate data base to provide the information on high risk, high adventure programming.

Step 4. With the assistance of the reference librarian or search consultant, the administrator selects the appropriate key words or descriptors for use in the search. In this example, two descriptive "sets" of "combinations" were used. The first set combined adventure with education, learning, or pro-

11. The search was conducted by Ms. Kenyon Fairey, a doctoral candidate at Indiana University, using the University Library.

gram. The second set combined outdoor education or recreation with risk. In this case, the articles selected were those that were referenced under a crossing of these two sets of descriptors.

Step 5.   The reference librarian and the administrator (in this example, the graduate student) use the computer terminal and feed in the appropriate sets of descriptors. Depending on the amount of information provided, the administrator may need to expand or reduce the sets of descriptors to obtain the appropriate information. Although the possibilities vary with the system or data base in use, the administrator may choose to tailor the information output to include only bibliographical references, to add abstracts of articles, or to index information. It also may be possible to have the information sorted alphabetically or by date of publication. In this case, there were eight articles that provided the most specific information on high risk, high adventure programming. As the costs are relatively low for up to 50 references, the entire information output was requested, including bibliographical references, abstracts, and indexing.

Step 6.   There are two methods of obtaining the output from this system. If the administrator needs the information immediately, an "on-line printout" may be obtained in a matter of minutes, although a somewhat higher fee is charged for this service. The second method is to obtain what is called an "off-line printout," which is printed at the resource center and mailed directly to the person requesting the information. In this case, the second method was chosen, and the information was received in six days.

Time and cost obviously are concerns for the administrator. In this example, approximately one hour was required from the time the graduate student entered the library until the entire process was completed. For almost any search, approximately one to three hours may be needed, depending on the amount of material available on the topic and the efficiency of the reference librarian and the data source. The fees for the service include such items as telecommunications charges, computer time, royalties to vendors, surcharges by the agencies, and cost for actual printed copy. The total cost for this search was $10. The available material on this topic, as delimited by the descriptors chosen, was relatively small. In most cases the average approximate cost would range from $15 to $25 for similar searches. Example pages of the output of this search are shown in Figure 3.1.

Figure 3.1. Example of on-line information request

```
                    EXAMPLE OF
            ON LINE INFORMATION REQUEST

FILE1:ERIC - 66-81/FEB
     SET ITEMS DESCRIPTION (+=OR;*=AND;-=NOT)
     ---  ----- -----------
? SS ADVENTURE(W)EDUCATION/TI,ID,DE OR ADVENTURE(W)LEARNING/TI,ID,DE OR ADVENTUR
E(W)PROGRAM?/TI,ID,DE
     1      59 ADVENTURE(W)EDUCATION/TI,ID,DE
     2       0 AT NTURE(W)LEARNING/TI,ID,DE
     3      15 ADVENTURE(W)PROGRAM?/TI,ID,DE
     4      67 1 OR 2 OR 3
? SS OUTDOOR EDUCATION OR RECREATION?/TI,ID,DE
? SS (OUTDOOR EDUCATION OR RECREATION?/TI,ID,DE) AND RISK/TI,ID,DE
     5    1899 OUTDOOR EDUCATION (UTILIZATION OF THE OUTDOOR ENV
     6    2995 RECREATION?/TI,ID,DE
     7     752 RISK/TI,ID,DE
     8      28 (5 OR 6) AND 7
? C 8 NOT 4
     9      20 8 NOT 4
? C 8 AND 4
     10      8 8 AND 4
? PR 10/5/1-8
PRINTED10/5/1-8
? T 10/8/1-2
10/8/1
EJ220024
  THE MANAGEMENT OF RISK.
  DESCRIPTORS:  *ACCIDENT  PREVENTION/  ACCIDENTS/    EMERGENCY  PROGRAMS/
*EMPLOYMENT QUALIFICATIONS/ EXPERIENTIAL LEARNING/  *OUTDOOR  EDUCATION/
*PROGRAM ADMINISTRATION/ RECREATIONAL ACTIVITIES/  *RISK/  *SAFETY/  STAFF
DEVELOPMENT
  IDENTIFIERS: *ADVENTURE EDUCATION

10/8/2
EJ187732
  THE LEGAL SYSTEM AS A PROPONENT OF ADVENTURE PROGRAMMING
  DESCRIPTORS:  *INJURIES/   *LEGAL  RESPONSIBILITY/  *TORTS/  *READINESS/
*RECREATIONAL ACTIVITIES/ *OUTDOOR EDUCATION/ LEADERSHIP RESPONSIBILITY
  IDENTIFIERS: *RISK RECREATION

? LOGOFF
```

continued

Figure 3.1/continued

1293

Print 10/5/1-8
DIALOG File1: ERIC - 66-81/Feb (Item 1 of 8) User 5953 2mar81

EJ220024 RC503718
The Management of Risk.
Meyer, Dan
Journal of Experiential Education, v2 n2 p9-14 Fall 1979
Language: English
Document Type: JOURNAL ARTICLE (080); NON-CLASSROOM MATERIAL (055)

Defining the nature and extent of risk associated with adventure education, this article notes the risk/est activities and delineates three main causes of accidents: unsafe conditions; unsafe acts; and judgmental errors. Careful program organization, staff selection, routine safety inspections, and emergency plans are also addressed. (SB)
Descriptors: *Accident Prevention/ Accidents/ Emergency Programs/ *Employment Qualifications/ Experiential Learning/ *Outdoor Education/ *Program Administration/ Recreational Activities/ *Risk/ *Safety/ Staff Development
Identifiers: *Adventure Education

EJ187732 SP507219
The Legal System as a Proponent of Adventure Programming
Rankin, Janna S.
Journal of Physical Education and Recreation, 49, 4, 52-3 1978
Reprint Available (See p. vii): UMI
Language: English
A survey of the law with respect to high risk or adventure programs and activities indicates that the probability of an agency being found liable due to negligence is generally less with more venturous activities than with more traditional programming. (Author)
Descriptors: *Injuries/ *Legal Responsibility/ *Torts/ *Readiness/ *Recreational Activities/ *Outdoor Education/ Leadership Responsibility
Identifiers: *Risk Recreation

EJ187731 SP507218
Adventure Programming and Legal Liability
Frakt, Arthur N.
Journal of Physical Education and Recreation, 49, 4, 49-51 1978
Reprint Available (See p. vii): UMI
Language: English
It is not only probable but appropriate that liability in risk recreation should ensue when there is (1) failure to explain hazards, (2) failure to restrict participation to participants who have the maturity, physical conditioning, and skill level necessary, and (3) failure to provide professional leadership and instruction. (Author)
Descriptors: *Injuries/ *Legal Responsibility/ *Torts/ *Outdoor Education/ *Recreational Activities/ Leadership

Responsibility/ Readiness
Identifiers: *Risk Recreation

ED187501 RC012057
Utilizing Adventure Education to Rehabilitate Juvenile Delinquents.
Gollns, Gerald L.
New Mexico State Univ., University Park. ERIC Clearinghouse on Rural Education and Small Schools.
Mar 1980 75p.
Sponsoring Agency: National Inst. of Education (DHEW), Washington, D.C.
Contract No.: 400-78-0023
Available from: National Educational Laboratory Publishers, Inc., 813 Airport Boulevard, Austin, TX 78702 (Stock No. EC-084, $7.00).
EDRS Price - MF01/PC03 Plus Postage.
Language: English
Document Type: PROJECT DESCRIPTION (141); ERIC PRODUCT (071)
Geographic Source: U.S./ New Mexico
Journal Announcement: RIEOCT80
The use of adventure based education is a new and relatively unresearched but apparently successful practice in the rehabilitation of juvenile delinquents. Courses offered by schools, state social service systems, juvenile courts, youth service bureaus, and other agencies are generally patterned after the standard Outward Bound course and involve the mastery of such outdoor pursuits as mountaineering, sailing, or river rafting. The gamelike atmosphere, the organization of participants into primary peer groups, the use of the outdoors, the nature of the problems posed, and the style of instruction are five elements of adventure education which impel a juvenile delinquent to alter his destructive ways. Programs are usually designed as cost-effective diversions to long-term institutionalization or as supplements to existing youth serving agency programs. Both types of program involve referral, orientation, the outdoor expedition itself, and thorough follow-up. Many exemplary programs exist throughout the country. Adventure based practitioners face several major issues: program follow-up; course management and staffing; and evaluation. This document includes an outline of steps in the development of an adventure education rehabilitation program; a sample program schedule; suggested teaching methodology; and a reprint of an article emphasizing the need for adequate follow-up activities. (Author/SB)
Descriptors: *Adventure Education/ *Affective Objectives/ Cost Effectiveness/ Delinquency/ *Delinquent Rehabilitation/ Experiential Learning/ *Outdoor Education/ Program Design/ *Program Development/ *Program Effectiveness/ Rehabilitation Programs/ Risk/ Self Concept
Identifiers: Outward Bound/ *Program Follow Up

DIALOG File1: ERIC - 66-81/Feb (Item   5 of   8) User 5953   2mar81   1294

ED187500 RC012055
Legal Liability--Adventure Activities.
van der Smissen, Betty.
New Mexico State Univ., University Park.   ERIC Clearinghouse on Rural Education and Small Schools.
Mar 1980   50p.
Sponsoring Agency: National Inst. of Education (DHEW), Washington,D.C.
Contract No.: 400-78-0023
Available from: National Educational Laboratory Publishers, Inc., 813 Airport Boulevard, Austin, TX 78702 (Stock No. EC-086, $5.75).
EDRS Price - MF01/PC02 Plus Postage.
Language: English
Document Type: NON-CLASSROOM MATERIAL (055); ERIC PRODUCT (071)
Geographic Source: U.S./ New Mexico
Journal Announcement: RIEOCT80
   The adventure of adventure education comes in the testing of oneself, in putting self against the environment and in striving to overcome through personal skill. Unfortunately, instead of perceiving the risks in terms of physical and psychological challenges, many schools and other organizations perceive them in terms of liability suits. The aspect of legal liability involved in most of the court cases involving the adventure field is that based on negligence, usually defined in five broad areas: (1) personal liability, which results from the actions of an individual with a direct relationship (program leader, volunteer, service person) to the participant; (2) standard of care, in which care for a safe environment is not appropriate standard of care for the activity, in which considerations provided; (3) conduct of the activity, in which considerations are made as to the adequacy of instruction, the relationship of maturity and condition to safe participation, and safety rules and regulations; (4) environmental conditions, in which the landowner is held responsible for hazards on his property; and (5) contributory negligence, in which the participant himself must assume responsibility for his own actions. The final portion of this document describes how to handle the sequence of events following an injury and lists four methods of financial risk management (avoiding the activity, insurance, retention of the risk, and reduction of injuries). (DS)
Descriptors: *Accountability/ *Adventure Education/ Court Litigation/ Guidelines/ Insurance/ Laws/ Leadership Responsibility/ *Legal Responsibility/ *Outdoor Education/ Public Relations/ *Risk/ Safety
Identifiers: *Negligence

ED179322 RC011505
Earlham College Wilderness Program. Instructors Manual.
Steeples, Douglas; And Others
1975   158p.: Not available in paper copy due to small print size

EDRS Price - MF01 Plus Postage. PC Not Available from EDRS.
Language: English
Document Type: TEACHING GUIDE (052)
Geographic Source: U.S./ Indiana
Journal Announcement: RIEAPR80
   The major resource for instructors in training for the Earlham College Wilderness Program, this manual covers the philosophy, academics, teaching methodology, and logistics of the program. It is designed as a field manual for the month-long programs (either mountaineering or canoeing) offered to Earlham students and contains information most applicable to the field situation. The manual is organized in three sections: Program Philosophy and Policy, Instructional Materials, and Logistics. The first section lists program goals, discusses the role of the instructor as specific instructor responsibilities ranging from the participant-leader in the expedition group, and outlines inspection of student gear to the communication of program philosophy. The second section contains information on group dynamics with emphasis on the stresses of the wilderness expedition; covers essential wilderness skills and safety and survival procedures; and presents background information on Western Ontario, where the Wilderness Program is conducted, including regional geology, plant and animal life, history and culture of the Ojibway Indians, and the significance of the region in the fur trading era. The final section gives detailed procedures (specific to the Earlham program) for outfitting, caravan travel, and check-in at the end of the expedition. (JH)
Descriptors: *Adventure Education/ Camping/ Curriculum Guides/ *Educational Philosophy/ Experiential Learning/ Group Dynamics/ *Educational Philosophy/ Higher Education/ *Instructional Materials/ Leaders Guides/ *Outdoor Education/ Regional Characteristics/ Risk/ Safety/ Skill Development/ *Teacher Responsibility/ Teacher Role/ *Teaching Methods
Identifiers: Canoeing/ *Earlham College Wilderness Program IN/ Expeditions/ Mountaineering/ Ontario

continued

Figure 3.1/continued

DIALOG File1: ERIC - 66-81/Feb (Item   7 of   8) User 5953   2mar81   1295

ED172994 RC011452
Adventure Education.
Mortlock, Colin
1978   44p.; Not available in hard copy due to small print
size of original document
  Available from: Old Fisherbeck, Ambleside. Cumbria. United
Kingdom. LA22 0DH ($5.40)
  EDRS Price -- MF01 Plus Postage. PC Not Available from EDRS.
  Language: English
  Document Type: NON CLASSROOM MATERIAL (055);   REVIEW
LITERATURE (070)
  Geographic Source: United Kingdom/ England
  Journal Announcement: RIENOV79
  Adventure is the most dynamic form of education currently
available and as such should move from its peripheral position
in British education to become a part of the core curriculum.
This move will require that school administrators better
understand the philosophy and content of Adventure Education
and that staff receive more rigorous training for their
demanding jobs. The objective of employing adventure in
education is to help people mature through experiences which
promote: physical, cognitive, and emotional growth; respect
and love for others; and awareness of and respect for the
environment. Adventure encompasses a wide range of activities
(rock climbing, skiing, night journeys, man-made obstacles.
etc.) which share with other outdoor pursuits a framework
consisting of the need for safety in potentially dangerous
situations; the need for technical, physical, and personal
skills; and the goal of enjoyment and satisfaction. Of all the
outdoor pursuits adventure is uniquely able to provide
satisfaction because it presents the most meaningful
challenge, i.e., it involves risk, a healthy degree of fear,
and uncertainty about the final outcome. Until such time as
adventure education for all students is a practical
possibility, it is important to consider subjects such as
drama, art, music, and sport which may provide, through
different means, some of the challenges of adventure. (JH)
  Descriptors: Activities/ Administrative Policy/ Adolescents/
*Adventure Education/ Cognitive Development/ Curriculum
Development/ Definitions/ *Educational Philosophy/ Elementary
Secondary Education/ Environmental Education/ *Experiential
Learning/ Individual Development/ *Outdoor Education/ Physical
Fitness/ Program Guides/ Relevance (Education)/ *Risk/ Safety/
*Self Actualization/ Skill Development/ Teacher Role
  Reviews/ Teacher Education/ Teacher Role
  Identifiers: *Great Britain

ED148818# SP012114
  Cowstails and Cobras. A Guide to Ropes Courses, Initiative
Games, and Other Adventure Activities.
  Rohnke, Karl
  1977   160p.
  Available from: Project Adventure, P.O. Box 157, Hamilton.
Ma. 01936. ($6.50)

Document Not Available from EDRS.
  Language: ENGLISH
  Document Type: CLASSROOM MATERIAL (050)
  Journal Announcement: RIEMAY78
  This document is designed as a resource book for senior high
school physical education teachers to aid in the development
of initiative and adventure activities involving rope
exercises. Goals of these exercises are defined as: (1)
increasing personal competence; (2) increasing mutual support
within a group; (3) developing an increased level of agility
and physical coordination; (4) developing joy in one's
physical self and in being with others; and (5) developing
increased familiarity and identification with the natural
world. The author discusses exercises appropriate for
coordination, cardiovascular warmup, limberness, distance
covering, and other preliminary activities. Procedures for
instruction in falling techniques, spotting, belaying, and
knot tying are discussed. Construction of a rope course, group
activities, winter activities, and games and nongames are
detailed. Practical considerations on weather, scheduling,
coeducation classes, and safety are noted. (MJB)
  Descriptors: *Adventure Education/ Curriculum Enrichment/
*Curriculum Guides/ *Outdoor Education/ *Physical Activities/
Physical Education/ Risk/ *Secondary Education
  Identifiers: *Rope Exercises

Why plan?

Why are some
administrators
reluctant to plan?

What are the
differences between
strategic and
operational planning?

How do mission
statements, goals,
objectives,
philosophy, policy,
and procedures
interrelate?

Why are they
all considered
essential elements
of effective
planning?

Chapter 4

Planning:
An Administrative Responsibility

Few people would consider taking a trip without having a travel plan that indicated, at the very least, where they were going and how they were going to get there. Most probably, they would want considerably more information than that, if they could obtain it. This type of preparation is important because having a detailed travel plan can make the difference between wandering around wasting one's time, money, and energy, or focusing one's efforts so that these resources can be used to the greatest possible advantage.

Planning is an essential element in life. Indeed, whether one is attempting to do something as complex as placing a man on the moon or as simple as making a luncheon engagement on time, actions are usually planned in some manner. Planning is one of the few factors that can determine whether a person will be successful in achieving his goals.

The idea that planning is an extremely important factor in every aspect of life is not new. To the contrary, planning is an old idea, the truth of which remains constant and convincing in modern culture. Whether you look at the achievements of medical science or the innovations spurred by a capitalist economy, planning is in evidence. Meals are cooked according to plans called recipes, buildings are constructed according to plans called blueprints, finances are managed according to plans called budgets, even one's waking hours often are lived according to a plan called a schedule. Planning clearly is interwoven in the fabric of everyday life.

While planning seems to be undeniably entrenched in life in general, nonetheless, large voids seem to be ruled by intuition or reaction rather than reason. These voids, while harmless in some instances, can have grave consequences in others. Management of human services is such a case in point.

Managing a department is much like taking a trip. If resources are to be used to their best advantage, an administrator's efforts must be guided by a plan or he will find his department wandering in a thousand different directions that neither forward its own goals nor contribute to the greater good. Unfortunately, planning is the exception rather than the rule in many operating units. Although preparing a detailed plan is the obvious course of action when you are anticipating some things such as a trip, it is not always the conscious choice when you are managing a department. In the hustle and bustle of everyday happenings many administrators get so caught up in the trivia of the daily routine that they never take time to plan. As a consequence, a department or program often fails to change with the changing needs of the clientele, thereby diminishing its role in society and making itself expendable. The end result is that it self-destructs, leaving space in the environment for a more productive and dynamic organization.

THE LITANY OF THE NONPLANNER

The arguments against planning are usually the result of fear or bias rather than logic. Nonetheless they keep many administrators from playing a role that is becoming more and more vital to an organization's success. Where planning was once the last resort of an organization in trouble, it is now the hallmark of one that is growing and prospering.

By examining the arguments of the nonplanner, the administrator can confront the obstacles that have caused her to neglect the important responsibility of planning in her professional life.

Argument 1: Planning Is Too Difficult

Without a doubt planning is a difficult process. The planner must utilize imagination, creativity, and careful analytical procedures, and most importantly must be committed to the process itself. The fact that planning is difficult does not negate its potential worth. It simply means that the process takes time to learn. It also means that you must be patient when trying to overcome the frustration and hard work that comes with learning something new. It is easier to say something is too difficult and give up on it—as the nonplanner prefers to do—than it is to work it out.

Argument 2: Planning Takes Too Much Time

Planning always consumes too much time if you are not committed to doing it, but so will any other effort to which you have not given high priority. If you view planning as useless, planning is likely to be a waste of time. If, on the other hand, you consider it as valuable, it is likely to be a wise investment. In short, the use of time relative to planning is directly related to your state of mind about the potential or worth of the planning process.

Argument 3: Planning Is Not Practical

Planning has its limitations, especially in an environment that changes rapidly without warning. In such an environment it is impossible to make accurate assumptions about the future, consequently it is impossible to make accurate plans. Most environments, however, do not change quickly, nor are they unpredictable. The key to accurate prediction is accurate observation and logical analysis, two tools that are poorly developed in most individuals. The problem of impracticality, then, is not directly related to planning as much as it is to poor observation and analysis. Developing the potential of these two tools should eliminate this argument effectively.

Argument 4: Planning Does Not Help in a Crisis

Planning is not an emergency tactic. It is a means of avoiding trouble, not getting out of it. Organizations that employ planning must recognize that it is a way of controlling the future, not a way of reacting to the present. Those who attempt to do otherwise most assuredly are disappointed.

Argument 5: Planning Limits Flexibility and Creativity in Decision Making

Planning is a process used to determine direction, not decisions. It provides the parameters of the decision-making process, not the exact line of thought. If anything, planning provides greater flexibility than intuition and luck, because the alternatives and consequences of a particular action can be measured against a known set of expectations. In other words, the administrator rather than some unknown element is in control when a decision is made in accordance with a plan.

These five arguments do not exhaust the number of objections that are commonly raised by administrators when discussing the pros and cons of planning, but they do represent the types of biases and prejudices that prevail on the topic. Old rules and old ways die slowly. If administrators truly intend to guide the course of their own actions and those of their departments or programs, they have to believe firmly that planning is the single most important function an administrator can perform to ensure continuity and success.

WHY SHOULD THE ADMINISTRATOR PLAN?

Managing a department or program is much like working a giant jigsaw puzzle. The administrator starts with a set of vaguely related parts, organizes them into seemingly compatible units, and presents them in a unified and coherent whole. The ease with which the transition is made, from disassociated parts to a recognizable whole, is directly dependent on the administrator's ability to organize and direct the situation toward a valued goal or objective.

The only way to accomplish this efficiently is to understand and effectively use the planning process. The following are several points that should clarify and affirm this position.

Planning Can Help Order Chaotic Situations or Seemingly Impossible Ones

At first glance, almost any situation can appear chaotic or even hopeless. This can occur because you are overwhelmed by a set of circumstances outside your sphere of experience or because you are caught off guard by a combination of events suddenly occurring outside your normal environment. The only way to combat either of these situations is to order the environment into a recognizable and workable entity. Planning can do this, because it provides a means of viewing the situation in manageable parts that can be put back together once they are isolated from the whole.

Imagine, for instance, wanting to build a pool in a town overburdened by taxes and worn thin by inflation. Most administrators would laugh at the thought. For them, building a pool would appear to be an insurmountable task, an impossible accomplishment that they are unwilling to try. To those who plan, however, nothing is impossible, primarily because they are never faced with one huge, foreboding obstacle. Instead, they look out over a series of small, negotiable tasks, each one designed to bring them closer to their goal.

For the planner, then, a goal is a sure thing several steps away. For the nonplanner it is an uncertainty, almost definitely out of reach.

Planning Can Highlight Opportunities and Indicate Problems

The world is becoming a more and more difficult place with which to cope each day. The barrage of information, the constant distractions, even the pace of living make it almost impossible for us to keep the fundamental elements within our environment from blurring together. This becomes a problem when an administrator cannot clearly differentiate those things within his sphere of interest from those things in the surrounding space. Without a clear notion of what he is doing or on whom or what he is supposed to be having an impact, he easily could lose sight of his mission and hence his ability to guide his department safely into the future. He also could find himself plunging headlong into a situation that is not at all compatible with existing circumstances.

Planning can help him cope with this situation because it requires him to focus energies and thoughts on the accomplishment of a particular goal. Focusing his attention in such a manner allows him to examine and project every aspect of his work to its outer limits. In so doing, he may discover opportunities or problems that were obscured from view by either an overriding desire to reach his goal or a misconception about what actually was occurring. The likelihood of success is greatly increased by locating potential opportunities and capitalizing on them and by eliminating problems that could be potentially debilitating.

The entire process is much like running a long distance race. If the runner's thoughts are exclusively on the finish line, chances of winning the race are simply based on being faster than anyone else on the track. The thought process, in this instance, does not take into account any of the external factors that can affect performance. If, on the other hand, the runner plans each leg of the race, deciding the position and pace to be maintained throughout, the runner will have far greater control over whether he wins the race than if he relied on sheer speed. This is true simply because he is totally aware of the situation and has set out a course to eliminate the potential hazards and capitalize on the potential opportunities.

Planning Allows Greater Latitude in Decision Making

Having a plan means having a goal. Having a goal means wanting something. Maybe the administrator would like to acquire a new secretary or a new faculty member.

Perhaps she would like to increase enrollment in the high school sports program or improve attendance at Friday night football games. Whatever it is, if she has a plan she has a way of getting what she wants via a specific course of action. It does not mean, however, that the success of the project is guaranteed. To the contrary, it only means that the road has been laid to the goal. The obstacles encountered on the way are still an administrative problem, although coping with them is easier because direction and standards have been provided by the plan.

There are those who fear that planning will stifle their creativity. What these individuals fail to realize is that it is impossible for them or anyone else to create in a vacuum.

If it is ludicrous to think that one could create a modern dance without a repertoire of steps to choose from and improve upon, why is it not just as ludicrous to expect an administrator to be creative in decision making without the necessary facts and understandings? Simply defined, creativity is the "recombination of *known* elements into something new,"[1] not the development of something from nothing. The latter case is what would be necessary if you attempted to be creative without the information provided by a plan.

Planning Can Help Chart New Directions and Accomplish Change

A business that fails to change with the changing needs of its clients eventually goes bankrupt. Consequently, most businesses are quick to detect changes and chart new directions accordingly. If a human service organization fails to change with the changing needs of its clients, it, too, eventually goes out of business, although it does not have to be as responsive or change as rapidly to survive.

Perhaps the lack of this kind of sensitivity on the part of a public service agency can be explained by the fact that its eminent survival has not been as closely dependent on the profit column as the survival of a business would be. With the economic climate changing, however, the financial responsibilities of private and public enterprises are becoming more and more similar. The public agency must find a way not only to be more responsive to its clients' needs, but to anticipate them the way a business does if it hopes to continue in the future as a working entity. As mentioned elsewhere in this chapter, this can be done with a certain degree of effectiveness through the use of a plan.

Although planning cannot guarantee a specific future, it can increase the probability that a particular future will be realized. Every premise of a plan is the result of asking: Where do we want to be? Where are we now? and How are we going to make the transition from one state to the next? These questions are just another way of asking: How are we going to do a better job of meeting our clients' needs? That question is the bottom line of any plan a human service organization formulates.

Planning Focuses Energy and Gives Direction

The old saying, "A house divided against itself cannot stand," is just another way of saying that a group of individuals without a clear focus or goal eventually will disas-

1. John Ciardi, "What Every Writer Must Learn," *Saturday Review* (15 December 1956): 7.

sociate from one another and begin competing for resources to forward their own ends rather than those of the group. In a department in which the chief administrator fails to formulate a plan or fails to share the plan with his subordinates, no unity exists. This occurs because there is no common goal to which everyone can relate. In such an environment each individual will create his own goal. The end result is chaos.

In a department or program that has a clear focus, each member knows exactly what must be achieved and what is expected of her. With this knowledge comes a sense of purpose and a sense of importance, two ingredients that contribute to a positive and productive working unit.

Planning Provides a Clear Understanding of "Who We Are" and "Why We Are Here"

A written plan is a visual manifestation of what is desired and how it will be achieved. It represents the organization's personality, perceived purpose, and how much energy will be expended to fulfill that purpose. It provides a constant reminder of the organization's values and goals and serves as a clear statement of these things to those outside the operating unit. In essence, a plan helps to distinguish the trivial from the important so that one can move unencumbered toward perceived goals.

STRATEGIC PLANNING: WHAT IS IT?

Ellis and Pekar open their discussion in *Planning for Nonplanners* with a commentary on our culture that is worth noting, for it has a great deal to do with the erroneous view many hold about planning. The world, they say:

> ...has never appeared as hostile, bewildering or unstable as it does today. Yet everyone wants to formulate concrete plans for the future. The problem is that often these plans focus on numbers rather than on the strategic issues that are the key to success of an organization.
>
> One need only review the national cancer program to uncover a perfect example of this type of nonthinking. With considerable fanfare and ballyhoo, President Nixon assured us that if we would spend $40 billion over 20 years on medical research a cure for cancer would be found. Why is it generally believed that we can do this? Well didn't we put a man on the moon in nine years? Didn't we build the Panama Canal when everyone else failed? Weren't we responsible for harnessing nuclear power in four short years? And after all, are we not the greatest nation on earth for getting things done?
>
> ...Despite the medical profession's doubts and lack of knowledge, the spending goes on. What have we found?[2]

The point of their statement was not to belittle the efforts of the medical profession in its quest to find a cure for cancer. It was to attack two beliefs that have distorted not only the understanding of planning and what it can accomplish, but also the manner in which the concept is applied.

Most persons would agree that it is impossible to solve a problem or reach a goal simply by investing large sums of money in a particular project, yet the notion permeates most thought in regard to planning. Trapped in a financial tug-of-war, many

2. Darryl J. Ellis and Peter P. Pekar, Jr., *Planning for Nonplanners* (New York: AMACOM, 1980), pp. 2-3.

aspirations and achievements are translated into dollar figures. How many times, for instance, do administrators lament, "How do they expect us to produce a quality program if they are only willing to fund 50 percent of our asking budget?" How many times do they say, "That program can't miss. They have more money than they'll ever be able to spend"?

Determining the quality of a program by the size of its budget is a dangerous practice, not only because it can create both good and bad reputations that are unwarranted, but because it limits one's ability to think clearly. Artificial constraints are created whenever a person is forced to evaluate an idea solely on the basis of whether it is considered financially feasible, rather than whether it will bring the organizational goal closer to accomplishment. Such thinking greatly reduces the number of alternatives that are possible in any given situation, and this in turn greatly reduces the likelihood of finding the "perfect" path to the goal.

While problematic, the dependency on financial feasibility alone is not as disruptive to the planning process as is the notion that every goal is a simple problem with a simple solution. This oversimplification, or one-dimensional thinking, is a tremendous liability when a person is attempting to develop a plan, because the eventual success of any course of action is related directly to the accuracy of the assumptions made about the future. When a problem is oversimplified, the image of the future is distorted. This causes the planner to make assumptions that are not necessarily true. Because plans are courses of action based on what the planner thinks the environment will be like beyond the present, he cannot afford to complicate or compromise the predictive phase of the planning process by failing to analyze completely all aspects of the goal. To do so is to doom the plan to failure from the beginning.

Present thinking defines planning as "the process of translating corporate objectives into the policies and resources allocations that will achieve those objectives. The process usually entails (1) establishing corporate goals and objectives, (2) assessing likely trends in the economic, political, technical, and competitive environment, (3) identifying potential opportunities and threats, and (4) developing strategies, policies, and resource allocations to cope with the threats and take advantage of the opportunities."[3] This definition implies a dynamic multidimensional process that focuses on maintaining, improving, or initiating strategic issues that are vital to an organization's success. In addition it implies a process that requires decision making on a tactical as well as a conceptual level. In the business world these levels are differentiated as **strategic** (conceptual) and **operational** (tactical) **planning**.

STRATEGIC AND OPERATIONAL PLANNING

Planning is a cyclical event that operates on at least these two levels. If an administrator became concerned about decreasing the incidence of theft or vandalism in a locker room, for instance, she might devise a plan that would increase the number of attendants on duty at any given hour. Such a course of action would be known as an

---

3. J. M. Lyneis, *Corporate Planning and Policy Design: A Systems Dynamics Approach* (Cambridge, Mass.: 1980), p. 3.

operational plan, because it deals directly with the resolution of a problem or the attainment of a specific goal. If, on the other hand, she were trying to decide whether the locker room facilities should be included among the services she should provide her clientele, she would be operating at the strategic planning level. At this second level, the administrator is committed to making decisions about the purpose of the organization, why it exists, what it hopes to accomplish, and how it intends to fulfill its role. In short, it is a long-range look at what the organization is all about.

Strategic Planning: The Administrator's Primary Task

According to Drucker, the primary task of any administrator is the task of thinking through the mission of the business, that is, of asking the question: What is our business and what should it be?[4]

Consider the following question: Have you ever tried to define what business you are in? Your answer is probably no, for like the rest of us, you probably assume you are in the business of recreation or physical education. The issue is: Are you really in the business you think you are? A moment's reflection might change your mind, as it did the minds of the farmers in the following case:

> In the early stages of their planning, for example, the managers of one farming group believed they were in the business of raising vegetables, citrus fruits, and cattle. On reflection, however, they decided that they were in the business of packaging fresh convenience foods. You can see the radical change this made in their total planning process: Now they were thinking more of the consumer and the methods for packaging vegetables that would reduce the amount of preparation at the point of use. It is quite a different approach from concentrating on techniques of harvesting vegetables and packaging them almost directly from the fields. This type of thinking turned out to be so profitable that the managers made a further intensive study of what business they should be in and decided that it was the business of land utilization. Maximizing the land assets that they own does not preclude their continuing to provide fresh convenience foods, but it also opens up new opportunities. For example, they now ask themselves whether a particular piece of real estate should be used for vegetable farming, citrus growing, or cattle raising—or whether it should be devoted to real estate development, say, for home sites or recreation.
>
> Similarly, this farming group decided that it was not in the subbusiness of cattle raising, but in that of preparing and processing meats for the end user. Consequently, it moved away from raising cattle and selling it on the hoof direct from the ranches to establishing its own feed lots. Eventually, it probably will go into meat processing. In the field of citrus growing, it is not simply raising oranges, lemons, and grapefruit; it is in the business of providing citrus juices and fresh fruit to the user in the most convenient form. The group has become involved in various ways of processing the fruit and in a total new marketing concept as well.[5]

Defining one's business is an extremely meaningful task in the planning process, for more than any other process, strategic planning represents that point in time during which the upper managers of an organization formulate a system of thinking

---

4. Peter F. Drucker, *Management: Tasks, Responsibilities, Practices* (New York: Harper and Row, 1974), p. 611.

5. Keith J. Louden, *Making It Happen* (New York: American Management Association Inc., U.S.A., 1971), pp. 60-61.

that they hope will direct the organization's safe progress into the future. For those who view such questioning as unnecessary academic prattle, many lessons are to be learned from the histories of enterprises in which the owners chose to say their business was obvious, such as, "We run railroads":

> During the 1960's, it became increasingly apparent that such thinking was too limited. Many organizations that seemed to know their business have disappeared from the scene. We must therefore recognize that today's business however bright its growth prospects may appear, may not even exist in only a few years. Although this is difficult for most of us to perceive, the lessons of history are so numerous and so vivid that they cannot be ignored.
>
> Consider the dry cleaning business, which only a few decades ago was viewed as having unlimited potential. How could a service industry that could offer the low-cost, safe, and quick cleaning of everybody's garments not continue to grow? Yet, synthetic fabrics and modern detergents long ago have reduced significantly the growth prospects of the industry.
>
> Similarly, many movie companies did not survive the advent of television, despite the fact that movies themselves have survived. The companies that did survive turned their expertise to producing movies for TV as well as for theaters and changed the kind of movie that they were making so that they would not be so directly competitive with a medium that they could not conquer. Thus, the surviving movie companies changed their view of their business and began to sell old movies to television as well as to produce new ones for TV. One can only imagine what might have happened had the movie companies viewed TV as an opportunity rather than a threat. The television industry is now larger than the movie industry, and it is easy to surmise that the many now-deceased movie firms might have been corporate giants had they viewed their business as that of "entertainment" rather than of "making movies."[6]

One can wonder where various organizations will be 10 or 15 years from now if those who administrate them continue to believe they are simply in the business of "providing recreation or physical education."

Although the determination of the business mission is, in the broadest sense, the essence of strategic planning, it is not the only item on the agenda. A strategic plan includes:

1. *A statement of the organization's purpose* that outlines the business or businesses in which the organization is involved, what portion of the market it hopes to control, and the unique contribution it hopes to make.
2. *Selected strategies* that are aimed at accomplishing its purpose and achieving the place it wishes in the market.
3. *Goals* that target what the organization wants, and provide a standard against which progress can be evaluated.
4. *A description of the environment* that is necessary for the organization to achieve its goals.
5. *The allocation of resources* that must be made so that the organization can move closer to its goals.

---

6. William R. King and David I. Cleland, *Strategic Planning and Policy* (New York: Van Nostrand Reinhold Co., 1978), pp. 47-48.

6. *Key decisions* that must be made to integrate the efforts of all operating units so that they contribute to the fulfillment of the plan.[7]

To accomplish this, Louden suggests that the members of a planning team ask themselves the following questions:

A. What businesses are we in? What segment of each do we serve? How big are they, and what percent of the market do we represent? What is our acceptance by customers? What is their image of us? What are the trends in each business—sales, products, prices, uses? What is our profit trend?
B. What areas closely related to our businesses are logical directions for expansion on the basis, principally, of our current know-how, facilities, and marketing practices?
C. What closely related areas are possibilities for expansion except that we don't have the required know-how, facilities, and marketing practices?
D. What are our management capabilities? This requires a management audit and inventory at all levels, basically to determine the following for each man: how he is performing on his present job, what his strengths and weaknesses are, what can be done to make him more effective, what his potential is, when he will realize it, and what help he needs to realize it.
E. What are our resources in technological skills at all levels?
F. What are our facility and financial resources and capabilities? What financial leverage do we have?[8]

Operational Planning: The Outward Workings of an Organization

Once the strategic plan has been established and the organization's direction is set, the administrator can begin to establish short-term goals and action programs that are known as operational plans. Generally, operational plans are resource allocation programs that establish budgets, manpower, and time constraints for a particular course of action. They represent the nuts and bolts of the planning process.

Operational plans, however, are much more than just courses of action set forth to achieve goals. They represent a means of determining, as well as filling in, the gaps that are present between the todays one has and the tomorrows one envisions through the strategic plan. Through a needs assessment the operational plan helps to determine the priorities of the organization so that it can move sensibly and sensitively from its present condition to a more desired one.

To accomplish this, Kaufman suggests that we move from needs identification to gap resolution in the six steps that are summarized below:[9]

Step 1: Determine gaps between current results and desired results, place them in priority order, and select the one or ones you wish to resolve first.
Step 2: Determine what would be required to resolve the gap and the number of ways this can be accomplished. Behavioral objectives are extremely useful during this stage because they assist the administrator in identifying those things that are required to obtain the desired results successfully.

---

7. Louden, *Making It Happen*, pp. 71-72.

8. Ibid., p. 72.

9. Roger A. Kaufman, *Needs Assessment: Concept and Application* (Englewood Cliffs, N.J.: Educational Technology Publications, 1979), pp. 37-44.

Step 3: Select the strategy or strategies that will be used to resolve the need (gap). Selection should be made on the basis of whether the strategy or strategies are: "the most likely to meet the performance requirements; are the most efficient as well as effective; and will work by themselves as well as with the other selected methods-means."[10]

Step 4: Implement the selected strategies. This is the stage at which the operational plan becomes a working reality. All plans are made functional at this point.

Step 5: Evaluate performance effectiveness. During this stage the results of each action are measured against the requirements that were translated into observable terms in step two.

Step 6: Revise strategy, if necessary. If there is still a gap between current result and desired result, the strategy will be modified at this point. If everything is working out as planned, the next gap is targeted for resolution.

THE DYNAMICS OF PLANNING

Planning is a multifaceted function comprised of many different management processes, each of which must be understood thoroughly if the planning function is to be performed efficiently and effectively. Below is a descriptive listing of each of these management processes, as they occur within the planning function. Such a listing should assist in the development of plans for any operating unit.

Determine an Organization's Mission Statement

Mission statements are considered summit decisions because they bind the operating units of an organization together by a common thread and act as a supreme guideline for all other organizational decisions. In the broadest sense mission statements identify:

1. The *role* of the organization
2. The *image* it wishes to project in the social, political, and economic environments
3. The *policies* the organization will operate under
4. The nature of the *business* the organization is in
5. The *strategies* the organization will use to achieve its mission

Mission statements are usually the result of value judgments made at the administrative level. Although it is impossible to validate the correctness of any decision based on a value or to guarantee its future certainty, an administrator can increase a mission statement's flexibility and responsiveness to internal and external factors by making sure that it is written in terms that:

1. *Clearly define what the organization does and does not do.*[11]
2. *Restrict the expansionist tendencies of an organization.* This refers to situa-

10. Ibid., p. 41
11. King and Cleland, *Strategic Planning and Policy*, p. 48.

tions in which an organization moves into an area that is potentially profitable, even though the area is clearly beyond the organization's capabilities and expertise because its mission statement is too broad. A classic example would be that of a recreation department sponsoring a "Smoke Enders Clinic," even though it has no expertise in this area, simply because the topic is popular and because the department's mission statement stresses its role as a provider of healthful activities.

3. *Refer to both services and target markets.* This is done to keep the scope of the mission from becoming too wide. Rather than to say that you "provide educational services," it is more meaningful to say you "provide educational services to improve a child's understanding of physiological effects of exercise."

4. *Avoid restrictive or detailed language* that limits management's flexibility in a changing environment.

5. *Explain what the business is, why it exists, and the unique contribution it can make.*[12] An example of such a statement follows:

> We are in the business of providing recreational opportunities and the concomitant amenity services to the residential and nonresidential populations of a college community. The provision of recreational opportunities and amenity services refers to facilitating the availability of any physical activity for recreational consumption.

Establish Goals

Goals are broad, enduring statements that express some desired result or vision. A perfect example of such a statement of belief is found in the Preamble of the Constitution of the United States:

> We the people of the United States in order to form a more perfect Union, establish Justice, insure domestic Tranquility, provide for the common defense, promote the general Welfare, and secure the Blessing of Liberty for ourselves and our Posterity.

While most goals are not as lofty or timeless as these, they are nevertheless important, for they help their creators to determine what is important to the organization and what it strives to achieve. Without such statements, there is little basis for purposeful behavior. When writing goals, remember that they should:

1. *Support the organization's mission statement.* A goal that does not support the organization's mission statement is counterproductive. One that is in conflict with it can help bring about the demise of the organization.

2. *Be acceptable to the staff of the organization.* A goal that lacks organizational support is doomed from the beginning. To avoid this possibility seek the support of everyone involved before making the goal public.

3. *Be broad.* Broad goals are flexible goals that will endure over time in a changing environment. Goals that cannot stand the test of time are not worth having.

4. *Be clearly stated.* Goals should be written in clear, concise language that every-

12. Ibid., p. 47.

one can understand. This will minimize confusion and increase the likelihood that the goal will be achieved.

5. *Be within the realm of possibility.* Creating a challenge for oneself and others can be highly motivating. Creating a situation that is unlikely to be resolved is demoralizing. Avoid goals that appear out of reach. They can cause the loss of enthusiasm and commitment of a staff before the program even gets started.

Define Objectives

An **objective** is a concrete, measurable expression of a desired result that an organization can use to evaluate its progress toward a desired goal. Objectives are extremely valuable tools because they force an administrator to define in explicit terms exactly what he hopes to accomplish by a specific date. Without observable objectives it becomes extremely difficult to:

1. Decide what strategies should be used to attain desired goals.
2. Understand exactly what is expected.
3. Evaluate whether a program or course of action is efficient or effective.
4. Ascertain the exact direction, behavior, or response to be measured.

When writing objectives be sure to:

1. *Use words that are explicit, not vague.* To state as an objective that a client should enjoy a particular recreational activity is too vague because one cannot be sure what the word *enjoy* means. Does it mean, for instance, that the client should laugh the entire time the activity is going on, or that she should want to do the activity again? The exact meaning is not clear, because the word enjoy represents much more than just one action or idea.
2. *Refer to the context of a particular goal or planning category.* Objectives indicate the desired results of a particular endeavor. This must be stated in the body of the objective, or it will lose its impact. Remember, if objectives are interchangeable across planning categories, they are not explicit enough.
3. *Establish small units of work so that the largest deadlines occur within a reasonable time frame.* Objectives represent stop points in a particular action during which an operating team can take stock of its progress and revise its course of action, if necessary. If the stop point is scheduled to occur at a point in time that is too distant from the start, the advantage of being able to evaluate progress within a time frame during which revision is possible will be lost.
4. *Designate desired results that are achievable within a specific time frame.* Time is an important element in the expression of an objective because it provides closure. If the time frame for an objective is not realistic, the operating team will experience a sense of frustration. If this occurs often enough, the team will begin to ignore the objectives on the basis that the objectives lack purpose. Staff will act this way especially if they view the achievement of objectives as secondary to their job fulfillment.
5. *Provide links between the objectives that are specified in a particular course of action.* Objectives are not formed in a vacuum nor do they exist in isolation.

They are part of a series of measurable steps designed to achieve a predetermined goal. Each objective in a series should be linked together by a common thread that distinguishes one set of objectives from another.

Develop an Organizational Philosophy

An **organizational philosophy** refers to the values, attitudes, and traditions of an organization. Taken literally, it is the system of beliefs, concepts, and attitudes on which the organization is founded and on which it stands. Thomas Watson, Jr., chairman of IBM, emphasized the importance of company philosophy as follows:

> This is my thesis: I firmly believe that any organization, in order to survive and achieve success, must have a sound set of beliefs on which it premises all its policies and actions.
>
> Next, I believe that the most important single factor in corporate success is faithful adherence to those beliefs...
>
> In other words, the basic philosophy, spirit, and drive of an organization have far more to do with its relative achievements than do technological or economic resources, organizational structure, innovation, and timing. All these things weigh heavily on success. But they are, I think, transcended by how strongly the people in the organization believe in its basic precepts and how faithfully they carry them out.[13]

What is included in a philosophy statement is up to the founders of the organization or those in charge. Whatever is written, however, must be deeply believed in and followed, for it reflects heavily on the credibility of the organization.

Establish Policies and Procedures

Once objectives are established, the administrator is faced with the task of translating the plan into operational terms known as policies and procedures. These two terms, although used interchangeably, represent two distinct sets of concepts and practices.

Policies

Policies are position statements made by upper-level managers for purposes of outlining specific decision areas in the organization. Said another way, policies represent specific limits on the decision-making power that middle management can exercise. Although policies are meant to limit decisions, they are not written in restrictive terms that specify the exact manner in which the decision is made or carried out. Instead, they are written in terms that allow the manager to react to the internal and external factors that are at work in a particular situation. The following is an example of a policy that might be found in a physical education or recreation department (see Appendix I for a full outline). Note that it only indicates, in general terms, what the decision area is, who is authorized to make the decision, and the outer limits of the decision-making area.

6000 Program Delivery

2400—Use of Facilities

---

13. Thomas J. Watson, Jr., *A Business and Its Belief* (New York: McGraw-Hill Book Co., 1963), p. 3.

Recreational space should be available to all members of the community. The coordinator of recreational services therefore is authorized to provide gymnasium space to the following groups, in the priority order listed, during regular operating hours:

Physical Education Department
Athletic Department
Recreation Department
Recognized Clubs and Civic Groups

Procedures

Procedures represent the detailed instructions of a plan. Written within the limits of accepted policy, procedures indicate an authorized method for reacting to a specific situation. Because each detail of the action is prescribed, procedures serve as an effective means of standardizing any operation. The following is a procedure that might have been devised for the facilities policy, given previously. Note the difference in detail.

2430.10—Making Application for Recreational Space

Gymnasium space will be available to bonafide groups specified in the priority system only on the presentation of an application that must be:

1. Filed in duplicate with the coordinator of recreational services
2. Filed at least ten days prior to the date or dates in question
3. Filed after: July 1, for the fall semester; December 1, for the spring semester; and March 1, for the summer session

Procedural detail is critical in any operation, because it is at this level that many aspects of the plan become a reality. It is also at this level that the best laid plans can go awry, because procedures that are translated incorrectly from their governing policies and goals can result in a negative outcome. This fact should be kept uppermost in your thinking when writing procedures. To ignore it is to invite disaster.

The following are counterproductive procedures, although on first observation this may not be clear. After you analyze their content in regard to the policy and goal that supercede them, however, it should become apparent to you that the procedures are contrary to what is prescribed.

2390.10—Handling Complaints

Complaints on any issue may be received only in writing. Individuals wishing to file a complaint should be instructed to submit the details of their complaint on Form RD 206 for further consideration.

2390.20—Recording Complaints

Complaints will be classified "major" and "minor" according to the gravity of the situation (for detailed explanation see procedure 2390.50). "Major" complaints will be forwarded to the appropriate supervisor upon receipt. "Minor" complaints will be held in the central office until the next regularly scheduled department meeting or until five similar complaints are received, whichever comes first.

These procedures seem quite plausible until you compare them to the following goal and policy, which they were written to implement.

Goal: It is the goal of this department to be responsive to every resident and to make each member of the community feel that his or her input is important.

2390—Policy With Regard to Complaints and Suggestions

Every member of the community is considered a vital contributor in the dialogue between the public and the department. All input should be seriously analyzed and acted on. Each person should be advised of this consideration and apprised, in an appropriate manner, of the action that is to be taken. At no time should suggestions go unheeded or unnoticed nor should participants be discouraged in their attempt to communicate their feelings and thoughts.

The procedures ignore and in some instances countermand the desire of the planners to keep a positive avenue of communication open between the public and the department, as outlined in the goal and policy provided above. The outcome of such a situation can undermine all other efforts to forward the original plan and reach the desired end.

Procedures should be reviewed periodically to be sure that they are in tune with the prevailing philosophy of the department and are in keeping with the course of action outlined in the master plan. In this way they will serve to enhance rather than detract from the forward movement of the unit.

CONCLUSION

Learning to plan is not as difficult as making the commitment to plan. For the administrator who decides that the rewards are worth the energy, commitment to planning will not be a burden, it will be the only rational action. For these individuals, a goal is a reality at the end of an ordered path. For others, it is a stab in the dark.

How are
qualified staff
selected and hired?

How is a
personnel search
conducted?

What can be
done to improve
staff morale?

What are the
traits or qualities
of a good
administrator?

What procedures
can be instituted
so that a staff
will be evaluated
effectively and
fairly?

Chapter 5

Personnel Development and Management

An administrator's success often is measured in terms of the competence of his staff and their ability to perform their assigned duties successfully. This being the case, a thorough understanding of the processes of selection, utilization, motivation, and evaluation of personnel is essential to administrative success.

SELECTION OF PERSONNEL

The potential for job success generally can be predicted not only on the basis of an individual's professional qualifications and experience, but also on the basis of his potential satisfaction with the job. Loosely translated, this means that the administrator not only must engage the services of a talented individual, but also must take care to match the demands of the position with the interests and expectations of the professional who is to be employed. To do less, to ignore the ambitions or the expectations of the potential employee, or to glaze over certain unattractive tasks required by the position, will ensure only the likelihood of future failure both on the part of the employee and the administrator.

The first step in engaging competent, highly motivated staff members who have the potential for success is to develop an accurate description of the tasks that must be accomplished. In this way the administrator and the applicants have a clear understanding of what is desired from the outset.

Developing the Job Description

Before an administrator can consider recruiting or employing personnel, he must have a clear delineation of the type of position to be filled. Regardless of whether the position has been created in response to growing user demands, expanding program offerings, or simply as a result of staff turnover, this process must commence with a careful assessment of the goals and objectives of the program and the professional resources presently available for their attainment. The difference between the available services and those needed to attain specified goals should form the basis for the development of the position or positions sought.

Consider, for instance, the community school described in Chapter 2. Having thoughtfully redesigned their equipment storage and utilization procedures, the directors of athletics, physical education, and recreation came to the realization that all their needs could be served better through the employment of an equipment manager. They decided, therefore, to pool their resources to create such a position, and also to designate a single individual from each of their staffs to serve as an equipment coordinator and liaison for their unit.

After determining the general program requirements, an administrator can begin to design job descriptions that best suit these needs. The following steps should prove helpful in that process.

I.   In consultation with staff members, advisory committees, and the next superior administrative unit, write concise descriptive phrases that delineate both the general and specific responsibilities of the position. Be sure to avoid generalities that are open to wide interpretation. Use words such as organize, supervise, assist, provide, and the like to describe observable behaviors. Include all responsibilities regardless of their unattractiveness or minor importance, because more often than not, job dissatisfaction is related to those aspects of the job that were not made known to the employee during the application process. The equipment manager at Edwin Eden Community School might be expected to:
   A.   Distribute and collect all athletic equipment and audiovisual aids according to established policy.
   B.   Type, file, and duplicate as required by position.
   C.   Enforce all rules, regulations, and policies set by the administrative units.
   D.   Organize and maintain accurate records on all equipment and audiovisual aids.
   E.   Care for, repair, and generally maintain all equipment, uniforms, and audiovisual aids.
   F.   Conduct annual inventory and collect and prepare equipment order requests.
II.   Assign priorities to these descriptive phrases and indicate clearly which are major and which are minor responsibilities. For example, the job responsibilities noted above might be listed in the following order of importance:
   A.   Distribute and collect all athletic equipment and audiovisual aids according to established policy.
   B.   Care for, repair, and generally maintain all equipment, uniforms, and audiovisual aids.
   C.   Enforce all rules, regulations, and policies set by the administrative units.
   D.   Organize and maintain accurate records on all equipment and audiovisual aids.
   E.   Conduct annual inventory and collect and prepare equipment order requests.
   F.   Type, file, and duplicate as required by position.
III. When applicable, review job titles and descriptions that may be provided by other

sources such as civil service. Incorporate descriptions that are appropriate.

IV.   Write a concise job description that clearly describes the responsibilities of the position as outlined in steps I, II, and III. The job description for the equipment manager at Edwin Eden Community School might read as follows:

> The equipment manager will have full responsibility for the organization and conduct of the equipment room to include: the distribution, collection, care, repair, and general maintenance of all equipment, uniforms, and audiovisual aids. He will be required to organize and maintain accurate records on all equipment, uniforms, and audiovisual aids, with such responsibility to include the conduct of an annual inventory and the preparation of purchase requests. Additionally, the equipment manager will type, file, and duplicate materials as required by the position, and will perform other related duties as assigned.

V.   Based on the job description and other factors as they apply (e.g., state law governing teacher qualifications, civil service requirements attached to specific recreation job titles, operating policies of a school, college, or governing body of a municipality), determine the minimum qualifications for the position. Usually there are convenient sources such as civil service that can be used as a guide during the initial phases of this step. Requirements cited in other sources may serve as the backbone of the requirements being developed for certain positions. The requirements for the Eden School equipment manager might be:

A.   Minimum of an associate's degree with major emphasis in physical education or an allied field.

B.   Experience in or familiarity with the care and repair of all types of athletic equipment and audiovisual aids.

C.   Ability to use common office machinery.

VI.   Determine the salary available for the position.

VII. Develop a single-page job description that clearly and succinctly puts forth the information developed in I, II, III, IV, V, and VI above (Figure 5.1).

VIII. Request the necessary approval of the position vacancy and the job description from higher administrative authorities. Once this has been granted, the search may begin in earnest.

Conducting a Thorough Search

In general, the more thorough the search, the greater the pool of well-qualified candidates from which one can choose. It is wise, therefore, to send notices of a position vacancy and job descriptions to:

1.   *Members of the present staff.* Perhaps someone within one's own district or department would be interested in and qualified for the position. This is particularly true of administrative or supervisory vacancies, which may be of interest to a person who is seeking the opportunity for career advancement.

2.   *College placement centers.* Virtually every college maintains a placement service for the benefit of its graduates. When you are seeking a person who recently has completed his degree requirements, this is an invaluable resource.

Title

Equipment Manager

Qualifications

Associate's degree with major emphasis in physical education or an allied field

Experience in or familiarity with the care and repair of all types of athletic equipment and audiovisual aids

Ability to use common office machinery

Job description

The equipment manager shall have full responsibility for the organization and conduct of the equipment room to include: the distribution, collection, care, repair, and general maintenance of all equipment, uniforms, and audiovisual aids. He or she shall be required to organize and maintain accurate records on all equipment, uniforms, and audiovisual aids, with such responsibility to include the conduct of an annual inventory and the preparation of purchase requests. Additionally, the equipment manager shall type, file, and duplicate materials as required by the position, and shall perform other related duties as assigned.

Salary

$4.15/hour

Letters of application and references should be forwarded to

Dr. Margaret Quaranta, Principal
Edwin Eden Community School
Burnett Park, Ohio 19317

Deadline for applications

March 1, 19XX

Figure 5.1. Sample job description

3. *Selected college departments.* Many colleges do not offer specialty programs that provide a graduate with in-depth training in a specific area. Finding those departments that offer specialties in the area you are seeking may provide you with a number of exceptionally well-qualified candidates.

4. *Professional associations.* Associations such as AAHPERD and NRPA carry inexpensive advertising sections for prospective employers within their publications. In addition, most associations provide free placement services at their national and regional meetings for the benefit of their members.

5. *Major newspapers.* Several major newspapers carry periodical listings of positions available in education. The *New York Times*, for instance, every Sunday carries relatively inexpensive advertising for educational opportunities.

6. *Special recruitment services for minority groups.* A number of groups provide special placement services for members of minority groups. Among these are:

National Black Alliance Newsletter
Black Women Employment Program
Equal Employment Opportunity Commission

Office of Indian Education Programs
Puerto Rican Congress
Women's Educators

Appraisal of Applicants

It would be nice to state that the well-designed and circulated job description will result in applications only from those persons who come reasonably close to meeting the stated requirements, but this is simply not the case. Human nature being what it is, the applicants more likely will range in ability from clearly unqualified to greatly over-qualified. The important point here is that somewhere in the mass of applications are several that approximate the needs of the job. The trick is to sift them out efficiently.

The first response that a prospective employer is likely to have with regard to a candidate is through the letter that accompanies the candidate's application. Given the impact of first impressions, it is wise for the administrator to recognize the letter's effect and to establish criteria against which to evaluate it, rather than allowing the letter to remain an unconscious and highly subjective influence. Such qualities as a candidate's grammar, style, clarity of expression, and ability to state factually her own strengths and background without appearing boastful or including unnecessary detail can and should be evaluated. Although a well-done letter does not necessarily indicate a high level of professional ability, a poorly written or carelessly typed letter certainly may be indicative of traits considered undesirable in an employee.

Compare the resumes of the candidates with the requirements of the position, and eliminate those that fail to meet the stated criteria. Having selected those candidates who appear to meet the criteria, further subdivide them into groups according to the degree to which they meet all of the primary and secondary responsibilities of the position.

Having categorized the candidates in this manner, carefully examine the references of the best-qualified group. It is essential that persons who are listed as references be contacted personally during this process. Rarely, if ever, does anyone write a negative reference or cite major shortcomings in a letter. A person might feel more comfortable, however, and be better able to provide a clear picture of the applicant in a personal conversation with the prospective employer. A relatively inexpensive telephone call can save a great deal of later difficulty. If a simple checklist were developed that listed the main qualities sought in an applicant, then the responsibility for calling the references could be shared by the entire search committee. Figure 5.2 is an example of a general checklist that could be made more specific, if necessary, to meet the details of any given position.

Personal Interviews

No person should be offered a contract without a personal interview. Because the responsibilities of an individual in a human service profession center primarily on face-to-face interaction with a variety of publics, and also because the ability of any given employee to interact cooperatively with co-workers can affect the success of the entire program, a personal interview with the applicant serves as one of the most important phases of the selection process.

Quality	Excellent	Good	Fair	Poor	Comments
1. Skill and Knowledge					
2. Diligence					

3. Relationships
      Superiors
      Co-workers
      Subordinates					

4. Self-expression
      Verbal
      Written					

5. Adaptability					
6. Experience					
7. Organizational Ability					
8. Overall Impression					
GENERAL COMMENTS:					

Figure 5.2. Evaluation form for telephone follow-up on written references

Interviews should be planned in advance. Although some flexibility is important, certain factors should be held constant for all interviewees:

1. Provide a private area that can be kept free from distractions for the interview. Ringing telephones, staff members coming in with problems, and rattling typewriters all detract from the concentration and depth of thought of both parties.

2. Plan for several major points to be covered in each interview, and be sure that all interviews cover these topics. This will allow a common basis for comparison. All candidates for the Eden School equipment manager's position, for instance, might be asked to discuss the manner in which they would organize and maintain the equipment room, their knowledge of equipment maintenance and care, how they would pursue the matter when equipment is mistreated or lost, and other similarly pertinent issues.

3. Provide the candidates with enough information concerning the position, working environment, and other important factors that they may evaluate and discuss their own potential contribution intelligently. Providing this information in advance of the interview is likely to be most fruitful. Examples of printed materials that would be of interest to a prospective employee might include: Activity, class, or athletic contest schedules, program descriptions, curriculum guides, and publicity flyers.

4. Put the candidate at ease. Try to use open-ended questions that call for a full answer or explanation rather than a simple yes or no response. Listen carefully and use soliciting statements such as "go on" or "that's interesting" or "how do

you feel about...?" Such questions often will provide the opportunity for greater insight into a person's knowledge and expressive ability.

5. Allow ample time for the interview. Nothing is more discourteous or less effective than a rushed interview. It is also useful to allow the interview format to shift naturally by varying the locale. For instance, you could meet in an office, tour the facilities, and conclude over lunch, thus gaining a much more complete view of the candidate.

6. Provide an opportunity for the candidate to meet privately with other members of the staff. This allows the staff to evaluate the candidate as a potential co-worker, and at the same time provides the candidate with an impression of the working conditions. One efficient and inconspicuous manner of accomplishing this is by asking another faculty member to provide the candidate with a tour of the facilities. Remember, both parties probably will be more comfortable and open if the administrator is not present, and the additional insight obtained in this manner may prove invaluable in ascertaining the candidate's compatability with the rest of the faculty. This process would necessitate a brief follow-up conference with those staff members who were involved in order to compile and summarize their impressions.

Hire the Best

Once you have completed the previous steps in the selection process, you will be able to compile and compare the results. Discuss the candidates with as many members of the professional staff as is reasonable in order to select the best-qualified person. In making this selection, remember that it takes more than professional skills for a person to become a valuable staff member. The personality of the candidate and the degree to which she will "fit in" with and complement the remainder of the staff are critical elements that must be given serious consideration.

Another issue that is often overlooked but is equally important is the possibility of a candidate's being overqualified. On the surface the idea of hiring a person whose qualifications and experience are well beyond those required by the position may appear to be a perfect way to upgrade a program, but the results are too frequently quite the opposite. A person who is overqualified, if hired, soon is likely to find the position less challenging than desirable and the salary less than could be obtained elsewhere. He may even view himself as better qualified than other staff members who are earning larger salaries. The resultant morale problems easily could affect the entire professional staff. The best candidate almost certainly will be the one who best matches all aspects of the job description.

The person who is finally selected should be notified as soon as possible. Although a verbal offer of employment provides a degree of personal contact and warmth that should not be overlooked, neither should you neglect to include a well-written letter of offer (Figure 5.3) with the contracts normally provided for a signature (Figure 5.4).

You also should develop a letter to be sent to all unsuccessful candidates, thanking them for their interest and encouraging their continued professional involvement (Figure 5.5).

Dear Mr. Torres:

We are pleased to confirm that we are prepared to recommend to the Super-intendent of Schools and the Board of Education your appointment as equipment manager with terms as noted on the enclosure.

Will you please advise us in writing as soon as possible of your decision regarding this offer? Upon receipt of your letter of acceptance, we will forward our recommendation to the school administration. Upon final approval by the Board, you will receive a formal contract.

We look forward to your association with Edwin Eden School and hope that we may soon hear from you affirmatively.

Very truly yours,

Margaret Dougherty, Chairperson
Department of Physical Education

Doris Lindsay
Director of Recreation

Jackson Toby
Director of Athletics

Enclosure

Figure 5.3. Letter of offer

Edwin Eden Community School

Contractual terms of appointment to be recommended to the Board of Education for:

Edwin Torres

Response requested on or before:	1 July 19XX
Title:	Equipment Manager
Department:	Physical Education/Recreation/Athletics
Percentage of Time:	Full-time — 40 hours/week
Salary:	$4.15/hour
Effective Date:	1 September 19XX
Expiration Date:	31 August 19XX

Figure 5.4. Contractual terms of appointment

Administrators at times will receive unsolicited requests for employment from individuals. Frequently these requests will arrive after a position has been filled or when no position is available. It is advisable, therefore, to maintain a standard form of response such as the one shown in Figure 5.6 that can be used for such occasions.

Dear _____:

We have carefully considered all applicants for the position of equipment manager at Edwin Eden Community School, and have recommended the appointment of Mr. Edwin Torres. Mr. Torres has a strong academic background and broad experience in the field and we are very proud that he will be joining the staff.

We would like to express our sincere appreciation for your interest in the position and wish you the very best of luck in your professional future.

Very truly yours,

Margaret Dougherty, Chairperson
Department of Physical Education

Doris Lindsay
Director of Recreation

Jackson Toby
Director of Athletics

Figure 5.5. Letter to unsuccessful candidates

Dear _____:

Thank you for your letter concerning (a) possible vacancy(ies) in the Department of Physical Education at Edwin Eden Community School.

At the present time, we have no vacancies in your area of expertise. As an Affirmative Action employer, however, we shall maintain copies of your application for two years in the event that any position should arise for which you are qualified.

Once again, thank you for your interest in Eden School.

Very truly yours,

Margaret Dougherty, Chairperson
Department of Physical Education

Figure 5.6. Form letter for unsolicited job applications

MORALE

The simple act of hiring outstanding personnel will not guarantee the success of a program. Unless all members of the professional and support staff are willing and able to devote their best efforts to the program, the results probably will be mediocre at best.

Morale is, in essence, the degree to which the members of a group are willing to work together for a common purpose or goal. Despite the acknowledged effects of morale on group effectiveness, many administrators overlook their own critical role or, worse yet, view it as a function of some uniformly applied recipe. They think that you simply can add three parts salary negotiations, one part working conditions, and one part positive feedback and out pops a happy, conscientious employee. Unfortunately this is not the case. Unless careful attention is paid to the deeper and less obvious factors in the process of human interaction, staff morale probably will remain low regardless of the attractiveness of the salary scale or the amount of praise accorded to each individual staff member.

Factors Affecting Morale

The development and maintenance of morale are dependent on the interplay of several principles of social psychology and group dynamics, a variety of job-related factors, and the nature of the group in question. Although it is unlikely that any of these are totally independent variables, they must be understood individually before they can be applied collectively.

Psychosocial Factors

George C. Homans explains social behavior in terms of several propositions and empirical statements that he draws from his own research and that of other social scientists.[1] These provide a structure through which an administrator can investigate and interpret virtually all forms of human group interaction. For the purposes of this text we shall examine Homan's propositions briefly and then apply them to the specific job-related factors that tend to exert a major influence on morale.

1. The more an individual's actions are rewarded, the more likely he is to repeat those actions.
2. The recurrence of the circumstances associated with a rewarded action make more probable a repetition of the successful action.
3. The greater value an individual places on the result of a particular action, the more likely she is to repeat that action.
4. The more frequently an individual has received a particular reward, the less value he is likely to attach to any further units of that reward and, therefore, the less likely he is to repeat the rewarded behavior.
5. When an individual does not receive an expected reward or receives unexpected punishment, she is more likely to become frustrated and more likely to act in an aggressive manner. Under such circumstances, the results of such aggressive behavior tend to be viewed as rewarding by the individual.
6. When a person's actions result in an expected reward, or the individual does not receive some anticipated punishment, she is more likely to be pleased and more likely to act in a positive manner. This is particularly true when the reward is greater than expected.

1. George Caspar Homans, *Social Behavior: Its Elementary Forms* (New York: Harcourt Brace Jovanovich, Inc., 1974).

7. In choosing between alternative actions, a person is likely to choose the one in which the value multiplied by the likelihood of success is greater. Action is, therefore, a joint function of success and value.

Homan's propositions rely heavily on the concepts of value and rewards. It should be remembered that, when applying these propositions to situations involving morale, the administrator must be concerned with those values that the employees in question perceive as being rewarding. The rewards that the administrator thinks employees *ought* to value are irrelevant.

Job-Related Factors

Salary and Compensation

There is no doubt that salary and other compensation-related issues have major effects on morale. In many cases, however, salaries are determined at a higher administrative level than that of the department chairperson or athletic director. Recreation directors generally are responsible for setting the salaries of their employees, but regardless of an administrator's role, she must see that staff members receive fair compensation for the work they do. When an administrator does not personally set the range of salaries, she must provide advice and guidance for those who do. If salary increases are to be forthcoming, they must be justified in terms of the cost of living, comparable salaries in the area, and most importantly, productivity.

Even if an administrator's influence in the development and implementation of salary guides is of a secondary nature, there are other matters of compensation over which he most probably will have more direct control.

1. *Equal compensation for equal work.* This is particularly true in the establishment of coaching salaries and in the development of compensation schedules for part-time employees such as an arts and crafts instructor, lifeguards, or trainers. Both moral and legal obligations exist to provide equity in this area. Whether the compensation is monetary in nature or takes the form of released time or both, the criterion for receiving compensation should be the type or quality of the work done or both.

2. *Merit pay.* Merit pay can be a source of tremendous dissatisfaction, if it is not carefully applied. Too often merit raises are accompanied by claims of favoritism and grievance actions by one or more of the non-rewarded candidates. One essential element in the establishment of a system of merit pay is a clear statement of the criteria on which it is awarded. One method of selection is to give all members of the faculty a list of the criteria for merit, and to have them list in rank order a specific number of persons whom they consider most deserving of the awards. The administrator simply collates the anonymous ballots and develops a ranking based on a point value for each relative position (e.g., five points for first, four points for second). In most cases, faculty accurately rate their peers and at the very least, recognize the fairness of the system.

3. *Nonfinancial compensations.* Sometimes compensation can be provided without changing an individual's salary. Extra secretarial assistance, released time,

increased or more convenient office space, or additional program assistants can often be strong rewards that serve the dual function of increasing program efficiency as well as raising morale.

Responsibility

Responsibilities for decision making and opportunities for leadership insofar as possible should be shared among all members of the faculty and staff. The more a person feels that he is responsible for the development or implementation of some integral segment of the program, the more likely he is to value and place a premium on the quality of his own performance and the success of the total venture. Simply stated, employees become ego involved when they feel that they have a piece of the pie. That some individuals, due to their particular abilities, gradually take on more responsibility and larger roles is inevitable. The opportunity however, for all to share in the decision-making or leadership process has proved to be a significant morale factor.

Autonomy

A wise administrator provides her personnel with a fair opportunity to achieve their potential. As professionals, most persons in an administrative group have clear ideas of how they can accomplish their jobs best. Some have had a great deal of experience in the area. In fact, some have more experience and a greater knowledge of their specific area of expertise than does the administrator. Treat these individuals like the experts they are. Reach agreement with them on desired objectives, and expect them to attain the objectives thus determined, but provide as much latitude as possible in the manner by which the objectives are achieved. Accountability and administrative control can be maintained through a formal reporting procedure that will occur regularly at intervals most appropriate to the task. This manner of developing autonomy is common practice in recreation departments, wherein the director establishes the basic policies and guidelines, but leaves the specifics of program development to those who must implement them.

Individual autonomy should be encouraged and supported within each administrative unit. Such practices not only improve morale but also help to develop among the staff a kind of possessiveness and attitude of involvement with the program that leads them to place a higher value on program success than might otherwise be the case.

Feedback

Along with the responsibility for making decisions regarding the program and the autonomy with which to carry out certain of those decisions, employees should receive feedback regarding the results of their efforts. Feedback goes beyond the traditional evaluations that are administered on some regularly scheduled basis and that are usually a function of the employment contract. Feedback is the provision of objective data and other information regarding process and product that lends itself to joint analysis and discussion by the administrator and the employee. This sets up further opportunities for shared decision making, while allowing the evaluation of performance in an atmosphere of mutual involvement and support.

In providing feedback, the administrator should take the approach of stating the observed element (for example, that 67 percent of the potential population registered for recreational tennis classes, or that 46 percent of the eighth graders scored below the 50th percentile on the PCPFS fitness test), and should discuss it with the appropriate persons in order to determine whether it constitutes a problem and what actions might be taken regarding it. This feedback process can and should be used on topics ranging from interpersonal relations to program results, and will result in a stronger feeling of sharing and involvement on the part of the entire organization.

The Nature of the Work Group

An atmosphere of acceptance, cooperation, and support among the members of the staff is absolutely essential to the success of the administrative unit. Too often, new staff members are "turned off" by the unwillingness of their senior colleagues to try new ideas or expend extra effort in the pursuit of professional excellence. Worse yet, hard work sometimes becomes the target of open derision. Most professionals have witnessed departments in which two or more factions are so busy jockeying for power that little or no productive work can be accomplished. Situations of this nature usually cause a high rate of turnover among the good members of the staff and result in a progressively deteriorating situation.

An atmosphere of acceptance and enthusiasm is essential. It must begin with the administrator and be felt and shared by each member of the staff. The more secure each staff member can feel in his own right, the more accepting and interested he can be in the professional efforts of his colleagues. If each person knows he performs a vital departmental role, in general he will be more willing to help and encourage others. This is particularly true when all parties realize that their roles are complementary, rather than mutually exclusive.

The congeniality and unity of the administrative unit most easily can be controlled through the hiring process. If new members are carefully selected for their ability to blend with and complement the group personality, and if care is taken to avoid unnecessary overlap among the skills and interests of the individual members of the group, the administrator can prevent many of the petty jealousies and role conflicts that become so difficult to remedy.

The Role of the Leader

One function of an administrator is to orchestrate separate factors into a unified program. He must be able to view the administrative group and the conditions under which it functions, and make whatever changes are necessary to develop the desired level of staff morale. Often this involves the skillful application of the principles of social behavior, or the modification of one or several of the conditions under which the group functions. One factor, however, cannot be negotiated and often cannot even be described fully, yet it is vital to the success of any administrative enterprise. The example set by the administrator gets at the very heart of personnel management. A loyal working team with sincere faith in its leader will rise above a multitude of technical administrative blunders. Without that kind of relationship, the administrative process can become a constant series of power plays, unpopular decisions, and arguments. In short, one can spend more time trying to justify authority than in exercising it.

Most of the personal qualities by which administrators are judged are controllable. Many seem to come naturally to successful leaders. All of them, however, are worthy of observation and should be cultivated.

Personal Dedication

Nothing succeeds like hard work. Nowhere is this more true than in the field of administration. Given the same personnel, facilities, and budget, some administrators orchestrate them into a harmonious unit, while others are forced to cope with a dissatisfied and underachieving work group. Often this problem can be traced to the personal dedication and diligence of the administrator. Most successful administrators arrive at work early, get their own work done efficiently and accurately, and give freely of their own time and efforts in activities of importance to the working unit. This kind of behavior leads to certain predictable responses from employees. For example, complaining about being overworked to an administrator who is working harder and longer than you are is difficult. Playing the martyr simply does not come easily under those circumstances. In fact, when the administrator is clearly dedicated to the unit, is willing to make sacrifices for the common good, and clearly carries her full share of the work load, the entire work group tends to try harder and mind it less. On the other hand, a lazy administrator who sits in her office and makes decisions affecting employees she seldom sees in circumstances that she barely understands will destroy employee morale more surely than pay cuts, equipment breakdowns, or any other factor.

Dedication cannot be claimed, promised, or discussed. It simply must be demonstrated in every aspect of one's administrative and personal life. It therefore must be sincere. If the administrator does not love administration and the type of activity for which she is responsible, she should find a different form of employment. The best she could hope for is mediocrity, and that simply is not good enough.

Courage

Not all administrative decisions are easy or clear-cut. Many times it will be necessary to make decisions that adversely affect someone or that place the decision maker under a great deal of pressure. The successful administrator must have the courage to withstand the pressure and accept the responsibility for all decisions, right or wrong, popular or unpopular. Every time an administrator yields to pressures or threats, he is allowing someone else to do his job. As soon as one staff member succeeds at this, others will try, and soon the administrator will merely be a pawn of other, more forceful individuals or groups.

Loyalty and Concern for the Staff

A good rule of thumb to follow in this regard is to see that the staff gets credit when things go well; when things go poorly, accept the responsibility. The administrator most certainly will want to discuss the matter privately with some or all the staff, but in public he should never allow the blame to fall anywhere but on himself. Administrators who pass the buck are usually unpopular with subordinates and superiors alike.

Loyalty and concern are usually the trademarks of a people-oriented administrator. Such persons honestly attempt to make the worklife of their employees more pleasant and productive. They show concern for individual, professional, and personal growth within the constraints of long-term unit objectives, and are willing to risk their own security to represent the feelings of their employees to higher administrative authority. Such behaviors on the part of the administrators usually result in similar feelings of loyalty and concern on the part of the entire work force and, hence, a uniformly high level of morale.

Communication

There must be an atmosphere of open, two-way communication between administrator and staff. Each must know what the other is thinking and feeling, if cooperation is to be maximized. Communication requires listening and asking, as well as telling. Sometimes the communication can take the form of a silent nod of approval, a few well-chosen words, or a lengthy session of listening to and discussing critical issues. One thing is certain, however. Where there is communication, opportunities for understanding and cooperation are increased.

How Much Morale Is Needed?

The fact that a strong relationship exists between morale and productivity is known to almost every administrator and employer. What is not so widely known, however, is the exact nature of this relationship. To assume that an increase in morale automatically yields an increase in productivity would be simplistic and inaccurate. In general, when work situations depend on a high level of interpersonal relations, a positive relationship does exist between morale and productivity. In situations where the work is more task-oriented, however, the reverse is true. It seems that the high levels of group interaction associated with high morale interfere with the direct time on tasks necessary for high efficiency and material output. The level of morale, therefore, that would be desirable in an accounting clerk whose primary duty is task-oriented paperwork would be lower than the level desired in a teacher or recreation supervisor whose productivity was heavily reliant upon successful interpersonal relationships.

Because the nature of human service professions such as teaching, coaching, and recreation requires an administrator to interact with a variety of persons, the wise administrator should make a conscientious effort to develop and maintain a high level of morale within his working group. Also, when hiring new staff members, he should give serious concern to the ability of the candidate to blend with and enhance this spirit of camaraderie and transmit her enthusiasm to others.

EVALUATION

Evaluation of subordinates is a universally accepted administrative task. It is accepted by virtue of the fact that administrators alone are held accountable by superiors and subordinates for the progress of an organizational unit. Clearly, individual basketball players are rarely, if ever, held accountable for a losing season. It is the coach to whom everyone turns for explanations. Consequently, administrators not only are assigned the duty, but they also are given the right to evaluate personnel in an effort to ascertain each person's effectiveness relative to organizational goals.

Briefly, the rationale behind a system of employee evaluation is based on the idea that effective appraisal of an individual's performance and future potential in the organization will improve his effectiveness on the job. It is believed, for instance, that the recreation leader who is appraised of his strengths and weaknesses and his potential for growth in the department can be expected to improve his performance; the understanding is that promotion might be the eventual outcome of such action.

Basically, the theory of performance evaluation rests on the assumption that employee motivation can be enhanced if the administrator:

1. Clearly outlines for the subordinate group the standards of performance that are considered acceptable by the organization.
2. Periodically reviews the performance of all personnel in accordance with the recognized standards of performance.
3. Individually shares this appraisal in a formal manner so that subordinates recognize the level of their work relative to the standards, and also relative, perhaps, to each other.

Although evaluation appears to be a rather simple and innocuous procedure, it is usually the most difficult of all administrative tasks to perform well.

The General Attitude About Evaluation

Evaluating a subordinate understandably is a task most administrators dislike, because the end result more often than not is conflict between themselves and their subordinates. The periodic review in its present form can be a devastating experience for both the subordinate and the administrator. "Subordinates often resent external evaluation, feel threatened by it, or become argumentative and contentious when they feel the evaluation is unfair, which they usually do."[2] No one likes to be told they are mediocre or ineffective, and very few individuals enjoy being the bearer of such bad news.

To avoid conflict many administrators acquire a nonchalance about evaluation. That is to say, they don't outwardly refuse to engage in the process, they simply engage in it superficially. They become proficient at writing noncommittal statements and glowing generalities. Wherever and whenever possible, they gloss over the truth and are less than candid with their subordinates. The basketball coach's complete lack of self-control with "bumbling officials," as he calls them, can be ignored in evaluations of his performance because he is a winner, and no one wants to upset the proverbial applecart. Similarly, the evaluations of a tennis instructor whose teaching tactics intimidate and demoralize youngsters can continue to be glowing, because no one in the community has complained.

2. Thomas Gordon, *Leader Effectiveness Training* (New York: Bantam Books, 1977), p. 238.

The Eventual Outcome

Minor grievances, however, have a way of becoming major abuses that cannot be ignored. Eventually, an administrator may be forced to act—the coach must be relieved, the tennis instructor replaced. The lengths to which the administrator has gone to avoid conflict may make the matter worse, and conflict may be inevitable, not only with the employee, but also with the entire subordinate group.

When an administrative action is delayed too long, action can come as a complete shock to the employee and the unit. Fears can begin to mount over suspected criticisms and future injustices. Eventually, the group can become enraged and take action to protect itself. The constant flow of communication between administrator and subordinate group is shut off, and the group provides only the information it believes will not intimidate its members or jeopardize their positions.

In such a case, the administrator's actions have completely defeated his purpose. Worse yet, he has lost one of the most important means of ascertaining the group's actions relative to organizational goals. Through his actions he has lost the ability to plan effectively.

Being nonchalant is not the way to avoid conflict, to ascertain the strengths and weaknesses of the organization, or to ensure the organization's healthy growth and progress.

The Traditional Methods of Evaluation

Conducted in the appropriate manner, the evaluation process can:

1. Foster personal growth
2. Improve group morale
3. Stimulate superior performances
4. Increase motivation
5. Identify the exceptional as well as the delinquent employee

This would appear to be no simple task. To ensure that these suspected benefits actually are attained, administrators over the years have constructed numerous evaluation systems. A review of many traditional evaluation systems reveals the following common themes:

1. *Evaluations usually are centered on job descriptions*—Job descriptions such as those described earlier in this chapter are usually the focal point of employee evaluation systems. They provide the basis for a standard of performance that is clearly visible to employee and administrator alike.
2. *Job descriptions are translated into a series of identifiable tasks*—An implicit contract exists between the administrator and the employee that defines the appropriate limits of what the administrator legitimately can demand of the position. Few would deny, for instance, that the athletic director would have stepped outside the bounds of legitimacy if he or she requested that the softball coach wash the team's uniforms after every game. If the administrative requests are restricted to what is considered legitimate, compliance is usually

automatic, and hence evaluation is appropriate. It is necessary, then, to translate the job description into identifiable tasks.

3. *A rating scale is superimposed on each task or job-related characteristic*—To standardize the process of evaluation, a rating scale is superimposed on each task or job-related characteristic such as loyalty or dedication. In this way the administrator has a means of evaluating the employee on each single item and of comparing his or her performance with others in the group.

4. *The evaluation process is standardized for all employees*—It is customary for the evaluation to be conducted at a specific point in time and in a specified manner so that it is evident to all parties involved that a formal appraisal of performance is being conducted. Many believe that this makes the system equitable for all involved.

5. *The rating is shared with the employee and other members of the administration*—A formal method of sharing the evaluation is usually devised for both the employee and other administrators who may be expected to use the information for further action (i.e., tenure, promotion, dismissal).

On cursory observation these themes would appear to form the basis of a fair and equitable means of evaluating a subordinate, a means that gets to the heart of the matter in an efficient and objective way and that can be conducted with little conflict. Closer examination reveals that this is not the case, and that clearly inherent within such an evaluation system is the potential for conflict, which so many administrators find repugnant and wish to avoid.

The bases for this conflict are pointed out by Gordon,[3] who has shown that:

1. Many job descriptions lack the necessary specificity to provide a clear delineation of the tasks expected of an employee. Room exists for considerable disagreement, therefore, regarding the performance or nonperformance of those duties.

2. Too many of the evaluated traits are ambiguous and open to widely divergent personal interpretation. Cooperativeness, creativity, and effort, for instance, are virtually impossible to define and delimit objectively, much less to evaluate.

3. Each administrator brings his own biases and opinions to the evaluative process. Therefore, different administrators are likely to produce a diversity of standards and relative ratings, even on similar or identical rating scales.

4. The "halo effect" or its negative counterpart, a continuing bad reputation, rarely can be avoided entirely.

5. Today's ratings are strongly influenced by tomorrow's effects. Initial ratings may be kept low so that there is "room for improvement." An individual may be downrated so that a future dismissal, if necessary, will be justified more easily.

Because the possibility of disagreements between the evaluator and the person being evaluated is tremendous, regardless of the tool or technique used, many people accept the path of least resistance. They attack only those deficiencies that are too great to ignore.

---

3. Gordon, *Leader Effectiveness Training*, pp. 239-240.

In short, traditional methods of evaluation tend to divert an administrator's attention. Instead of focusing on the laudable goals mentioned previously (such as stimulating superior performance, improving group morale, encouraging personal growth), the administrator's energies are diverted to a task that is dramatically opposed to her original purpose. The focus becomes one of finding and removing the weakest link in the chain. With this shift the administrator becomes a critic of an individual's work rather than one who assists a subordinate in achieving a superior level of performance.

A Matter of Perspective

The evaluation process does not have to be threatening or unpleasant, nor does the evaluator have to be a critic. With some changes in the present system, evaluation actually can be a means for stimulating superior performance through personal growth. It is all a matter of perspective.

If an administrator is forced into the role of a critic he eventually will come to believe that evaluations are conducted simply for purposes of deciding which coach gets rehired or which recreation leader is given a raise or is promoted. In so doing the process becomes rather arbitrary and capricious. The end result is that evaluations serve little purpose beyond providing the administrator with ammunition he can use to rehire or fire an individual. It is little wonder that from this perspective evaluation is viewed as a veiled threat by the employee, and as a distasteful task by the administrator.

By starting with the assumption, however, that the vast majority of professionals perform satisfactorily on the job, rather than the reverse, the administrator is freed from the role of critic. From this perspective it is no longer necessary to list and analyze employees' strengths and weaknesses to determine whether they are doing a satisfactory job, because it is assumed they are. This means that the department head no longer has to gather the shortcomings of the teaching staff for purposes of rank ordering their performance according to arbitrary shades of gray. Instead he can assist the individual members of the staff to become better teachers.

Using this perspective, the negative and damaging aspects of performance evaluation are eliminated. The administrator is free to create a nonthreatening atmosphere that can benefit both the organization and the individual. This perspective can be translated into a procedure quite easily.

The Evaluation Procedure From a New Perspective

There are two adjustments the administrator must make if she wishes to create an evaluation system that has the potential of making a positive impact on the employee and the organization.

Adjustment 1: Assume the Role of the Facilitator

Trust is an extremely important element in the evaluation process. If the employee does not trust the administrator it is highly unlikely that she will (1) place any credence in the opinion expressed in the evaluation, (2) provide the information necessary to do an accurate performance appraisal, or (3) abide by any of the recommendations. If the administrator wishes to create a trusting relationship between the subordinate group and herself, she must shed the role of critic and assume the role of facilitator. What this means is that the administrator must begin to perceive herself as one who assists an employee to perform at the highest possible level, not simply one who demands that performance.

Loosely translated, the administrator must help the employee set performance goals and then assist him to achieve them, perhaps by sending him to clinics or by rearranging a schedule or by helping him get into a graduate or specialty program. Whatever the case, the administrator must be geared to accelerate an employee's forward momentum, not to deter it.

Adjustment 2: Think Only in Terms of the Future

In keeping with the role of facilitator, the administrator must think in terms of the future rather than the past. Dwelling on specific aspects of past performance serves no other purpose than to create a situation that places the employee on the defensive. By thinking in the future tense one can help the employee formulate goals, thereby maintaining the administrative facilitator role.

Once the administrator has accomplished this mind-set (of playing the role of facilitator and thinking in the future tense), conducting the evaluation from a positive perspective becomes a simple task. The followng is an outline the administrator can use as a guide when initiating his own system.

Stage 1: Invite the Employee to Set Up the Ground Rules

Administrators receive their authority to act in a specific capacity from a higher administrative level. The power to perform the job he is authorized to do, however, usually comes from the subordinate group. This being the case it would appear that an evaluation system conceived by both the administrator and the subordinate group more likely would make an impact than one conceived by the administrator alone. In keeping with this idea the administrator should arrange a meeting with the employee in order to:

1. Familiarize the employee with the type of performance planning session he would like to conduct.
2. Explain that a rating based on past performance is not congruent with the perceived mode.
3. Identify his role as the facilitator.
4. Ask for input on the evaluation process. Determine those procedures that the employee feels would give him sufficient assistance to perform at a higher level.
5. Arrive at a final evaluation process that is mutually agreeable to the employee and administrator.

Stage 2: Define the Employee's Job in His Terms

Every job has a job description similar to the type constructed at the beginning of this chapter. While appropriate for recruiting purposes, the typical job description does not provide the detailed information needed to conduct a thorough evaluation.

If the administrator wishes to help the employee set goals that will provide direction and increase motivation, she must become familiar with the job as the employee perceives it. Therefore she should:

1. Discuss the formal job description with the employee, giving her perspective of each point.
2. Ask the employee to discuss each term in a descriptive manner, listing the specific responsibilities that must be assumed to comply with each demand in the job description. For instance, a typical statement in the job description of an equipment manager would be written something like this: "The equipment manager is responsible for the care, repair, and general maintenance of equipment."

    This statement provides a general description of what the equipment manager is expected to do, but it does not reflect the importance of conducting such a service. Rewritten in more descriptive terms the statement might read as follows: "The equipment manager must maintain all equipment in exc_llent operating order so that a maximum number of pieces are available to maximize participation in instructional classes, ensure the safety of the athletic teams, and provide increased recreational opportunities for those students who borrow equipment through the lending service."

    It becomes immediately apparent that the equipment manager makes a far greater contribution to the organization than one is led to believe by reading the statement in the job description.

    The administrator can help the employee describe her job in detail by asking "how" and "why" questions (such as "Why is that responsibility important?" or "Why do you give that job priority?" or "How do you meet these specific demands?").

    Another important aspect of reviewing the job description from the employee's perspective is determining what the employee feels the job *ought* to entail. Many times what the employee feels the job ought to entail and what it actually does entail are two different things. Realizing these differences the administrator may be able to resolve minor grievances before they have a deleterious effect on the employee's performance. This point is demonstrated in the case of the softball coach who was expected to maintain the practice field that her team used. In a review of the coach's job description it became apparent to the athletic director that a major portion of the coach's time was spent doing custodial work and that a number of accidents suffered by members of the team were the result of their helping the coach prepare the fields or from unsupervised horseplay engaged in while the coach was occupied with custodial tasks. It became apparent that these and other incidents that had led the athletic director to believe that the coach had little control of the team were, in fact, directly related to a responsibility that was an inappropriate extension of the coach's job description.
3. Rewrite the job description utilizing both the administrator's and the employee's perspective.

4. Using the job description, determine a set of performance standards. Both parties should contribute to this aspect of the planning by answering questions such as "How do I know when the job has been performed well?" or "What makes me think the job can be performed better?" A typical answer from a teacher might read: "I feel I've done a good job when my students are excited about learning or when they've acquired a new skill."

These statements must be converted to observable behaviors if they are to be useful. The comments made above concerning "excitement about learning" could be translated to the following observable behaviors:

Do all students participate on a regular basis?
Do the students come to the gym early so that they can play before class begins?
Do students linger after class is dismissed so they can practice what they've learned?
Do students request extra help so they can perfect a skill that was learned recently?
Do students ask to learn new skills?
Do students make a point of showing the teacher and others a skill they've just acquired?

These and other statements or questions help clarify what determines a "good job" in everyone's mind.

5. Determine goals based on the level of performance the employee hopes to attain in a specified period.

6. Determine a plan for helping the employee achieve the performance goals set in the previous step.

Stage 3: Meet With the Employee on a Continuous Basis

A plan to help the employee achieve her performance goals should include periodic meetings and casual contacts to determine the status of the plan. In other words, the administrator should meet with the employee not only to determine the employee's progress, but also to determine the effectiveness of her assistance in helping the employee to meet the goals. During these meetings the plan should be altered if necessary so that it remains a dynamic rather than static element in the employee's personal growth.

Evaluation is vital to an organization's growth, but it is only as effective as the administrator who uses it. A wise administrator will spend her evaluative energies improving the organization by helping the organization's personnel to improve, not by simply trying to weed out the weakest link.

How is a
budget developed?

What alternative
budgetary forms
can be used?

What type of
record keeping
is necessary
for sound fiscal
operation?

How can additional
sources of revenue
be developed?

Chapter 6

Financial Administration

We are living in a period of extreme cost consciousness. Spiraling inflation in the 1970s drastically reduced the purchase power of the dollar, thus greatly increasing the cost of developing and administering all forms of human service programs. Virtually every candidate for public office includes in his platform a promise to lower taxes and reduce governmental spending. Although all governmental and tax-supported programs have come under scrutiny, cost consciousness is particularly acute in the areas of sport, physical education, and recreation, as these often are considered to be discretionary areas or "frills." It is in these areas that the first cuts are often made. Recreational staffing is reduced; physical education requirements are eliminated, thus reducing staff and equipment needs; and many of the so-called "minor" activities are eliminated.

The problem is compounded by the rapid growth of fitness and sport clubs in the private sector. These facilities generally provide a narrow range of program options in a plush atmosphere for a high price. Such programs are acceptable for those who are willing to pay the type of membership and daily user fees that they charge. A paradox develops, however, when people begin to expect to see carpeted locker rooms and expensive training equipment in the same public programs that are suffering drastic cutbacks in budget and staffing.

It is essential that all administrators be extremely cost conscious. Like it or not, programming and finances are inextricably tied to one another. Neither can be accomplished fully without careful consideration of the other. Furthermore, administrators must realize that all decisions in these areas of necessity will be based on three types of factors: (1) administrative—functions of organization and finance, (2) technical—decisions based on the application of the body of knowledge in the field, and (3) political—questions regarding how each decision will affect the opinions of significant others.

Although a careful, cost-conscious approach to the manipulation of these factors does not necessarily reduce the effects of inflation or eliminate outside pressures for program reduction, it does allow one to take advantage of the administrative and political processes, as they exist, to maximize both the financing and the financial efficiency of individual programs.

Financial administration is a continuous process composed of the following four components:

1. Planning—program analysis and budget preparation
2. Authorization—presentation of budget to appropriate higher authority
3. Execution—application of budget to daily program operation through appropriate accounting procedures
4. Recapitulation—analysis and evaluation of this year's budget program with appropriate application to future planning

The execution of this year's budget of necessity occurs in the same time period as the planning and execution of next year's budget. Since recapitulation is an ongoing process, it tends to overlap all other phases. The overlapping relationship of the four phases may be seen in Figure 6.1. The degree of overlap and the target dates for the accomplishment of each phase depend on local guidelines. Most organizations and governmental bodies maintain their budgets on a fiscal year policy. The fiscal year runs from 1 July to 30 June, and during this period the execution phase of the budget is accomplished. In a fiscal year program, the planning and authorization phases for any given year have to be completed prior to 30 June.

OPERATING VERSUS CAPITAL BUDGETS

The **operating budget** provides a detailed analysis of the cost of administering a program for a given year. It is implemented during the execution phase of the financial management process and includes such items as salaries, equipment, supplies, rental and leasing costs, and advertising costs.

The **capital budget** is a separate budget containing long-term proposals for major items of equipment and construction projects. In general, the capital budget includes items that are of considerable expense, have an anticipated life span of several years, and require extraordinary funding procedures such as special fund drives, bond sales, borrowing, or long-term savings. Examples of items common to capital budgets would be a new swimming pool, an addition to an existing building, a new bus or van for departmental use, or the development of a new recreational area.

TYPES OF BUDGETS

There are three primary types of budgets in common use today: **line item**, **program**, and **zero-base**. Regardless of which type is employed, a factor known as incrementalism often plays a major role. That is, a tendency exists in many organizations to assume that any given program will be funded at essentially the same level as in previous years, and that the function of the proposed, or asking, budget is to justify any proposed increase in funding. The actual size of a year's increase or decrease is a

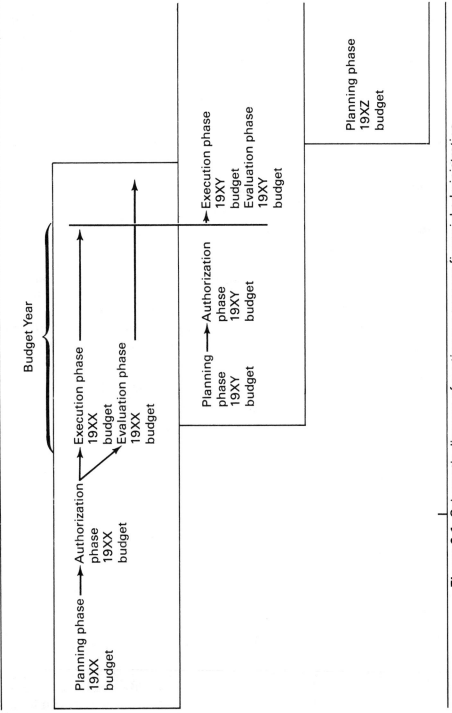

Figure 6.1. Schematic diagram of continuous process financial administration

function of several factors: (1) the total funding available to the granting authority and the relationship of these funds to those available in the previous year, (2) the size of the increase granted to the requestor in previous years, and (3) the percentage of last year's total budget represented by this year's increase.

Incrementalism tends to result in a gradually increasing budgetary base, but allows only minor or marginal changes in the total program. Although incrementalism simplifies the budgetary process and reduces the threat of major program cutbacks, because it is predicated on available resources rather than on program realities, it makes major program changes harder to justify on the basis of changing values and objectives. The administrator, therefore, runs a risk of developing a homogenized level of mediocrity and status quo.

Line Item or Object Class Budget

The use of line items or object classes is the oldest and still the most common form of budgetary organization. In it, all items of expenditure are grouped into specific, numerically coded classes and subclasses called line items. A specific dollar amount is then budgeted to each line item and the spending for that line item is limited to the amount authorized. An example of the object codes used in a line item budget may be seen in Figure 6.2.

A line item budget effectively focuses attention on individual expenditures, thus providing a very clear picture of the amounts programmed and expended within each budget category. It does not provide any illustration of the relationships between the expenditures and the program itself, however. It is often difficult, for instance, to determine from which aspect of the program (e.g., instructional programs, aquatics, open recreation) a given expenditure in object code 210, "Supplies," is being drawn. As a result, the administrator justifies the budget in terms of actual costs for specific items rather than on the value or anticipated outcomes of the program or both. Although on the surface this is an advantage for the administrator in that the specific costs of a given program need not be made known, nor must the program be justified in terms of cost-output relationships, budget cuts also are not directly attributable to programs and, hence, are sometimes easier to justify at higher administrative levels. In fact, if the approving agency is forced to impose budgetary reductions or to approve less than the amount asked, and if they wish to avoid the appearance of a substantial reduction in desirable programs, they almost are forced to apply the reduction to administrative and housekeeping expenses such as part-time salaries, overtime, maintenance, and advertising. In the long run, cuts of this nature can have an even more devastating effect on a program.

Program Budgets

In a program budget, expenditures are grouped according to departmental functions or programs. Separate budgetary categories might be established for such things as a tiny tots swimming program, football, or general administration as opposed to supplies, repair, advertising, and part-time salaries. Program budgets thus direct one's attention to programs and services rather than to individual expenditures, as is the

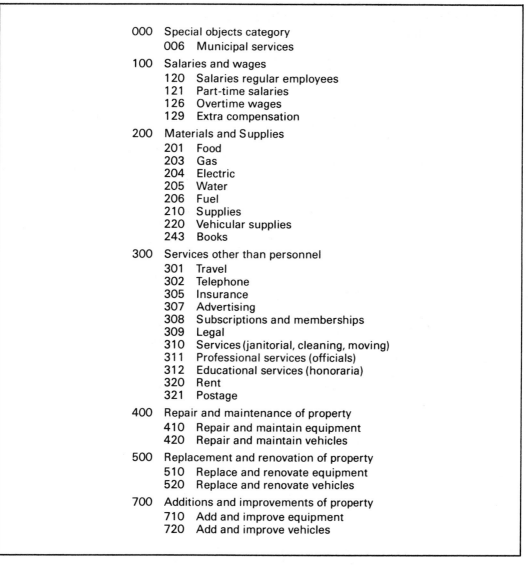

000   Special objects category
    006   Municipal services
100   Salaries and wages
    120   Salaries regular employees
    121   Part-time salaries
    126   Overtime wages
    129   Extra compensation
200   Materials and Supplies
    201   Food
    203   Gas
    204   Electric
    205   Water
    206   Fuel
    210   Supplies
    220   Vehicular supplies
    243   Books
300   Services other than personnel
    301   Travel
    302   Telephone
    305   Insurance
    307   Advertising
    308   Subscriptions and memberships
    309   Legal
    310   Services (janitorial, cleaning, moving)
    311   Professional services (officials)
    312   Educational services (honoraria)
    320   Rent
    321   Postage
400   Repair and maintenance of property
    410   Repair and maintain equipment
    420   Repair and maintain vehicles
500   Replacement and renovation of property
    510   Replace and renovate equipment
    520   Replace and renovate vehicles
700   Additions and improvements of property
    710   Add and improve equipment
    720   Add and improve vehicles

Figure 6.2. Object codes for expenditures

case with line item budgets. They provide a clearer picture of the manner in which the funds are actually used and are a better means of comparing costs with philosophy, goals, and results.

In developing a program budget, the administrator first identifies the major departmental functions and programs and then determines all the costs associated with each. The cost determination is frequently accomplished by developing a line item breakout for each program, thus combining the features of both line item and program budgets. The administrator thereby can examine line item costs within and among the various departmental functions while still retaining a clear picture of the total cost of each program (Figure 6.3).

200 Physical Fitness	
Equipment	$ 3,000.00
Supplies	500.00
Personnel	9,000.00
Maintenance	2,000.00
Utilities	1,000.00
Towel service	800.00
	$16,300.00
300 Instructional Programs	
310 Dance	
Records	$ 100.00
Instructor	1,000.00
Facilities	700.00
Equipment	300.00
	$ 2,100.00
320 Karate	
Instructor	$ 1,200.00
Equipment	1,000.00
Facilities	300.00
	$ 2,500.00
400 Open Recreation	
Personnel	$12,000.00
Equipment	500.00
Maintenance	2,000.00
Utilities	700.00
	$15,200.00
500 Sports Program	
510 Baseball	
Coaches	$ 2,700.00
Trainer	1,000.00
Equipment	2,500.00
Transportation	1,000.00
Field maintenance	700.00
Officials	1,000.00
	$ 8,900.00
520 Basketball	
Coaches	$ 2,200.00
Trainer	1,000.00
Equipment	1,200.00
Uniforms	1,500.00
Officials	1,000.00
Timers	350.00
Transportation	1,000.00
	$ 8,250.00

Figure 6.3. Planning phase budget sheet (program budget)

Zero-Base Budgets

The zero-base budget format was introduced in the industrial sector in the early 1970s as a means of avoiding the incrementalism that so often accompanied line item and program budgets. Since that time, it has gained rapid acceptance in both industrial and public administration and, unless replaced by a newer and better alternative, probably will become the norm in the near future.

In essence, zero base budgeting views each year's budget as an isolated entity. Each year, therefore, the entire budget must be planned and justified from ground zero. All of the primary functions and programs of the administrative unit must be described, analyzed, costed, and evaluated in terms of their output and achievement of accepted performance criteria. This process is referred to as the formulation of **decision packages** and is the first step in zero-base budgeting. Each decision package should include:

1. The purpose or goals of the activity
2. An explicit description of what is to be done and how it is to be accomplished
3. The costs and effects of alternative funding levels
4. Output or performance criteria
5. Alternative methods by which the stated purposes and goals can be accomplished

The key elements in the decision packages are the identification of the effects of alternative funding levels and the identification of alternative program approaches. Herein lies the primary difference between zero-base budgeting and all other formats. The identification of alternative funding levels provides a variety of options beyond the usual one of total approval or disapproval. The administrator must identify the effects not only of funding as requested, but also of no funding, reduced funding (usually five to ten percent), and increased funding (usually five to ten percent). Further, she must identify and evaluate alternative methods of accomplishing the same goals. The intent is to provide both professional and financial substantiation for the approach selected as well as to provide alternatives for the consideration of higher-level administrators.

The second major step in the development of a zero-base budget is the ranking or prioritization of the individual decision packages. The packages are normally ranked in order of descending value to the requesting organization. The priorities are consolidated and reordered at each subsequent level of budgetary authority in accordance with the needs and objectives of the total organization.

Although zero-base budgeting is clearly more complex and time consuming for the administrator than are the line item or program formats, it offers the distinct advantage of tying costs and financial adjustments directly to program goals and outcomes. Thus, the programmatic effects of budget reductions can be pinpointed. When the program is well managed, productive, and of a reasonably high priority, with zero-base budgeting one has a far greater chance of receiving adequate funding.

PREPARING AND PRESENTING THE BUDGET

Regardless of the format used, there are several general steps that are essential to the systematic development of a successful budget. Although the specific manner in which each of the following tasks is approached and presented may vary according to budget format and organizational policy, the value of each and, indeed, the order of their application should remain constant.

Reexamine Departmental and Organizational Goals and Purposes

A good budget outlines the programs and activities necessary to attain the stated goals and purposes of the organization. Just as it is illogical to expect an archer to hit a target that she cannot see and for which there is no reference point, it is fruitless to design programs without a clear understanding of the purposes for which they are designed and the results they are expected to achieve. Because organizational objectives can and should vary with experience, resources, and clientele, it is essential that they be reexamined before a budget is prepared. For a thorough analysis of goal setting and planning see Chapter 4.

Assess the Present Status and Departmental Programs

Before planning for the future, it is essential to have a clear understanding of one's present position and past performance. It is necessary, therefore, to identify each departmental program and function, to ascertain the present level of each in terms of costs and equipment, and perhaps most important, to evaluate the results of the program in terms of its contribution to departmental objectives. The cost analysis may be accomplished through an examination of cost and property management documents as well as previous years' budgets. The effects of the program should be determined in consultation with appropriate staff members and should be evaluated in light of the relative expense of the program as compared to other departmental projects of greater or lesser importance and magnitude.

Design Programs for the Budget Year

In planning the programs and functions to be accomplished during the upcoming budget year several factors should be considered:

1. Which of the present programs should be retained and which should be dropped?
2. Of those programs that will be retained, which ones should be modified and what modifications should be made?
3. Given the goals of the organization and the amount of financial support that can reasonably be expected in the coming year, what new programs or projects should be added?
4. What adjustments, if any, will be needed in the overall administrative and support structure of the organization?

A detailed discussion of program development may be found in Chapter 4.

Attach Costs

Many administrators begin their budgetary planning with this step. However, only through a careful process of program analysis and planning can an effective budget be developed.

In this step the administrator must estimate the cost of every aspect of the organizational mission. Because the programs and activities already have been determined, the administrator only needs to examine each program or activity in terms of its costs for such items as staff, equipment, and supplies. Probably the most effective way to accomplish this task is to view each program as a separate budget account and utilize a line item format to guarantee a thorough analysis of all possible expenses. Cost estimates should be based on past expenses and present costs, as reflected in catalog prices, salary scales, estimates of inflationary effects, and salary increments.

Examine Alternative Programs and Funding Sources

Regardless of whether an administrator is required to make a formal presentation of alternative programming possibilities, it is reasonable for him to assume that the question will be asked in some manner before final budgetary approval is granted. The wise administrator therefore will examine alternative approaches to the accomplishment of unit objectives. Is there a much less expensive program that offers almost as many advantages as the one proposed? Can responsibility be shared with another agency or department? Have all sources of additional funding been considered? Is there some way of reducing the cost of some particular program or project? A complete discussion of alternative funding sources is found later in this chapter.

Formulate the Written Budget

Once programs have been carefully developed and evaluated and the costs have been estimated, formulating a written budget can be a simple matter of following directions. Most organizations maintain budget manuals, which provide a standardized set of policies, instructions, and forms for use in the preparation of budgets. This manual should provide a detailed explanation of the required budget format as well as specific guidelines for the completion of all required forms. The primary issue at this step is one of written presentation.

Regardless of the format used, the fulfillment of several criteria will greatly enhance the quality of a budget and its likelihood for successful adoption:

1. The budget accurately should reflect the philosophy, priorities, and policies of the organization.
2. The budget should provide a detailed and realistic description of all proposed expenses and sources of income.
3. Prior to completion, the budget should be reviewed and analyzed carefully by key members of the unit staff.
4. The budget should meet all essential program requirements.

5. Cost estimates should be as realistic as possible. Budget padding and underesti-mation should be scrupulously avoided, as they serve only to give the total pro-gram less credibility.

6. Be sure that the budget allows some degree of administrative flexibility to deal with unforeseen emergencies.

7. Be sure that the professional staff has had an opportunity to provide input. Nothing is more embarassing than the discovery of major omissions or internal conflict after publication of the budget.

8. One program should not be expanded at the cost of another to satisfy a per-sonal interest or a highly vocal pressure group. Decisions of this sort should be based on a needs assessment, not personal inclination.

Present the Budget

Many organizations make provisions for formal hearings or presentations of the budget. This is a critically important step in which the administrator is required pub-licly to present and defend the purposes, activities, and accomplishments of her pro-grams as well as the costs involved. This procedure calls for thorough preparation, explicit information, and sound documentation. Even when formal hearings are not required, the wise administrator will arrange for an informal presentation with the advisory committee or granting authority or both. A program and the budget to support it are often better understood when the written presentation is reinforced verbally. Further, if the preceding steps have been followed in the formulation of the budget, then the hearing should be viewed as an excellent public relations vehicle. The better the preparation, presentation, and justification, the more difficult it will be for anyone to reduce funding levels.

Some general guidelines to remember regarding both formal and informal hearings include:

I. Prepare thoroughly. The administrator will be asked to answer questions regard-ing all aspects of the program and budget.

II. Be confident and decisive. If the administrator does not appear sure of the pro-gram, how can he convince anyone else?

III. Be sure that the written budget proposal is provided to all persons who will be present.

IV. If the hearing is to be a formal one, try to avoid a crowded agenda or one that contains highly emotional and controversial issues.

V. If the hearings are open to the public, be sure some supporters are in the au-dience. Most people only attend such hearings when they have an axe to grind. The result may be a skewed sampling of public opinion at a critical time.

VI. Use a logical format when making the presentation. Present the total picture but limit the boring facts. Your presentation could include the following elements:
    A. Department
    B. Purpose
    C. Goals
    D. Present progress in meeting goals

E.   Objectives for coming year
F.   Plan for meeting objectives
G.   Budget proposal
H.   Rationale
I.   Alternatives if budget is not funded
VII.   Use audiovisuals whenever possible to present major ideas.
VIII.   Do not make the mistake of restricting public relations efforts to formal hearings. An effective, ongoing program of public relations is one of the strongest weapons in the battle for funds. A complete discussion of the role and techniques of public relations may be found in Chapter 10.

THE EXECUTION PHASE

The execution phase of financial management takes place during the entire fiscal year, during which time the approved budget is applied to the daily operation of the department or unit. Although efficient budget control and application are officially administrative responsibilities, they can be accomplished only with the understanding and cooperation of the staff and the clientele. Unless there is total cooperation and input in such matters as planning, record keeping, and conservation, financial effectiveness and efficiency are severely restricted.

Maintaining Financial Records

During the execution phase the administrator needs to maintain an up-to-the-minute awareness of and control over the budget through the application of basic financial accounting procedures. Most large organizations, particularly those that are governmentally controlled, have financial policies that clearly spell out the accounting forms to be used. Regardless of the forms used, proper accounting should provide:

1.   An accurate record of all financial transactions.
2.   A representation of the pattern of all transactions with regard to programs or object codes or both.
3.   An effective means of transmitting information regarding the status of individual accounts to appropriate persons.
4.   An accurate form of documentation regarding organizational compliance with pertinent laws and regulations.
5.   A method of supervising expenditures to ensure compliance with budgetary limitations.
6.   An effective tool to be used in the analysis and evaluation of budgetary planning and fiscal procedures.

The two most commonly used accounting forms are **cost accounting** and **accrual accounting**. A cost accounting system requires the maintenance of separate records for each departmental program or activity that has been identified in the budget. This method is particularly appropriate for use in conjunction with a program budget format because it focuses attention on the cost of operating each individual program or service and as a result allows greater control as well as more obvious cost-benefit analysis.

Accrual accounting is by far the more common form and is used in most human service organizations. In an accrual accounting system a complete statement of expenditures is produced at regular intervals (usually monthly). These statements are often computerized and provide an immediate visual comparison of the budgeted sum, amount committed, and the amount actually expended for each budget category. The administrator can tell without any additional calculation how much money has been spent on salaries, equipment, telephone, or travel at any given point in time and how much of the budgeted amount remains to be spent in each category. See Table 6.1 for an example of an accrual accounting statement.

In addition to an accounting form that provides a means of summarizing financial transactions, the administrator also must employ a system for continual record keeping or bookkeeping. A general or daily expense ledger accomplishes this purpose, and provides a continuous sequential record of all transactions. Each entry minimally should include the budget account charged, the date, the nature of the transaction, the amount debited or credited, and the appropriate voucher number. The general ledger provides an accurate, up-to-the-minute record of the total departmental expenditures as well as an effective means for cross-checking the monthly accrual accounting statements. See Table 6.2 for an example of a daily expense ledger.

Table 6.1. Sample Monthly Account Report (Selected Budget Categories Only)

Object Code	Description	Purchase Order No.	Entry Date	Actual Payments	Commitment Balance	Amount Budgeted
210 Supplies			8/31	$ 517.43	$6524.03	$7041.46
	Duplic/Mailing	418507	9/02	10.00		
	A. Meeks Co.	702343	9/07	47.60		
	Atra Sporting Goods	702346	9/21	191.70		
	Lincoln Hardware	418512	9/21	29.66		
	BX Office Equipment	702343	9/22	188.00		
	Dance Record Co.	418508	9/24	8.96		
	EZ Athletic Equipt. Co.	418519	9/29	829.75		
	Object code total		9/30	$1823.10	$5218.36	$7041.46
304 Telephone toll charges			8/31	$ 72.64	$ 327.36	$ 400.00
	August charges		9/01	41.14		
	Object code total		9/30	$ 113.78	$ 286.22	$ 400.00
410 Repair and maintenance equipment			8/31	$ 48.03	$ 301.97	$ 350.00
	Object code total		9/30	$ 48.03	$ 301.97	$ 350.00

Table 6.2. Sample Daily Expense Ledger for Account No. 27-9587

Requisition Date	Requisition Number	Description	Income/Expense	Balance
				$3724.48
5/30	Q418597	Meeks Office Supplies	$ 36.55	3687.93
5/30	Q418598	Master Lock Co.	45.00	3642.93
5/30	765838	Vencil, Inc.	152.62	3490.31
6/3	Q418599	GBM Repairs	22.25	3468.06
6/4	765839	General Sporting Goods	876.51	2591.55

Selection and Purchase of Equipment

Supplies and equipment usually are purchased according to one of the three general procedures that follow. The procedure used for any given purchase is related directly to the dollar value of the expenditure. Although the exact ceiling cost of each procedure varies according to local law and organizational policy, the general framework tends to be relatively consistent.

Low dollar direct purchase items. Items in this category normally range from no cost to $50 or $100. Purchases of this type generally can be made directly from the vendor and require only the authorized signature of the responsible administrator.

Purchase from approved suppliers with approval. Items in this category normally range from $50 or $100 to $1000. These purchases generally can be made only from a list of approved vendors that usually is developed at the municipal or state level. These purchases also require approval from the next higher administrative or budgetary authority.

Purchases for which bidding is required. Competitive bidding usually is required on purchases that cost more than $1000. State and federal laws are very explicit regarding the necessity and procedure for gathering and selecting bids, and it is absolutely essential that any and all laws regarding competitive bidding be followed meticulously. Although all such laws clearly require that the contract be awarded to the lowest responsible bidder, the buyer is allowed to make the determination regarding the responsibility of the sellers with regard to their relative abilities to meet the terms of the contract. In some states such as New Jersey, however, the rejection of a low bidder for lack of responsibility requires that the rejected bidder be given formal notice and the opportunity for a hearing. It also should be noted that no state will allow the rejection of a low bid in favor of one that has been altered or modified in any way.

Regardless of the method by which a particular order is placed, the purchasing process can be divided into five basic steps:

Assess needs. This is a continuous process that is best accomplished through the maintenance of a perpetual inventory. Keeping a careful record of all equipment on hand, with appropriate postings each time new items are added or old ones are used up or must be replaced provides easy reference to the total quantities needed as well to the patterns of their use and replacement. In addition to the simple replacement of equipment and supplies, the administrator must plan for the needs of new programs and in addition must adapt quantities to the expected growth or decline in program enrollments.

Set priorities and timetables. At this point one must categorize all possible purchases according to need. Which are essential, important, nice to have, or unnecessary? Can any be constructed locally? When are the various items needed? Early buying or buying in quantity is best, but an administrator's ability to buy in bulk or in advance is directly related to the amount of storage space available. It is necessary therefore to develop schedules for ordering and receiving all items in order to combine maximal economic efficiency with the realities of use and storage.

Determine costs. The process of cost determination allows one to examine alternative brands, styles, and models prior to reaching a final decision regarding purchase.

Whether the items are to be purchased directly or placed on bid, certain elements should be observed:

1. Be explicit in the specification of requirements. Standardization of equipment throughout the department and purchasing from open stock can increase the efficiency of equipment use and reduce purchase costs.
2. Specify delivery requirements.
3. Determine whether substitute items will be accepted and how wide a range of substitution will be tolerated.

Review costs and place orders. While price is without question a major factor in the ultimate selection of both the equipment and the vendor, it is often not the main factor. Serviceability, ease of maintenance and repair, and most especially, the quality of the product cannot be ignored. Likewise, the reliability of the vendor is of prime importance. A bargain is not a bargain if it arrives two weeks after it was needed or if an unacceptable substitution is made and the discrepancy cannot be rectified in time for the scheduled use.

Carefully check, catalog, and store equipment as it is delivered. All deliveries should be examined immediately for shipping damage as well as for adherence to the ordering specifications. Any discrepancies must be documented and reported promptly and properly or any opportunity for correction may be lost. Newly purchased items should be marked and cataloged for identification and inventory and stored according to the manufacturers' recommendations.

SOURCES OF FUNDING

Physical education, intramurals, interscholastic athletics, and public parks and recreation programs are legitimate functions of the municipal government and, hence, are normally included within appropriate portions of the municipal budget and supported, at least in part, by tax monies. The exact amount of revenue that any given program can be expected to derive from these general funds will be a function of the total amount available and of the relative value ascribed to the program. Regardless of the support provided by general funds, most administrators will be compelled to seek additional sources of income to provide the best possible program. Even where the general funding is sufficient to meet normal budgetary needs, opportunities for the enhancement of facilities and programs through special funding sources must be given serious consideration.

Fees and Charges

Fees and charges are commonly assessed for a variety of privileges and services. Use of recreational swimming facilities or public golf courses, attendance at athletic contests, and participation in special instructional programs not directly associated with the school curriculum—all things considered to be outside of regular program efforts—are frequently subject to a user or entrance fee. Although the specific activities that are subject to charges and the size of the fees required vary greatly in accordance with state and local laws, several general guidelines should be followed:

1. Develop an organizational philosophy with regard to fees and charges. Is the purpose to increase revenue, meet expenses, encourage more regular attendance, or something else?
2. Establish and follow a clear set of policies. Will all activities be subject to a fee? Should all persons be charged equally? Will discounts be available? See Chapter 4 for a discussion of policymaking and its relationship to philosophy.
3. Be sure that all policies and procedures for the collection, utilization, and recording of fee income are in strict accordance with local and state laws and regulations.

Concessions

The term **concessions** generally is used to refer to all individuals or groups, not affiliated with the program, who are allowed to sell merchandise or services on public property in return for a fee. This fee is usually either some agreed upon percentage of the income from the concession or a flat fee. Among the more common forms of concessions are: vending machines in school and recreational facilities, refreshment stands at athletic contests, and the provision of golf carts at public courses. Concessions, like fees and charges, should be based on a philosophy and should adhere to carefully defined policies. Special consideration should be given to such things as the nature and terms of contracts, conditions for renewal, the roles and responsibilities of all parties, and the nature and type of concessions that will or will not be allowed.

Gifts and Endowments

Gifts in the form of money or property sometimes are provided by interested persons or organizations. Although such occurrences can be tremendous financial windfalls for a program, the gifts are frequently earmarked for a specific program or capital project and therefore carry restrictions as to their use. Before accepting such a gift, any and all restrictions must be clearly understood and investigated to guarantee both the willingness and the ability of the recipient to meet all conditions. A gift of $1000, for instance, if it were given on the condition that it be used to construct a new swimming pool on land that is presently the object of a matching fund grant, may not be acceptable.

Endowments usually are established in the form of a trust fund, the income from which is made available for specific uses. Again, all restrictions must be observed faithfully and thus should be carefully investigated.

The administrator should be alert to every possibility for the encouragement of gifts and endowments. In seeking to develop such opportunities, he may wish to emphasize the positive effects of gifts or endowments on programs, their tax advantages, or the possibility for creating a lasting memorial to some person of merit. Alternative sources of funding can help alleviate the pressure on a shrinking budget, but they also can pose problems. If an administrative unit were given a building in the form of a gift, for instance, the administrator would need matching monies to operate the facility. Without such additional funding, the building would be a white elephant. Caution is probably the best advice when deciding whether to accept alternative sources of funding.

Bond Issues

Federal and state laws allow individual towns and cities the privilege of issuing interest-bearing bonds to all interested investors through standard commercial brokers. All bond issues must be earmarked for specific capital projects and must be authorized by public vote or legislative act. Because each state imposes limits on the total debt that any given municipality may accrue at any one time, there is a great deal of local selectivity in the development of bonded projects. All governmental functions in essence are competing for a limited number of opportunities over an extended period of time. Careful planning and extensive justification are critical elements for success.

Grants

The federal government, most state governments, and an increasing number of private business and philanthropical organizations have programs of grants-in-aid to schools, recreation departments, and municipalities for a wide variety of uses. Some grants require the provision of matching funds by the recipient, and all demand careful justification and rigid adherence to explicit application procedures in order to qualify for an award.

There are a wide variety of funding possibilities. One such possibility involves governmental funding for the acquisition and development of public lands. Other possibilities include assistance from the private sector in the development of jogging and exercise trails or the provision of extensive curricular materials by numerous health-related organizations.

The wise administrator must keep abreast of all funding possibilities through careful and constant review of governmental and professional publications.

Although not intended to be exhaustive, the list in Table 6.3 illustrates the variety of funding and materials available through grant sources.

Table 6.3. Sources of Federal Grants

Federal Programs That Provide Grants	Purpose of Grants			
	Land Acquisition	Development of Facilities	Operation and Maintenance	Planning
U.S. Department of Agriculture				
Community Planning Service				X
Conservation Operations				X
Resource Conservation and Development	X	X		X
Small Watershed	X	X		X
Recreation Facility Loans	X	X		X
Food Service for Children			X	X
Urban and Community Forestry				X
Essential Com. Facilities Loans		X		
U.S. Department of Commerce				
Coastal Zone Management				X
Public Works and Economic Development		X		X
U.S. Department of Defense				
Corps of Engineers Planning Assistance				X
U.S. Department of Health, Education and Welfare				
Environmental Education		X	X	X
Office for Handicapped Individuals				X
Older Americans Act		X	X	X
Community Education				X
Rehabilitation Services		X	X	X
U.S. Department of Housing and Urban Development				
Community Development Block Grants	X	X		
Comprehensive Planning Assistance "701"				X
U.S. Department of the Interior				
Land and Water Conservation Fund	X	X		X
Urban Park and Recreation Recovery Program		X	X	X
Historic Preservation Grants-in-Aid	X	X	X	X
Technical Assistance — HCRS				X
Federal Surplus Property for Parks and Recreation	X			X
Technical and Professional Assistance — NPS				X
Young Adult Conservation Corps			X	
Youth Conservation Corps			X	
National Environmental Education, National Environmental Study Area, National Environmental Education Development				X

continued

Table 6.3/continued

Federal Programs That Provide Grants	Purpose of Grants			
	Land Acquisition	Development of Facilities	Operation and Maintenance	Planning
U.S. Department of Justice Juvenile Justice and Delinquency Prevention			X	X
U.S. Department of Labor Comprehensive Employment and Training Act (CETA)			X	X
U.S. Department of Transportation Bicycle and Pedestrian Facilities in the Federal Aid Highway Program	X	X		X
ACTION Retired Senior Volunteer Program The Senior Companion Program			X X	
Appalachian Regional Commission Community Development Grants	X	X		
Community Services Administration Summer Youth Recreation			X	X
Environmental Protection Agency Clean Water Act	X		X	X
National Endowment for the Arts			X	X
President's Council on Physical Fitness and Sports				X

What are the
steps in the
process of facility
development?

How can the
administrator
obtain community
support?

Who should be
involved in the
planning process?

What are the
operational
considerations
in facility
management?

What kinds of
policies are
needed?

Chapter 7

Facility Development and Management

FACILITY DEVELOPMENT

An administrator may go through an entire career without being involved in the development or renovation of a major indoor or outdoor facility. On those occasions when such involvement becomes necessary, extensive assistance is required and available in the form of expert consultants and skilled architects. Although detailed literature is in abundance concerning this subject, building materials and structural concepts are developed and modified so rapidly that the administrator cannot hope to develop and maintain the level of expertise necessary to function effectively without professional aid. Further, because each situation presents its own set of needs, resources, and geographic variables, no single set of criteria can be applied to all types of facilities in all circumstances.

Successful facility planning requires the coordinated efforts of primary decision makers, secondary decision makers, and definers. **Primary decision makers** are those persons who must shoulder the major decision-making responsibility for any given unit and are aware of all facets of the operation. **Secondary decision makers** are persons who are asked to exercise professional judgment with regard to elements of the facility in question. **Definers** are persons who are selected to represent the ideas and interests of the major groups that will be using the facility. Definers may or may not be participating members of such groups, however. For instance, if a tennis facility were being constructed for school and community use, the primary decision makers would include the physical education administrator, the recreation administrator, and the athletic administrator. Secondary decision makers would include coaches, supervisors, teachers, and support staff. The definers might include representatives of selected recreational leagues or instructional programs. In many cases persons with particular expertise in the area such as a local tennis professional, the manager of a highly successful tennis facility, or a representative of the United States Lawn Tennis Association also might be asked to serve as definers.

The primary and secondary decision makers and the definers are called on to interact at various points in the planning process. The primary decision makers are called on to coordinate the entire project. Secondary decision makers may provide general advice as well as share in selected administrative elements such as data collection or design evaluation. The definers generally are called on to provide feedback regarding proposals and problems and to serve as liaisons between the decision makers and the community. This interaction is accomplished best through a series of carefully defined steps.

This section presents those steps that are essential to the successful planning and development or major renovation of any facility regardless of its size, location, or intended use. These steps usually are accomplished in concert with a professional consultant, and are presented here so that the administrator will be better able to initiate and coordinate the project effectively and to utilize the resources at her disposal productively.

Projection of Needs

The first step in the process of facility development is a careful and accurate assessment of the present and future facility needs of the program. General questions to be investigated at this point are listed in Table 7.1.

The answers to questions such as these should provide a framework within which specific needs can be projected and evaluated. The process at this point takes the following form:

1. Given the constraints of the master plan, local climate and geography, the socioeconomic level of the clientele, and future program projections, what type of facilities are needed?
2. Given the demographic projections, how many people will the programs and facilities be required to serve? How are they likely to be divided in terms of such variables as age, sex, ability, and socioeconomic group?

Table 7.1. Outline for Needs Assessment

Question	Sources of Solutions
What does the master plan call for?	Municipal or school master plan or both
What are the future program projections?	Staff consultation—review of trends in other parts of the country, journals, research, and commercial ventures
What are the demographic projections for the target populations?	National and state census data and local planning board projections
What are the needs and desires of the clientele?	Open forums, zoning board rules and regulations, and projections from trends in the commercial sector
What are the projected administrative and staff needs?	Assess the present skills of the staff and the community support for the delivery system—assess growth potential

3. Given the proposed program developments, what facilities will be necessary to house the staff and provide the necessary ancillary services?
4. What level of funding will be required in order to meet the facility needs thus outlined?

Asset Analysis

The future cannot be dealt with effectively in the absence of a clear picture of the present. What facilities are presently available to the program? What other commercial, private, or municipal facilities are available to the community? How many people can the facilities reasonably be expected to serve? What is the condition and projected life span of the present facilities? What funds are currently available for capital projects? What level of support reasonably can be expected to be provided by the community? An example of the checklist to assist in the task of facility analysis is presented in Table 7.2.

Comparison and Synthesis

Having outlined both the future needs and the present assets of the organization, the administrator more simply and more accurately can project the specific facility development program. The question is, in what ways does the present base fail to meet the projected needs? The answers to this question will provide a reasonably clear picture of the nature and size of the facilities to be planned as well as a general idea of the functions that the facilities must serve.

Develop Policy

To plan a facility properly, one first must determine the purposes that it will be required to serve. A preliminary policy therefore needs to be developed regarding the use of the facility. Chapter 4 contains an explanation of policy development and the importance of this procedure in any administrative task. Specific policies that must be determined while planning new facilities include: Who will be the primary users? What types of activities will receive scheduling priority? What types of special events will be conducted? How will the facility be funded? Will there be user fees? To what degree must the daily operation of the facility be self supported?

Information and Feedback

Public information programs, such as those using information circulars, and personal contact with various constituent groups provide excellent means of gaining public input to the planning process, and help to ensure the development of the support that is critical to the success of the project. Information and feedback programs should be conducted at specific intervals in the planning process in order to ensure responsiveness to community needs and to encourage public support. The definers are an excellent starting point for the dissemination of information and also can serve to express the ideas and thoughts of their constituent groups to the appropriate decision makers.

Table 7.2. Facilities Survey and Evaluation Chart

Space Surveyed or Specific Features Within the Space	National Standard as Applied to the Situation Surveyed		Sq. Ft. or Number We Have	Percent of Standard We Have		Percent of Standard We Need		Amount or Number We Need to Meet Standard		Conclusions — Our Space Is:				Remarks
										Adequate		Inadequate		
	Now[a]	Future[b]		Now	Future	Now	Future	Now	Future	Now	Fut.	Now	Fut.	
Examples														
Girls' locker room[c]														
1. Area	2400 sq. ft.	3000 sq. ft.	1800 sq. ft.	75%	60%	25%	40%	600 sq. ft.	1200 sq. ft.			✓	✓	
Boys' shower room[d]														
1. Shower heads	33	40	22	67%	55%	33%	45%	11	18			✓	✓	
2. Walls	Smooth impervious material	Tile	—	—	—	—	—	—	—	✓				
3. Additional features, etc.														
Tennis courts[e]														
1. Number	20	25	12	60%	48%	40%	52%	6	13			✓	✓	
2. Fencing	Rear: 12 ft. high; Sides: 10 ft. high	All 12 ft.	—	—	—	—	—	—	—	✓				
3. Additional features, etc.														
Softball fields														
1. Number	No present national standard		2	—	—	None	—	—	8	✓			✓	Added future enrollment
2. Size (each)	275' x 275'		Each 310' x 300'	100%	—	None	—	None	—	✓				
3. Additional features, etc.														

[a]Now = Present program and enrollment

[b]Future = Projected program and enrollment

[c]National standard: 20 sq. ft. per student at peak load
Example: Now — 120 students x 20 sq. ft. = 2400 sq. ft.
Future — 150 students x 20 sq. ft. = 3000 sq. ft.

[d]National standard: 10 shower heads for first 30 people, 1 head for each additional 4 people at peak load
Example: Now (120 students) for first 30 = 10 heads
$120 - 30 = 90 \div 4$ = 23 additional heads
= 33 total shower heads
Future (150 students) for first 30 = 10 heads
$150 - 30 = 120 \div 4$ = 30 heads
= 40 total shower heads

[e]University national standard: 1 tennis court per 400 students of applied student population
Example: Now — $\dfrac{8000 \text{ students (a.s.p.)}}{400}$ = 20 courts
Future — $\dfrac{10{,}000 \text{ students (a.s.p.)}}{400}$ = 25 courts

Develop a General Plan

The general plan sets forth the basic needs and requirements that must be met by the facility. Properly set forth, the plan will serve as a very effective tool in the process of selecting an architect as well as in the later development of schematic diagrams and working drawings. The general plan is developed by the primary decision maker and represents his professional judgment based on input from the secondary decision makers and the definers with regard to the types of activities that will be conducted in the facility, the number of people served, the number and type of activity areas or teaching stations, the nature and quantity of service areas, and specific requirements with regard to security, safety, and supervision. An example of a general plan for a multipurpose recreational facility is presented in Appendix 2.

Select an Architect

The architect will be required to interpret the organization's needs and requirements, as put forth in the general plan, to integrate them into the design of the facility in a functional and aesthetically pleasing manner, and to do so within the financial constraints imposed by the proposed funding policy. In selecting an architectural firm, seek one that is experienced in the development of facilities for sport and recreation. Visit and observe first hand other facilities that the firm has designed. Make personal contact with other clients for whom it has designed facilities to gain further insight into the quality and effectiveness of its work. Before deciding, share the general plans with the candidates and ask them for feedback. What are their reactions? Do they seem to understand the organizational needs? Will they plan a facility to meet these needs or will they be governed by their own desires and opinions? Do they think that they can work within the constraints imposed by the funding program? What is their past record with regard to cost estimation and budgetary overruns? The answers to questions such as these may provide great insight into the selection of the person or persons who will ultimately play one of the most critical roles in the development of a new facility.

Develop a Schematic

A schematic is a graphic representation of the relationships between the major components of the new facility. The schematic should be developed in consultation with the architect and in general terms should consider such factors as the location of the facility, the type of building proposed, the nature and general size of the various components of the facility, the relationship of these components to one another in terms of location and traffic flow, and a preliminary cost analysis.

Information and Feedback

The information and feedback process should continue informally throughout the preliminary development phases.

Develop the Design

The architect develops the general design on the basis of the general schematic and the expressed needs of the organization. The preliminary design would include specifics with regard to site development, building design, and cost analysis. At this point the architect would submit drawings that clearly depict the size, relationship, and aesthetic qualities of the interior segments of the facility, as well as the structure and appearance of the exterior. In reviewing the design, consideration should be given to such factors as aesthetic quality, utility, ease of supervision, efficiency, ease of access, economy of space and resources, flexibility, and future growth potential.

Information and Feedback

The design phase generally includes the last formal feedback session, and, if all has gone well, should result in a strong expression of support from all decision makers, as well as from the definers who will represent the views of the public.

Develop Working Drawings and Specifications

The working drawings developed by the architect should provide total detail regarding the facility. They should provide specifications for every aspect of the proposed construction, and should enable contractors to submit accurate bids and construct the facility in the specified and agree-upon manner. Checklists that have been established for the evaluation of construction plans for various types of athletic facilities and service areas are included as Appendix 3 and Appendix 4.

Monitor Construction

The architect should monitor all phases of the construction process carefully in order to guarantee strict adherence to the agreed-upon standards. In addition to the architect's efforts, one or more professionals from the staff should be assigned to monitor the progress of the construction to catch any potential deviations or problems.

FACILITY MANAGEMENT

Administrators must bear the primary responsibility for the manner in which facilities are used. They must be prepared to deal with leaking showers, broken backboards, overflow crowds, scheduling conflicts, and myriad other problems that call for efficient and judicious action.

Unfortunately, no one yet has devised an effective system to eliminate problems. As long as one deals in a human service profession, and as long as there is some degree of dependence on facilities and equipment, uncontrollable variables and problems will occur. The wise administrator, therefore, will attempt to eliminate as many problems as possible, while taking steps to minimize the disruption caused by those that do occur. In facility management, this can be accomplished best through the application of a carefully developed set of policies and procedures.

A policy is a selected course of action to be followed in a particular situation. The administrator is permitted a certain degree of latitude or freedom of choice in the specific implementation of a policy. A procedure, on the other hand, is an interpretation of policy that explicitly designates the manner in which the policy is to be implemented.

Many municipal swimming pools, for instance, have established a policy that only residents of the community may gain admission to the facility. The procedures by which this policy is implemented could vary from the presentation of a driver's license or other verification of address on each admission, to the issuance of a full season badge to all residents who request one, or to any other reasonable means of implementing a residents-only policy.

The development of policies and procedures is the responsibility of the primary decision makers. Although many policies for the utilization and management of facilities will be developed in the pre-construction phase, program development and revaluation almost certainly will necessitate some degree of modification. The wise administrator will maintain close liaison with secondary decision makers and definers to assure the applicability and acceptance of new or modified policies and procedures. The relationship between the primary and secondary decision makers and the definers is shown in Figure 7.1.

Secondary decision makers shoulder a major portion of the responsibility for the implementation of policies and procedures. Their proximity to the firing line makes them an invaluable consultation source in the development process. They should have a first-hand sense of the importance of proposed policies, as well as a feeling for the type of procedures that will implement policies best.

Definers tend to view the situation from the perspective of clientele and very often will act as a pressure group to generate the development or change of particular policies and procedures that they consider to be ineffective or unpopular. Their views merit careful consideration and thoughtful discussion, as their support is vital to the ultimate success of the program.

Procedures for the Management of Facilities and Equipment

Chapter 4 contains a description of the process by which an organization's objectives are translated into policies and procedures. The most important thing to remember in policy development is that a policy is a selected course of action that makes it possible for an organization to achieve its goals in a manner that is consistent with its philosophy.

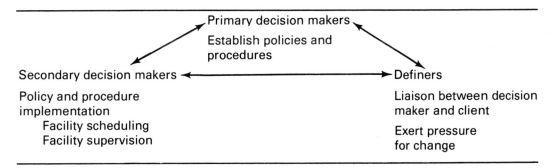

Figure 7.1. Relationships among primary decision makers, secondary decision makers, and definers

Although no set of policies would be applicable to all administrative situations found throughout the country or would take into account all situations that might give rise to the need for a policy, one can outline specific areas of facility management that almost certainly will require the development of policy. Remember, however, that all policies must be reflective of organizational goals.

What Is Available?

Before the administrator begins to outline specific policies for the utilization of facilities and equipment, he must have a clear statement of what is available and the general functions that the facilities and equipment are expected to serve.

Who Is Responsible?

Perhaps the most critical concern in facility management is the question, "Who is in charge?" The answer to this question varies with the particular function or level of supervision concerned. A number of individual policies therefore must be developed to answer questions such as the following:

Who exercises primary administrative authority?
Who assumes responsibility during normal use?
What kind of supervision is required?
Who plans and implements security?
Who is responsible for normal maintenance and repair?
Who is responsible for special repairs and renovations?

Who May Use the Facilities and Equipment?

The administrator almost certainly will be inundated with requests from every conceivable type of group and organization for use of any reasonably desirable facility. Without an established policy, decisions regarding the approval or disapproval of such requests are likely to be inconsistent and open to criticism and complaint. A clearly stated policy, on the other hand, should reduce the number of inappropriate requests and should provide a consistent means of dealing with those that are received. Questions to be answered include:

What classes of individuals or groups are eligible to use the facility?
What purposes or types of activities may be served?
What is the order of priority for use?
Who may use what equipment under what circumstances?
What is the policy regarding reservations?
    Who may make reservations?
    May the facilities be reserved for profit making functions?
    What is the procedure for application and approval?
    What special supervision is required?
    What are the restrictions regarding set up and clean up?
    Will there be fees or charges?

Will there be a policy regarding fees and charges for normal use?
What special provisions must be made for crowd control?

What Provisions Must be Made for Maintenance and Upkeep?

Everyone who uses facilities and equipment must accept a certain responsibility for their maintenance and upkeep. To that end, a few policy questions should be considered:

What provisions should be made for general policing?
    Who will do it?
    How often?
What are the general responsibilities of the maintenance staff?
How does one initiate a request for other-than-normal maintenance and repair?

Procedures

As stated earlier, a procedure is an interpretation of a policy that specifically defines its manner of implementation. For many of the policies that she develops, the administrator should establish one or more specific procedures by which it will be implemented. A policy that permitted a facility to be used by students and faculty only, for instance, might be implemented by a procedure that required the presentation of a valid identification card at the door prior to entry. This policy also might be implemented by a procedure that restricted facility use to the hours of the normal school day. Such procedures should relate directly to the organizational policies and should result in the most effective and efficient use of the facilities and equipment in question.

Although the majority of procedures are designed to facilitate the implementation of specific organizational policies, procedures are of value whenever the situation calls for consistency of action. Most notable among these situations are those that carry the potential for a great deal of public dissatisfaction with the program but over which the administrator has no direct control. At Lindsay Community Center, for instance, such a problem arose virtually every time the facility was in need of some type of repair. The director of recreation, as the individual with scheduling and supervisory authority, immediately would notify the maintenance department, which had the responsibility for all repair work. It then would take anywhere from two weeks to two years for the maintenance department to complete the requested repairs, during which time the recreation offices continually were bombarded with staff and client complaints. When constant follow-ups and secondary requests proved to no avail, a more direct set of procedures was adopted:

1. All needed repairs were to be reported by work order to the office of buildings and grounds within 24 hours of discovery or notification.
2. A prominent sign would be placed next to the facility in need of repair, stating the date on which the need was reported and giving the telephone number of the office of buildings and grounds as the number that interested persons should call to address any questions or comments.

As a result of this procedure two important things were accomplished. First, the recreation office no longer was forced to take the criticism generated by the inefficiency of another organization. Second, and in many ways more importantly, the increased pressure created by the procedure resulted in a shorter lag time between the reporting of a problem and the ultimate repair.

Thoughtfully developed and skillfully implemented policies and procedures are essential to the efficient management and control of facilities and equipment. Without them, administrative efforts, no matter how well intentioned, almost certainly are characterized by inconsistency, the absence of a clear relationship between goals and actions, and a great deal of adverse public reaction.

What are the
critical components of
a computer system?

How can the computer
be used to improve
operational efficiency?

How can computer
technology be applied
to instruction and
management?

How can the computer
assist in the management
of finances, personnel,
and facilities?

What special
administrative
considerations are
necessary in the use
of electronic data
processing?

Chapter 8

Computer Utilization

by John H. Holloway

The processing and storage of information are tasks common to all administrators and managers. The operations involved in these tasks are routine, repetitious, and in most cases cumbersome. Nevertheless, because of the increasing number of regulations mandated by federal, state, and local agencies, and because of the need for information that is inherent in the duties of management, many forms and quantities of data must be sifted, sorted, and retrieved by administrators on a daily basis. To maintain effectiveness the administrator must take advantage of suitable techniques to control this flood of information.

THE ELECTRONIC DATA PROCESSING SYSTEM

In most instances, the information needed to manage a successful program no longer can be maintained simply by utilizing clerks, filing cabinets, and adding machines. In today's fast-paced, fluid society these techniques are neither cost effective nor practical. The administrator, whether in the public sector or in private industry, must be totally aware of and committed to more advanced practices and concepts. The purpose of this chapter is to examine the applications of one system of information management—electronic data processing (EDP).

Using machines to process and store data is not an entirely new technological concept. This practice was introduced in 1880 by the United States Census Bureau. At that time a simple device was developed to collect and store population counts based on sex, age, and other vital statistics of the nation's inhabitants.

Mechanical processing technology grew slowly during the 60 years that followed. However, in the early 1950s the first commercially successful EDP device, known as the computer, was developed. Although computer science and EDP technology have grown in an almost geometric progression since the inception of these machines, the basic theory of the system remains unchanged.

A computer system is composed of four functional components. If EDP is to be an effective management tool, the manager or administrator first must understand each of these components. He or she must be familiar with the basic vocabulary of the science, and also must be cognizant of the uses, capabilities, and purposes of each component of the system. These four components are the **central processing unit**, **memory**, **input**, and **output**.

Central Processing Unit

The heart, or more appropriately the "brain," of the EDP system is the central processing unit (CPU). This component is responsible for the actual manipulation of data. When properly directed it is capable of performing tasks such as arithmetic operations at speeds approaching one-billionth of a second. In addition, the CPU is capable of storing data and the instructions for the processing of these data. The instructions are called computer programs, and will be described later in this chapter.

Memory

The second functional component of the data processing system is memory. As stated above, the CPU is capable of storing data (memory) on a temporary basis until it can be processed.

There are two primary types of memory, RAM and ROM. RAM, or Random Access Memory, is the amount of storage space provided within the computer for the task at hand. In essence it is your workspace. This workspace must be sufficient to run the program being used, as well as to manipulate and retain the data generated. All data held in the RAM is erased when the computer is turned off. For this reason, data often are transferred to magnetic tapes, disks, or punched cards for permanent storage. ROM, or Read Only Memory, is information that is permanently stored within the computer for the purpose of operating the system itself. The primary programming language that the computer uses is stored most often in the ROM. Unlike RAM, ROM is not erased when the computer is turned off.

Part of the mystique of data processing has been created by the abundance of specialized terminology in the field. This is particularly true with regard to the memory function, which routinely employs many simple but unusual terms. Once mastered, these terms provide a common basis for understanding and evaluating the working capacity of a data processing system.

A BIT is a BInary digiT. It is the smallest unit of information that a CPU can recognize. The amount of information that a given computer can recognize and manipulate at one time is expressed in BITs. Eight and sixteen BITs are the standard format for most personal computers. Eight BITs equal one BYTE, which is the equivalent of a single character (such as a letter, digit, or symbol). K is the standard unit of memory. One K equals 1024 characters. A personal computer with 64K of memory, therefore, stores approximately 64,000 characters or about 50 typed pages at one time.

As previously mentioned, when storage needs exceed the memory of the CPU, data can be transferred to tapes, disks, or punched cards. The standard storage mode for personal computers is the disk. **Floppy disks** are usually 5¼ in. in diameter and consist of a flexible plastic disk encased in a cardboard envelope. A floppy disk will store about 100,000 BYTEs, or the approximate equivalent of 80 typed pages. A **hard disk** is constructed from magnetically treated metal and is considerably more expensive than the floppy disk. It will store up to 150 times as much data as a floppy disk, however.

Input

The input function is the component that enters information into the CPU. As in the case of memory, data can be inserted into the computer by several methods. One way that this can be accomplished is with the use of a card punched in a pattern that can be interpreted by the CPU. Data also can be entered by using a typewriter-like keyboard. In the latter case an operator codes a magnetic tape or a disk that can be decoded by the computer. In all cases, the three input devices (card, tape, or disk) also function as additional data storage for the EDP system, as in the previous discussion of memory. Each input device can be filed and stored physically for later use. The obvious managerial advantage to this system is the ability to store millions of bits of information in an astonishingly small amount of space.

Output

The final EDP system function is output, and refers to information processed by the CPU. Output is retrievable in a variety of formats based on the capabilities of the hardware employed and the intended application of the user. Processed data may be obtained as a visual display on a video screen or auditorily through the implementation of a voice synthesizer. Other commonly produced forms utilize a printer to produce lists, labels, cards, and similar hard-copy materials. In some instances it is appropriate to place output on magnetic tape cassettes or disks to be stored for future use. The information generated in this manner can be reproduced in turn as hard-copy, printed matter or can be displayed visually, as described above.

Hardware Interfacing

Depending on the intended applications and on the financial limitations or other factors affected by the resources and goals of the user, there is a wide variety of options from which to choose when planning an effective EDP system. By exploring current literature devoted to the improvement of human service delivery modes, by visiting similar situations in which computers actively are being used, by visiting one of the many dealers specializing in personal computers, or by utilizing the services of state or federal agencies, the administrator has the opportunity to investigate those EDP arrangements that will be most useful based on the planned applications.

Many school districts and municipal governments have their own central computer. Remote schools or offices within the district can be supplied with individual terminals for input and output that would be connected by telephone wires to the central, or mainframe, computer. With minimal training the administrator can enter and retrieve the data needed in the daily management of her program.

In some cases several municipalities or school districts may use a time-sharing system. With this cooperative arrangement a central computer is electronically connected to terminals for input and output that are located within each separate organization. This mode of implementation is usually cost-effective. However, there are some disadvantages. If the CPU is out of service because of routine maintenance or mechanical or electrical failure, all of the participating units are without its services. Additionally, the various districts usually are dependent on the existing computer programs and output formats available at the central source. This necessarily limits the applications available to the users.

Recent advances in computer technology have resulted in the development and rapid acceptance of personal or microcomputers (PCs). Today's PC easily will fit on a standard office desk and will perform all the functions of room-sized mainframes of 15 years ago at a cost that is within reach of most organizational budgets. The decision as to whether to utilize existing mainframe equipment, purchase a terminal to tie into a central mainframe, or purchase a PC should be based on several factors. Among them should be:

1. *The amount of use expected.* If the computer will be used infrequently (only for biannual registration, for example), probably no reason exists to purchase expensive hardware. Arrange to use existing equipment, and pay for and retain the stored data (on cards, tapes, or disks).
2. *Accessibility.* If the mainframe computer must serve a variety of functions and if the needs cannot be met according to a reasonable time frame (for example, waiting periods of 30 minutes or longer to get "on-line" pose a problem), a PC that is always at your exclusive disposal may be needed.
3. *Availability of programs or software.* Is software available to do the exact functions needed? Will the software run on the available CPU? Will someone in the organization have to program the unit or is programming assistance available? At what cost?
4. *Comparative costs.* What is the relationship of the anticipated use to the cost of hardware, software, programming assistance, and time on the mainframe? Is the amount of use likely to increase or decrease over time? Which option offers the greatest flexibility for the least cost?

Programming

In order for the computer to process data it first must receive a list of instructions, or programs. These are part of the computer system software. The user has the option of using programs that have been developed commercially and are available through software vendors, using custom-designed programs written by a trained individual, or a combination of the two. Commercially produced software packages are designed to fulfill certain tasks. Most commercial programs offer a degree of flexibility, but the user still may need to adapt some of her needs to the program. Most business-related software falls into one of four categories:

1. Word processing—simplifies the composition, correction, modification, and storage of textual material
2. Financial modeling and forecasting—serves those functions normally accomplished with a calculator, spreadsheet, and pencil; uses an electronic worksheet

to create models, display and compare data, and make "what if" comparisons, predictions, and a broad range of mathematical computations quickly

3. Mail list and data base management—serves as an electronic filing system to maintain records and recall data based on any appropriate index feature (e.g., a simple mailing list could be recalled by an alphabetic listing of last names, by a numerical sequence of zip codes, by telephone area codes, by streets, or for that matter, by those persons named John who live on Eighth Avenue)
4. Accounting—accounting packages facilitate the development and mainte-nance of general ledgers, accounts receivable and payable, invoicing, inventory control, and payroll

Computer programmers and some software dealers can make minor modifications to commercially packaged programs to tailor them to the unique needs of a given organization. Although this involves an additional expense to the user, it is often far less costly than the development of custom software when the commercial package alone will not suffice. Programmers can develop software to meet the needs of any organization or situation. Unless the programmer is a staff employee, however, the cost of such a service is likely to outweigh by far the minor inconvenience of adapting to one of the many predesigned products. By employing appropriate programs the administrator is able to apply the computer to an endless variety of managerial and instructional tasks.

In utilizing the computer system one must remain cognizant of an important fact: nothing is intrinsically intelligent about the computer. The CPU simply follows the directions of the program. In addition, the CPU and the program generate output based on the nature and quality of the input. If the program has not been designed or written properly, or if the input is not accurate, the output in turn will be invalid and unusable. This concept is best expressed by an axiom known to data processing personnel as "garbage in = garbage out" (GIGO).

COMPUTER APPLICATIONS

The applications of EDP to managerial tasks are growing each day. EDP is presently being employed by recreational and school administrators alike to assist in program development, inventory control, security, energy conservation, financial transactions (budget development, payroll, purchase ordering), word processing, participant sched-uling, and countless other tasks. The list of user applications is constrained only by the imagination of the administrator and the financial limitations of the school district or governmental agency. Many of these applications are common to the management of a physical education department and a public recreation service. Other uses are designed for a specific program, however. These uses cluster into three major catego-ries: general administrative applications, physical education program applications, and public recreation applications.

General Administrative Applications

Many uses of EDP are common to all management positions, whether they be in industry, commerce, education, or public service. A partial listing of these common applications includes:

Personnel Management

1. Staff listings showing vital statistics (name, address, age, sex, staff position, and so on)
2. Staff evaluation records showing previous ratings linked to job descriptions
3. History of job assignments or positions of each employee
4. Individual work and vacation schedule listings
5. Data files based on employee interest and skill surveys

Fiscal Administration

1. Storage and processing of data needed for annual budget preparation
2. Automatic budget development and printing by department
3. Maintenance of inventory records for accounting procedures and security control
4. The allocation and distribution of resources
5. The generation and processing of purchase orders
6. Daily business accounting procedures
7. Automated energy distribution and control

Activity Programming

1. The scheduling of participants based on their activity selections
2. The integrated scheduling of activities and staff based on expressed needs and available facilities

Personnel information is ideally suited to the storage and data retrieval capabilities of the computer system. Facts about employees that are maintained normally include: name, birthdate, address, sex, level of education or training, facts regarding professional certification, work experience, special interests, job classification and salary, and any other personal facts deemed necessary. These data can be furnished by asking each staff member to complete an appropriate personal information form, which can be coded for input into the computer system. After the forms have been completed they can be stored, modified, or recalled, when necessary.

The advantage of having this information in the computer memory file becomes obvious when one sees how it can be applied in an administrative unit (whether a school district or recreation department) that employs a large number of persons. Suppose, for example, that a senior high school physical education department supervisor is seeking a certificated individual within the school district who is skilled in lacrosse to assist in an after-school recreation program. Instead of the supervisor having to search manually through the files of the hundred or more individuals employed by the school district, the computer can be instructed to print a list of all personnel who have expressed this talent on the special interest portion of the personal information sheet. By using this initial listing, the supervisor's task of completing the search is simplified greatly.

Budget preparation, purchase ordering, and payroll accounting are among the fiscal transactions that can be handled by electronic data processing. Each of these functions can be effected through a variety of strategies, as prescribed and dictated by the needs of the manager. To determine the amount of money needed to operate an entire school system or recreation department a budget must be developed showing the anticipated expenditures for each individual program (see Chapter 6, "Financial Administration"). Using information from staff members and administrators, input data can be generated and supplied to the computer system for storage, sorting, tabulating, and printing.

The purchasing and ordering of supplies and equipment can be linked to budget development. When these operations are electronically automated in a computer system, the administrator has an efficient accounting procedure capable of monitoring the entire flow of financial transactions. Input data can be produced for each item purchased. The data should include: the description and cost of the item, the name and address of the vendor, the department or individual who ordered the item, and when it was ordered, shipped, and received. This system not only provides the administrator with verification of the placement of all orders and the receipt of each item, but it also provides a current account balance and inventory for each department.

An additional and widely used EDP application for financial transactions is personnel payroll management. This becomes an automated accounting procedure when linked with each staff member's personal file. A current and accurate payroll system can be developed by using input data such as: step on the salary guide, length of service within the unit, expended sick and personal days, tax and pension information, and other related facts.

Resource allocation is another major responsibility of all administrators. These resources normally include items such as: physical space within a building or on the grounds, equipment and supplies, and other related goods and services needed to operate an effective program. The process of procuring and distributing these resources can be done in an organized and effective manner when combined with participant scheduling, budget preparation, and purchase ordering. In addition, when this information is placed in the data bank of the computer system, the administrator has the opportunity to develop an efficient inventory control program.

Inventory control is a system that allows an administrator to know the location of each resource item and the number of items available for distribution. For example, the equipment manager of an athletic program should be responsible for knowing the whereabouts of each piece of equipment. This task becomes more complex and more difficult to control as the number of teams and participants expands. It is greatly simplified, however, with an EDP system.

In the example given above, the process begins at the start of the athletic season when the manager takes an inventory of equipment on hand. All items (e.g., football helmets, shoulder pads, and uniforms) are coded as input data for the CPU. Eventually the computer memory file will contain a complete listing of each item available for all activities. Before the start of the season the manager is able to provide each coach with a printed list of each item of equipment supplied for that sport. As the coaching staff and manager issue each item to the athletes, this information can be fed back to the computer. At the conclusion of the season, the manager can retrieve the list indicating which athlete received each piece of equipment. As the items are returned, they are compared with this list to account for each piece of missing and damaged equipment.

Linking this inventory control data to the memory file containing purchase order facts offers the equipment manager many advantages. The reordering of missing or damaged items is simplified because the original purchase information can be retrieved easily from the CPU. In addition, by knowing the expected lifetime of each piece of equipment, the CPU can predict which items will be ready for replacement and automatically enter this fact in the budget preparation file for the following year.

Scheduling was one of the first administrative applications of EDP in the school system. Today this function has been expanded and refined to include not only pupil scheduling in general, but also to assist the department supervisor to place students in special activities within the instructional unit. EDP also is commonly employed by the recreation administrator to assign participants to planned activities. Participants in either the school or recreation setting can be assigned to activities or courses by using EDP in a variety of methods. No matter what process is used three distinct steps normally are involved in the total application.

The first operation in the scheduling procedure is the participant's course or activity selection. In this step the registrant completes the required information on an input instrument. This device is normally a computer card that is filled in by the program applicant. The data requested usually include: name, address, sex, age, and activities or courses elected. The data on each card are then fed into the computer in preparation for the next phase of the process.

Using the above selection data the administrator can determine the number of participants requesting each of the activities offered, which in turn will allow him to calculate the number of sections needed for each subject or activity. Based on the data and the administrator's knowledge of the skilled personnel and rooms or stations available, he can develop the master schedule. This plan relates activity offerings to appropriate facilities, times or periods, and instructors. Although the master schedule could be developed manually by the administrator, utilizing EDP allows it to be generated automatically as part of the scheduling operation.

The final phase of scheduling is participant loading. This refers to the placement of individuals in activities, based on their initial selections and the configuration of the master schedule. To do this without the benefit of EDP is time-consuming and complex. When variables such as balancing the number of clients in each section and room, priority activity selection for certain clients, and sequential election of activities are introduced into the process, the task of scheduling can become monumental.

Use of a computer system for the scheduling operation is efficient, cost effective, and more accurate than manual manipulation of data. As in all computer applications, however, the administrator must begin with valid input and with a program properly prepared to consider both the major scheduling function and all of the variables described above.

The basic scheduling format outlined in this section can be applied to a recreation program or to an entire school to load all participants into all courses. It can also be modified to plan for pupil participation in a specific course area such as a physical education program. By describing the individual activities in which clients are to be engaged according to age level, sex, ability, and other factors, EDP can be used to develop a master schedule and load participants in a coherent and sequential manner. With proper evaluation techniques, the administrator has the technical capacity to plot the progress of each individual, team, or group of individuals, and to develop programs based on participants' needs, abilities, and interests. Thus it is possible, for instance, to reorganize a competitive schedule on a regular basis to provide the most equitable competition possible and to avoid the consistent mismatching of teams.

The computer applications described above are commonly used in physical education and recreation departments, primarily because the data employed in these operations are ideally suited to EDP procedures. There are additional uses, however, that deserve comment. For instance, many school districts, day camps, and other organizations that transport their clientele use computer processing to organize the transportation system. Setting up routes, determining bus stop locations, and all the other factors that must be considered in transportation planning can be done with a suitably programmed computer. Although this is a familiar application, other examples are not as commonplace.

Less widely employed computer applications include: security devices, energy conservation programs, and clerical assistance. Major computer manufacturing companies have developed and market electronically controlled door locks. To gain access to an area controlled by this type of lock an authorized individual must place a magnetically coded card into a slot in the locking mechanism. If a computer determines that the card is properly coded, the CPU automatically deactivates the lock. In addition, the computer memory can store data such as the date and time a particular door was unlocked and relocked, and which individual opened the door.

Another application for computer systems that is gaining more popularity each day is energy conservation. Computer technology can help achieve effective reductions in electric power consumption. With appropriate hardware and programs added to the central processing unit, room temperatures and lighting can be regulated automatically and individually. Different rooms can have different temperatures, depending on their use and occupancy. In addition, electric power can be reduced during peak load times when cost rates might be higher.

A final computer function that is becoming more prevalent is word processing. A word processor is basically an automated typing system composed of a keyboard input device connected to the CPU. The output hardware normally consists of a video screen and a printer. Using word processing, an operator types out the first draft of the document using the input keyboard. This manuscript or report then can be reproduced on the video screen so that it can be edited. Words or sentences can be altered or entire paragraphs and pages can be transposed throughout the document. The CPU is capable of making these modifications and then electronically retyping the corrected manuscript in its entirety. An added feature of this process is that the corrected copy can be incorporated automatically in the computer memory file.

Physical Education Program Applications

Many computer applications have been developed specifically for use in physical education programs. Some examples of these applications include:

Pupil Instruction Management

1. Participant scheduling based on activities offered within the department and the expressed interests and needs of the pupil
2. The development of individualized programs for pupils based on such goals as physical conditioning, weight control, and skill improvement
3. The development of a comprehensive and specific system of pupil evaluation that can be continuously monitored by the instructors and administrator
4. Instructional assistance through the use of EDP systems
5. Pupil interest counseling

Program Management

1. Activity and facility scheduling
2. The development of specific programs based on needs analysis data and available research
3. The individualization of activities based on pupil evaluation for the purpose of providing remediation and skill development
4. The requisition and distribution of equipment and supplies among staff members

In the preceding section, the process of participant scheduling was outlined. This application is of significant benefit in a physical education department that offers a great many activities during different times of the year to a large number of pupils. The basic scheduling format already described can be employed, and has the obvious advantage of monitoring the participant activity selections recorded in the memory storage file of the system.

EDP normally is used in testing programs to score examinations and to analyze the results. In addition, EDP can be employed to report and store pupil grades. The array of formats available to the administrator in processing and publishing evaluative data is widely varied, and it is up to the administrator to consult with test publishers, producers of software, and programmers to obtain the style of material most suitable to the needs of the user. However, the physical education instructor also can use this system to evaluate individual pupils on specific tasks. By utilizing an appropriate testing instrument, the instructor can monitor the progress of each student continuously and consequently can schedule future activities for that pupil based on the results of the evaluation.

The preceding paragraph described how two computer applications, scheduling and evaluation, can be linked to help ensure pupil progress. This system of using EDP to plan and monitor student growth commonly is known as computer-managed instruction (CMI). When the appropriate display terminals, data entry keyboards, and programs are employed to teach pupils directly, this process is referred to as computer-assisted instruction (CAI).

A pupil sitting at a video screen can type out instructions for an appropriately programmed computer to show a suitable lesson. The screen will display questions or tasks that the pupil must react to by typing a response on the keyboard. The CPU then can provide the pupil with instantaneous feedback, indicating that the answer was correct or directing the pupil to remedial material if the response was incorrect. This computer-assisted instruction can be used effectively by a teacher in such areas as personal hygiene, first aid procedures, and sports rules and strategies.

Attendance is an additional pupil instruction management example. Daily pupil attendance data can be stored in the computer and retrieved, when needed, in a variety of forms based on the needs of the user. Data may be displayed each day to indicate which pupils are absent, or it may be obtained from the memory file during the course of the school year to compile information for tasks such as state reports. Individual instructors can use this information to determine which pupils were absent from specific activities so that appropriate remediation can be employed.

Many schools have adapted their guidance programs to include computer technology. Software is commercially marketed to enable counselors to assist students with college and career planning. Pupils who have elected to attend colleges or universities can use the computer to obtain listings of institutions based on numerous criteria. These factors may include: majors offered, tuition costs, location, student population, activities, and other pertinent facts. Pupils who are in the process of making career choices also may use the computer system to assist them in making the correct selection. The computer can provide the pupil with a list of career possibilities after the student has supplied the CPU with personal input data such as interests, educational background, and aptitudes. In addition, this same technology can be used by the physical education department as an adjunct to the scheduling procedures. Using the foregoing EDP counseling techniques, pupil interests and abilities can be maintained in the memory file to assist the student in making activity selections appropriate to his or her talents and capabilities.

In the area of program development, EDP has been widely accepted as an aid in the conduct of research. The administrator who is involved in curriculum planning has many sources of assistance based on computer technology, and these include organizations that have been created to provide clients with a data-based information retrieval service. These organizations obtain documents from many sources. Each year they may obtain thousands of journal and newspaper articles in addition to theses and dissertations. When they receive a report, they microfilm and catalog it according to a precise subject description. Because these services receive and record many thousands of items in a year, computer technology is needed to store and recall this information.

If, as an example, a physical education supervisor has been given the responsibility of developing a new unit of instruction in cardiopulmonary resuscitation, an information retrieval service can be of great benefit. Not only can the organization provide the supervisor with specific technical information concerning the subject, but it usually also can furnish reports describing similar course development and implementation in other districts.

Some examples of information retrieval services include: ERIC (Educational Resources Information Center), which is associated with the National Institute of Education in Washington, D.C.; INFOBANK, which is a subsidiary of the *New York Times* in New York City; and, as a possible source of assistance in the example cited above, BIOSIS Previews. This is the BioSciences Information Service of Biological Abstracts, located in Philadelphia, Pennsylvania.

Public Recreation Applications

As in the management of the physical education department, several computer applications are unique to the administration of a recreation service. These uses include:

Fiscal Management

1. Forecasting revenues from fees, charges, and sales
2. Forecasting expenses for land acquisition, construction, maintenance, programs, personnel, and all other anticipated and unanticipated expenditures
3. Cost tracking

Personnel Management

1. Staff inventory of skills, talents, and other personal characteristics
2. Workload and performance standard determination
3. Factoring the staff/public ratio for events

Facility and Site Development

1. Site acquisition records
2. Construction costs and bidding data
3. Work order distribution and priority determination
4. Terrain and earthwork surveys
5. Space analysis with respect to function and participant capacity
6. Vacant facility and land surveys
7. Land use by geographic location

Demographic Studies

1. Population surveys of movement and trends
2. Distribution of population based on age, sex, education, and socioeconomic status
3. Recreational facility and activity placement based on projected population shifts and trends

Activity Development

1. Outputs showing areas or facilities where planned activities might be scheduled
2. Needs analysis of activities to be offered
3. Leisure counseling
4. Participant registration

The foregoing list is by no means inclusive of the spectrum of computer applications employed by a recreation department. The examples cited, however, can be expanded and refined by the administrator to suit the needs and goals of the program. In each case, the administrator must work with the computer specialist to develop the input modes, programs, and output arrays that are most suitable to the needs and requirements of the department.

As an example of how EDP might be adapted to public recreation one might consider the example of cost tracking and employee workload. In this case, a computer system can be utilized effectively to determine the cost of labor, equipment, and material when maintenance must be performed on a recreation facility or site. In addition, the program can account for employee time on the job and can maintain the records required to show expenditures of tax monies. Along with the accomplishment of these main purposes, the administrator has the advantage of gaining access to data that will show: inventory control on materials and supplies, time study information, equipment allocation and performance, and an accounting of expenditures for each facility or location.

The flow of data necessary to operate this system usually begins at the job site. The field workers are provided with work tickets (input) that are completed by them as they proceed through each job assignment This ticket can show the name of the worker, the location of the facility, the specific place within that site, the type of job (e.g., electrical or plumbing), the reason (e.g., preventive maintenance, storm damage, or vandalism), the time (travel to job, rest breaks, actual time on task), and the equipment required. Before being sent to the computer operator to be placed into the system, these facts can be checked and verified by the field supervisor.

After this input is entered into the CPU, it can be processed to provide a variety of output facts. For instance, monthly reports can be generated to show the cost of maintaining each facility. This is a benefit when the administrator begins to anticipate expenditures during the preparation of the annual budget. Work standards can be developed based on the time it normally takes to complete specific tasks. This information can be related to personnel distribution and evaluation. Data can be offered to show what types of equipment usually are required for specific jobs. In addition, the data can show when certain pieces of equipment are no longer profitable to be maintained or used. Finally, based on the reasons for maintenance that are indicated on work tickets, the administrator may be able to review patterns of vandalism for use by security personnel.

Utilizing cost tracking coupled with other appropriate fiscal considerations, the manager can use EDP to forecast the fees and charges necessary to operate each facility. Input data such as monetary inflation trends, facility capacity, attendance or usage trends, maintenance cost, and other factors can provide the manager with the output data necessary to determine participant fees.

The use of EDP to manage client flow is a widely accepted practice in recreation administration today. For example, many agencies use computer technology to register participants. This process can be initiated during the first year of participation by an individual. The initial registration card filled out by the client can provide the agency with such information as the client's name, address, sex, birthdate, and interests (as determined through automated leisure counseling). Once this initial form is filed, the procedure during subsequent years can be automated. Before each subsequent registration period, the computer can be used to generate mailing labels and develop forms to be sent to all previous participants. The client who receives the registration information in the mail simply has to sign the card and return it to the agency to signify his or her desire to re-enroll. Any changes in interest or personal status also can be noted on the form by the individual.

EDP-based registration allows the administrator to generate team and activity rosters automatically. With this process no opportunity exists for criticism from rival teams or other interest groups about favoritism or "stacking." Also, the computer can be programmed to move each child or adult participant to the next higher level of competition or activity each succeeding year or period of competition.

All of the computer applications described in the foregoing sections of this chapter are currently in use by school systems and recreation services. Some applications are common in most units, other functions are used more rarely. It is the responsibility of the administrator to decide which uses are most practical and effective in each given situation. The implementation of a computer system capable of performing many of the administrative tasks described above represents a considerable financial investment, and a genuine commitment must be made by all individuals responsible for the decision to employ EDP.

MANAGEMENT OF COMPUTER UTILIZATION

A practicing administrator, either of an instructional department within a school or associated with a public recreation agency, generally will not be involved in the actual management of a data processing center. These administrators and supervisors should possess an awareness of some of the factors that are necessary for the effective utilization of EDP, however.

For computer systems to achieve maximum effectiveness all users of the system need to adhere to a specific written plan. This operational strategy should indicate the precise objectives of the EDP department, and these objectives in turn should be linked to the objectives of the school district or governmental unit. This plan must detail the resources necessary to operate the computer system efficiently, including not only the actual hardware and software needed to meet the objectives but also the appropriate personnel. The operational strategy should include a managed schedule, based on the objectives and resources, that will provide for a continuous flow of applications and tasks throughout the system. Although this plan of organization is extremely important, other management factors also should be considered by the administrator.

For the computer system to be most effective in making predictions and in determining an array of measures of productivity, many individual tasks need to be combined as one functional operation. This concept of the unification of tasks should become a basic goal for all administrators who wish to utilize EDP. An example can be developed from the discussions of fiscal management described earlier in this chapter. By linking individual tasks such as budget preparation, ordering equipment, and inventory control, the administrator can produce a single operation that allows the CPU to monitor all phases of equipment acquisition, distribution, and replacement. Other applications, such as word processing, security, and related operations, can be added continuously to this function in order to enhance the capabilities and efficiency of the user.

In addition to the above principles, administrators always must be cognizant of one final management consideration. Provisions for the security of the entire computer system must be implemented and adhered to by all users. The hardware and software of a computer represents a considerable financial investment by the purchaser. To prevent damage to this equipment, only qualified, authorized personnel should be permitted to use the terminals. Even more significantly, security must be maintained because of the one major component of the computer system most vulnerable to tampering—the memory file. Stored within the memory are data that must remain confidential (e.g., student records), and data that are based on countless numbers of hours of research and clerical manipulations. These data files must be protected from inspection by unauthorized individuals and from damage, alteration, or theft.

The security of data usually is accomplished by secret access and task codes. These codes, comparable to an unlisted telephone number, are designed to allow only specific individuals to obtain or alter data. By typing the proper sequences of symbols on the input keyboard the operator can gain access to the CPU and instruct the computer to perform the desired operation. If the integrity of the system is to be preserved these codes must remain confidential.

Computer utilization by administrators and supervisors has a wide array of applications. Effective use is predicated on the administrator's basic knowledge of EDP principles, a keen awareness of his or her responsibilities, and an active imagination. If computer utilization succeeds it is because the administrator is actively involved in the implementation of EDP and has coupled this involvement with effective planning and fresh thinking.

Who may participate in programs of sport and recreation?

What are the responsibilities of the administrator with regard to sex equity and the participation of disabled persons?

To what degree can a person in authority infringe on the rights of the participant?

What is the responsibility of the administrator with regard to employee negligence?

What are the most common causes of negligence suits?

What administrative steps can be taken to reduce the likelihood of lawsuit?

Chapter 9

The Administrator and the Law

The entire field of sport, physical education, and recreation has undergone a number of significant changes in recent years. Some of these changes have occurred as a result of the increased leisure time now enjoyed by much of our population. Some undoubtedly can be traced to the effects of a tight national economy. Still others are attributable to the effects of the media in bringing about increased public awareness and interest.

In this chapter we examine another change agent that has been exerting an ever increasing effect in the world of sport: the law. Various laws concerning the recruitment, salary, and employment rights of professional athletes have been publicized widely. Their direct effects are limited, however, to the relatively small number of persons involved in the professional arena, and therefore will not be discussed here. We will concentrate instead on those laws that most directly affect the rights of the participant and thereby influence school and community programs.

THE RIGHT TO PARTICIPATE

In general the answer to the question "who may participate?" must be "everyone." Athough certain restrictions may be imposed on certain types of activities, several laws have been enacted that clearly are intended to provide equal opportunities for all persons.

The equal protection clause of the 14th Amendment to the Constitution provides that no state shall make or enforce any law that denies to any person the equal protection of the laws. This does not deny the power of the various governmental bodies to treat various classes or groups differently, but it does require that constitutionally valid justification be provided for any such differentiation. Racial classifications therefore have been regarded as emphatic violations of the equal protection clause. Classifications by size or ability, on the other hand, would be acceptable in certain activities in which these factors would affect the quality or safety of the experience provided.

Title IX of the Educational Amendments of 1972 provides that no person on the basis of sex shall be excluded from participation in, be denied the benefits of, or be subjected to discrimination under any education program or activity receiving federal financial assistance. Although most of the publicity regarding Title IX has centered on sport activities, it is important to remember that the law applies equally to arts and crafts, mathematics, and all other activities. Title IX expressly applies to all levels of education from preschool through graduate school, as well as to federally funded clubs and organizations such as municipal recreation departments.

The decision as to whether equal opportunity has been provided within a given program is based on a number of factors:

I.   Whether the interests and abilities of both the males and females have been served effectively
II. The equity of:
   A.   the provision and distribution of equipment and supplies
   B.   the scheduling of instruction, practice, and games
   C.   the opportunity for quality instruction and coaching
   D.   the assignment and payment of teachers and coaches
   E.   the provision of competitive, practice, and locker room facilities
   F.   the funding provided for all program levels
   G.   the provision of training and medical care and facilities

At present Title IX allows separate teams for the sexes and, with the exception of contact sports, allows a person to try out for a single-sex team if there is no comparable team available for members of his or her sex. If a program offers both a men's volleyball team and a women's volleyball team, each team can be maintained on a single-sex basis. On the other hand, if only a men's volleyball team is provided, interested women cannot be barred from the team by reason of their sex. Single-sex teams may be maintained in contact sports so long as the program as a whole can be shown to provide equal opportunities for both sexes. Therefore, if an organization developed a policy that it would provide only one league for males and one for females during each season, and that the sports would be selected on the basis of participant interest, it would not be necessary to allow a woman to try out for the men's spring softball league, even though the only woman's league available was in tennis. According to present interpretation of Title IX, the opportunities for each sex in this case would be equal, as each would have one league per season.

Instructional programs, with the exception of those for sex education, are expected to be conducted on a coeducational basis. Ability grouping is permitted only so long as the grouping method can be shown to be valid and does not constitute a form of de facto segregation. It would be perfectly acceptable, for instance, to base ability grouping in a softball program on a number of valid skill tests. Grouping on the basis of height and weight, however, or on participants' scores on a test of upper body strength probably would be more closely related to sex than to softball skill and therefore would be suspect.

The Education for All Handicapped Children Act (PL 94-142) calls for specially designed instructional programs (at no cost to the parent) to meet the individual needs of each handicapped child. Specific program guidelines are provided that require instruction to be provided in the areas of:

1. Physical and motor fitness
2. Fundamental motor skills and patterns
3. Skills in aquatics, dance, individual and group games and sports, including intramural and lifetime sports
4. Special or adapted physical education, movement education, and motor development

Section 504 of the Rehabilitation Act of 1973 (PL 93-112) states that no recipient of federal funds may discriminate on the basis of handicap in the provision of recreational programs, physical education courses, intramurals, clubs, or interscholastic athletics. The provision of separate or different activities for handicapped persons is acceptable only when the participant cannot take part in the normal program or when normal participation would be contrary to the person's health, safety, or interest.

The intent of these laws is quite clear. Handicapped persons must be afforded equal participatory opportunities. Further, they must receive the same quality of instruction as is provided to their non-handicapped peers. No longer is it acceptable, for instance, to provide periods of "free play" or to steer handicapped students into the more sedentary activities. As a rule of thumb, programs either should be open to the handicapped on an equal basis, or parallel programs should be developed to meet their needs.

The Architectural Barrier Act (PL 90-480) requires that any building or facility constructed wholly or in part with federal funds must be accessible to and usable by persons with physical handicaps. This law applies to gymnasia, locker rooms, and all other types of athletic facilities.

Federal versus State Law

The legislative acts described in this section have been enacted by the federal government and therefore apply to the entire nation. Most states have enacted similar laws that apply specifically within their borders. The issue of whether federal or state laws take precedence is fairly clear cut. Federal law takes precedence in all cases unless the requirements of the state are stricter. When the state law is more restrictive and is not in conflict with the federal law, state mandates take precedence. It is permissible for a state to require that *all sports*, whether contact or not, be coeducational and indeed some have done so. It is necessary therefore that administrators familiarize themselves with the applicable laws of their particular state, as well as with those enacted at the federal level.

Guidelines for the Provision of Equal Participatory Opportunities

The administrator should:

I. Familiarize himself with all applicable federal and state legislation.

II.   Establish and publish written procedures for such things as:
   A.   Team selection.
   B.   The development of new programs and activities.
   C.   Eligibility for participation.
   D.   Scheduling and funding.
III. Conduct periodic polls of his clientele to determine needs and interests, and develop programs to meet these.
IV.   Examine all facilities periodically.
   A.   Are they equally accessible to males and females?
   B.   Are they accessible to handicapped persons?
   C.   Plan necessary modifications.
   D.   Are the scheduling practices sex-biased?
V.   Examine all instructional, recreational, and competitive programs.
   A.   How many males, females, and handicapped persons are involved?
   B.   Are there reasons for any observed inequities?
   C.   What program or scheduling changes might bring better results?

TRAINING RULES

Training rules traditionally have been considered an unquestioned part of all programs of adult and youth sport. The most common regulations center on curfews and the use of alcohol, drugs, and tobacco. Although athletes and their parents have been increasingly vocal in their dissatisfaction with training rules, in those cases that have reached the courts, the right of a coach to enforce reasonable training rules usually has been upheld.

In general, challenges to training rules rely on one of the following arguments:

1. The rules infringe on those rights guaranteed by the First Amendment (i.e., the protection of one's freedom of speech and speech-related activities).
2. The rules violate the equal protection clause of the 14th Amendment (i.e., they arbitrarily and unreasonably separate people into different groups or classes). A prime example of such a rule would be one that required athletes to have hhshort hair. If the requirement is only for athletes and is not directly related to success or safety in the sport it very well may be invalid if challenged.
3. The lack of clarity or specificity of the rule leads to a violation of the right to due process, as described later in this chapter. The courts generally have allowed some latitude here. As long as the *type* of behavior expected is understood clearly by the participants, specific examples of all possible violations need not be provided.
4. The rule creates a circumstance of guilt by association. For instance, some training rules have set penalties for attending a party where alcohol was being consumed, regardless of whether the athlete in question was drinking. Carried to the extreme such rules prohibit an athlete from attending a wedding reception at which adults are drinking or from riding home from the supermarket with a parent who has just purchased a six-pack of beer. These rules traditionally have been overthrown by the courts.

The key issues involved here are the reasonableness of the rules and the fairness with which they are enforced. If a reasonable connection can be drawn between the rule and the safe or proper conduct of the program or team, if the rules are distributed to all affected parties, if the rules are not vague or dependent on administrative discretion or guesswork for their enforcement, and if a fair hearing is provided when instances of serious offense or severe punishment occur, one reasonably may expect that a court would uphold the rule and its enforcement, if necessary.

PERSONAL APPEARANCE AND DRESS CODES

An extension of the training rule controversy that frequently affects instructional and recreational programs as well as interscholastic sports is the question of personal appearance and dress codes. Court reaction in cases involving personal appearance and dress restrictions has been mixed. Despite the relative lack of predictability in such cases, however, several constants can be identified and should be considered carefully in the formulation and enforcement of appearance restrictions. Among these are:

1. The more vague or indefinite the rule, the less likely it is to be upheld by the courts.
2. Any and all restrictions identifiably must relate to the safety or quality of the activity.
3. The benefits of the regulations must be such that they clearly outweigh the restrictions that they place on the constitutional rights of the participants.
4. There can be no reasonable alternative courses of action that are less restrictive of the constitutional rights of the participant. For instance, although a restriction on hair length could be shown to relate directly to water resistance, and thus be a reasonable restriction on a swimming team, the use of a bathing cap probably would accomplish the same result without placing the same type of restriction on the rights of the participant.

Certain types of rules, however, pose little problem for the administrator. Rules that relate directly to the health or safety of the participants are rarely disputed and almost invariably are upheld by the courts. For instance, it is considered perfectly reasonable to require appropriate footwear for all participants in physical activities or safety glasses on the racquetball court or mouthpieces on the football field. Additionally, although it would be difficult to support a requirement that persons wear blue and white tank suits in a swimming pool, a requirement of a clean bathing suit and the prohibition of swimming in gym shorts or cutoffs probably would be supportable.

Guidelines for the Development and Enforcement of Training Rules and Dress Codes

1. Be sure that all rules serve an identifiable, valid function.
2. State all rules explicitly and briefly to minimize confusion and misinterpretation.

3. Be sure all rules are understood clearly by the participants. An introduction to these rules through written materials and frequent reminders avoids misunderstanding. Signs and posters also are helpful.
4. Rules are much more palatable when stated in positive rather than negative terms. This is especially true of rules that are published, posted, and frequently encountered. "Swimming Between 8 a.m. and 8 p.m. Only" is clearer and less oppressive than "No Swimming Between 8 p.m. and 8 a.m." or "No Swimming After 8 p.m."
5. Enforce training and dress rules according to established policies. The more discretionary the enforcement process, the greater the likelihood of problems.
6. When establishing a rule that in some way will infringe on student rights and freedoms, be sure to consider alternatives that might be less restrictive of those rights and freedoms.

DUE PROCESS: CAN PARTICIPATION BE WITHHELD?

Most courts clearly have affirmed that one's rights to full participation in all aspects of the educational experience are so fundamental that they cannot be denied without the due process of law. Although on the surface this is a straightforward guideline, indecision regarding the exact definition of due process has led to considerable confusion. The issue is so clouded that it frequently becomes the main source of contention in civil cases involving training rules, dress codes, and other circumstances in which administrative sanctions have been imposed. The definition of due process in fact is often dependent on the situation in which it occurred or should have occurred.

The due process clause of the 5th and 14th Amendments prohibits the deprivation of life, liberty, or property without due process of law; however, the courts will intervene when the right that has been denied is considered of sufficient importance to justify constitutional protection.

No one questions the need for short-term disciplinary measures to be imposed occasionally "on the spot" by anyone charged with supervisory responsibilities. Still, the greater the severity of the punishment and the more long term its consequences, the greater the requirement for the elements of a due process procedure and, hence, the greater the likelihood of legal action if the process is not provided. Such legal action would have to be predicated on the legitimacy of the claimant's entitlement to the right that he or she claims to have been denied. Participation on an all-star team, for instance, is a privilege reserved for those who have displayed unusual excellence and would not be considered a legitimate entitlement of all participants in a softball league. All players would be entitled to equal consideration for membership on the team, however.

Most problems that give rise to due process complaints can be avoided by giving careful attention to the following guidelines:

I. All persons must be presumed to be innocent until there is irrefutable proof to the contrary.
II. Before any disciplinary sanctions are imposed, the affected person should be provided with a fair hearing. In simple matters this might take the form of being

provided an opportunity to discuss the issue with the person imposing the sanctions. In more serious matters, such as when the penalty is expected to be long term, a more formal hearing process is necessary.

III.　The accused person always must be given notice of the specific charges against him. The relative formality of the notice would be a function of the severity of the charges and the anticipated punishment. In simple cases such as when a coach plans to bench a player for the upcoming game due to violation of a curfew, a verbal statement of the offense and the anticipated punishment should suffice. In severe cases with long-term effects such as when a municipal recreation director is contemplating barring an individual from any further participation in community-sponsored activities due to repeated violations of an alcoholic beverage rule, the notice should be written and include:

    A.　The time and place of the hearing
    B.　A statement of the specific charges
    C.　The basis on which possible sanctions would be justified
    D.　The possible sanctions

IV.　This notice should be provided sufficiently in advance of a hearing to allow for the preparation of an informed defense.

In summary, administrators must recognize the right of all persons to appear, be heard, and present an informed defense before being subjected to enforcement procedures or sanctions. The exact amount of due process required is a function of the particular circumstances involved and, most particularly, the relative severity of the sanctions imposed. The exact determination of the amount of due process afforded should be based on three factors:

1.　The severity of the sanctions anticipated.
2.　The relative cost of carrying out the due process procedures. Certainly a full trial procedure is too complex and costly for a situation involving a two-day team suspension.
3.　The relative likelihood of making an incorrect judgment in the absence of a full hearing. When guilt is obvious or admitted, and the sanctions have been clearly established, the need for a full hearing is minimized.

RISK MANAGEMENT AND LEGAL LIABILITY

In recent years an alarming increase has occurred in the number of lawsuits brought against professionals in the fields of sport, physical education, and recreation, and also in the size of the awards demanded in such cases. Whether these increases are a result of an increased public awareness of their legal rights, the willingness of insurance companies to make generous out-of-court settlements, an increase in public dissatisfaction with programs as they exist, or a combination of these factors, the result has been a rapid decrease in the availability of certain types of insurance coverage and a tremendous increase in the cost of the insurance that can be obtained. Because any person can sue any other person at any time, no one is guaranteed protection against lawsuits; however, those administrators who possesss a thorough understanding of the legal process and the elements of risk management can increase their chances of success greatly in any suit that may be brought against them.

Elements of the Legal Process

In recreation, physical education, and sport, tort claims center almost exclusively on personal injuries caused by the alleged negligence of instructional or supervisory personnel. A tort is a legal wrong for which one may seek recompense through court action. In order for a tort claim to be successful, four elements must be proved:

Duty—it must be shown that the accused person had a responsibility or duty to provide for the safety and welfare of the injured party.

2. *Negligence*—it must be shown that the accused person by act of either commission or omission failed to meet the standard of care that reasonably could be expected from any professional under the same or similar circumstances.

3. *Foreseeability*—it must be shown that, in the normal function of his duties, the accused person should have been able to predict or foresee the hazard that resulted in the alleged injury.

4. *Proximate cause*—not only must the negligence of the accused party be proved, it also must be proved that the specific act of negligence in question either caused or aggravated the injury for which recompense is sought.

If the plaintiff or injured party is able to prove these elements by the greater weight of evidence (as opposed to the "beyond a reasonable shadow of doubt" principle followed in criminal law), that person is entitled to an award in compensation for her losses. If, on the other hand, one or more of the elements are not proved, then the defendant is not held liable and no award is granted.

In addition, a number of legal arguments and defenses are particularly important in that they pinpoint several administrative and supervisory responsibilities with regard to risk management.

Contributory or Comparative Negligence

In a state that follows the principle of contributory negligence, if it can be shown that negligent actions of the plaintiff in any way helped to cause or aggravate the injury, the case would be dismissed. If, however, the doctrine of comparative negligence were in force as is the case in most states, the negligence of the injured party simply would diminish the size of the award he could receive by the percentage of his involvement. Table 9.1 graphically demonstrates the relative effects of contributory and comparative negligence.

Assumption of Risk

It is often contended that a person who chooses to participate in certain activities must assume the risk of accident or injury associated with that activity. According to an opinion issued by the New Jersey Supreme Court, this assumption has no validity

**Table 9.1. Relative Effects
of Contributory and Comparative
Negligence on Compensatory Awards for Damages**

Plaintiff	Percent of Responsibility for Own Injury	Damages Sought	Maximum Award Contributory	Maximum Award Comparative
Jane Jones	10	$100,000	0	$ 90,000
James Smith	45	250,000	0	137,500
Mary Sweet	0	125,000	$125,000	125,000

as a separate defense.[1] Simply put, no one assumes a risk of which they are not aware. If a defendant failed to make a plaintiff aware of the dangers involved in the activity in question, she may well have been negligent in fulfilling her supervisory duty. If, on the other hand, a plaintiff was informed of the risks and acted in a manner that increased the likelihood of his own injury, there may be grounds for a claim of contributory or comparative negligence. In either case, the term "assumption of the risk" is merely verbiage that has no place in today's law.

Permission Slips

When parents send their children to school, they have expectations regarding the type of activities in which the children will participate. If an activity is to take place that clearly is beyond the reasonable limits of these expectations, or involves transportation away from the school grounds, it is wise to secure a permission slip from parents. This form would state that the child has parental approval to participate in the specifically designated activity. In a recreational program, permission slips frequently are required before the child may participate at all. If the limits of the program clearly are specified, permission slips may be reserved for exceptional activities only.

Waivers

A waiver is a signed contract that frees the supervisor or administrative unit from liability in the event of an accident or injury in conjunction with some specifically named activity. Waivers have little legal value because the courts have tended to favor the position that a person cannot be protected by contract from the consequences of his own negligent actions. Further, no person legally can waive the rights of another; therefore, parental waivers on behalf of their child cannot prevent a later suit on behalf of that child.

Waivers are not without a certain administrative and legal value, however. They provide clear evidence that the participant or the parent or both were well aware of the nature of the activity and of the possibility of accident or injury—both of which are important elements in the establishment of a sound defense in the event of a lawsuit.

---

1. Meistrich v. Casino Arena Attractions, Inc., 31 NJ 44 (1959).

Risk Management

Risk management in simplest terms is a matter of understanding those circumstances in which accidents are most likely to occur and taking appropriate steps to minimize the probability of their occurrence. There are four primary categories of causal factors that are at the root of most preventable accidents. They are: faulty supervision, unsafe conduct of the activity, unsafe environmental conditions, and judgmental errors. These factors provide the basis for most negligence claims, and by controlling these factors an effective program of risk management may be developed.

Supervision

Because every educator is responsible for providing competent supervision and because effective supervisory practices can prevent many needless accidents, the quality or quantity of the supervision provided is brought into question in virtually all cases of tort negligence.

In essence, two types of supervision must be provided: general and specific. General supervision refers to the overall supervision of the class or group. It requires the supervisor to have complete knowledge of the subject matter, visual contact with the entire group, an alertness to dangers or deviations from normal procedure, and immediate accessibility when needed. Specific supervision is the direct supervision of one person or a small group, and generally is called for when the supervisor notes a danger or deviation from the norm or when he is introducing a new or particularly hazardous activity. As a general rule, participants need specific supervision until they can understand and appreciate the risks involved in an activity, evaluate their own performance, and understand and follow necessary safety practices.

Some general guidelines that the administrator can follow to help minimize the likelihood of accidents due to supervisory shortcomings are:

1. Hire only qualified personnel and be sure there are enough supervisors for the size of the group being supervised. Not only are poorly qualified teachers or supervisors liable for their negligent actions, the administrators who hire or supervise them are liable as well. When an applicable certification may be obtained (e.g., Red Cross Water Safety Instructor or United States Gymnastic Safety Association Certification), be sure your personnel have it. When no certification standards exist, set organizational criteria that unquestionably show administrative efforts to guarantee the quality of the person employed.

2. Never require staff members to teach or supervise activities that are clearly beyond their capabilities. When unfamiliar subjects must be assigned, provide ample time and support to assist each staff member involved in developing her skills and preparing the best possible program.

3. Develop the habit of writing all plans thoroughly and insist that all members of the staff do the same. Not only does the act of planning tend to alert the administrator to many potential hazards, but the plans themselves also can serve as valuable legal evidence of preparation and knowledge regarding the subject matter and of the ability and preparation of the participants.

4. Establish, publish, and rigidly enforce rules of conduct and safety for the gymnasium and all fields and facilities. Insist that these rules be adhered to faithfully and enforced by each member of the staff.

5. Never allow classes, teams, or recreational programs to be left unsupervised. Even going into an equipment room to gather material for the group creates a period of supervisory absence that, regardless of its brevity, can serve as a source of negligence in the event of an accident.

6. Never allow an unsupervised facility to be left open to the public. A gymnasium, for instance, is traditionally associated with a variety of dangerous activities. It is reasonable to assume that persons entering the gym will participate in many of these activities even though no supervisor is present, thus exposing themselves to unreasonable and often unexpected risks. When facilities are not in use, require that all equipment be put away and all doors secured.

Conduct of the Activity

With the possible exception of sports such as boxing and bullfighting, few activities are regarded as inherently unsafe. In the event of an accident, therefore, the question is whether the activity was properly conducted. Proper conduct of an activity includes: the selection of tasks that are appropriate to the age and ability levels of the participants; the provision of instruction that is both factually correct and sufficiently detailed to ensure the likelihood of success; the provision of a warning concerning any hazards and dangerous conditions as well as guidelines by which they may be avoided; and the provision of necessary protective measures and devices.

The following guidelines should be considered in the selection and development of programs and activities:

1. Comprehensive curriculum and program guides are indispensable. Not only do they reflect the choice and planning of activities on a given day, they also provide a record of the type and extent of previous instruction.

2. Remember, readiness is an individual matter. Pretesting and screening participants therefore have distinct value, as does careful recordkeeping of achievement and development.

3. Establish procedures for the acceptance of medical excuses and for allowing a person to participate after serious injury or illness.

4. Require all supervisory and instructional staff to maintain plans for alternative activities that can be conducted in the event that an outdoor activity must be suspended due to inclement weather. It is very difficult to justify an injury that occurred in a spur-of-the-moment substitute for a planned activity.

5. Be prepared to provide a sound justification that is consistent with organizational objectives for any and all activities conducted. Far too many injuries occur in activities chosen only because "the kids enjoy it."

6. Be sure all instruction is consistent with the latest techniques and information in the field and that the participants are warned clearly of any dangers and the ways in which these dangers can be avoided.

7. Be sure all appropriate safety equipment (e.g., gymnastic mats, catcher's masks, and eye guards for racquetball) meets appropriate standards, is readily accessible, and is required of all participants.

8. Reinforce the verbal warnings and requirements for safety equipment with clearly posted signs and written warnings (Figure 9.1).

9. Never allow anyone to participate in an activity for which he is not physically prepared and properly attired. Remember that proper attire in this case is a matter of safety and function rather than color and style.

Environmental Conditions

In addition to their responsibility for guaranteeing an appropriate activity that is properly supervised and implemented, administrators must guarantee the safety and appropriateness of the area in which the activity takes place and also the safety of any equipment used. Administrators or their employees should become aware of any potential environmental dangers through one of two primary ways. Constructive notice is the result of normal and appropriate safety inspections such as examining a field before use or inspecting a balance beam that has just been set up for a class or contest. Actual notice occurs when a situation is specifically pointed out by another person or persons, such as when a tennis court has been the source of player complaints due to erosion of part of its surface. In either case, there is a clear obligation to eliminate any environmental conditions that may interfere with the safety of the participants.

Specific guidelines for the provision of a safe environment would include:

I. Develop and implement regular inspection and maintenance schedules for all facilities and equipment.
   A. Assign individual responsibilities.
   B. Establish procedures for correcting deficiencies.

II. Be sure any new facilities exceed all applicable safety standards. Give great attention to such details as surfacing, free area around courts and fields, lighting, and the presence of obstacles or dangerous protrusions on walls.

III. Be sure all equipment meets or exceeds applicable safety standards and is designed properly for the purpose for which it will be used.

IV. When equipment must be installed, give careful attention to the question of who will do the installing. The use of local staff in the installation process often voids any guarantee that may exist and, in certain instances, may absolve the manufacturer of liability in the event of product failure.

V. Provide safety equipment for all participants and require its use. Post reminders for staff and for the participants to guarantee their awareness of the importance of protective equipment (Figure 9.1).

Judgmental Errors

The area of supervisory judgment is rather broad and encompasses a wide variety of situations in which the administrator may fail to apply common sense or prudent

Figure 9.1. Example of poster reminding staff and participants about protective equipment

judgment. Allegations regarding judgmental errors frequently center around the provision of first aid, when required, and around the mismatching of competitors in activities in which physical contact is probable. Guidelines for the reduction of risk in the area of supervisory judgment include:

1. Be sure all staff members have thorough, up-to-date training in first aid procedures. A wide variety of negligence claims center on allegations regarding improper application of first aid. One thing is clear. When necessary, first aid must be applied promptly and properly.

2. Establish and post a list of written procedures to be followed in all accident cases, and have emergency equipment and telephone numbers readily accessible.

3. Develop clear, thorough accident report forms that account for the circumstances surrounding the injury and subsequent first aid procedures (Figure 9.2). It often takes several years for a civil suit to reach completion. Unless accurate records have been kept, many important facts and the names of valuable witnesses can be forgotten.

4. Take whatever steps may be necessary to avoid mismatch situations in activities in which physical contact is likely. Students should be matched according to size and ability. Sex in and of itself is not a reasonable grounds for matching students. That is, a 100-lb girl attempting to block a 200-lb boy is no more or less mismatched than a 100-lb boy attempting to block the 200-lb boy. The importance of this factor is tempered considerably in interscholastic sports, due to the selectivity of the groups involved.

Legal liability and the accompanying demands for careful risk management are, without question, major areas of concern for all administrators. It would be a serious administrative blunder to view them only as problems to be solved, however. Properly handled, the elements of legal liability become a most effective weapon in program development. For instance, it is difficult to argue against the purchase of equipment that is necessary to meet acceptable safety standards or to ignore facility conditions that are clearly hazardous. Frequently, when other arguments fall on deaf ears, one can justify staff additions and in-service development on the basis of safety and recognized standards of professional care. The same professional standards that can be used to condemn poor programs in other words can provide the wise administrator with compelling arguments for program and personnel development and improvement.

REPORT OF INJURY TO STUDENTS OR PUBLIC

INJURED   Person: _____

                 Address: _____ Phone: _____

                 Age:_____

                 Association with program: _____

INJURY   Described: _____

                 Where taken: _____

                 Name of doctor or hospital:_____

                                                                    AM

ACCIDENT   Date: _____ Time:_____ PM

                 Exact address: _____

                 Exact location at address: _____

                 Describe accident: _____

                 _____

                 Cause of accident: _____

                 Name and address of witness:_____

DATE OF REPORT:_____ PREPARED BY: _____

                                                    _____

Figure 9.2. Sample accident report form

What are the objectives
of a planned public
relations program?

What are the steps in the
development of a positive public
relations program?

How can relevant publics be
identified and targeted?

How can an organizational image
be identified and delineated?

How can the administrator
assess the image projected
by the organization?

What should be considered
in the development of
printed material, verbal
contracts, and special events?

Chapter 10

Public Relations

Organizations, like individuals, are judged by the impressions they make on those around them, and public impressions play an extremely important role in determining whether an organization will survive or perish. This connection is especially apparent in financially difficult times when everything comes under careful scrutiny or attack. Organizations that are held in low esteem in a tight economy almost assuredly are doomed, regardless of how important they were in the past or consider themselves to be to the future. One only has to consider the rapid decline of the American automobile industry in the late seventies to realize how devastating public reaction can be to an organization that depends on public support and confidence.

Although an organization may be subject to the pressures of public opinion, it need not be totally at its mercy. In fact, an organization has much more control over its fate than most persons realize, particularly if it has learned to exercise control over public opinion. Administrators always have been confronted by the reality that the public forms an opinion of their organization whether they want them to or not. What these administrators subsequently have come to realize, however, is that they can favorably influence these opinions by selectively projecting only positive impressions. Toward this end many administrators have adopted an interventionist policy that calls for the continued and systematic evaluation of public opinion for purposes of developing, maintaining, and when necessary, altering the organization's image to ensure favorable public support. This policy is known as positive and productive public relations.

WHAT DOES PUBLIC RELATIONS MEAN TO THE ADMINISTRATOR?

According to Public Relations News, public relations is "the management function which evaluates public attitudes, identifies the policies and procedures of an individual or an organization with the public interest, and executes a program of action to earn public understanding and acceptance."[1] What is implicit in this definition and quite obvious even to the novice is that administrators involved in the public relations process are expected to:

1. Determine the organization's image from the public's point of view
2. Relate this image to the organization's hierarchy
3. Make suggestions to improve, maintain, or change the image
4. Execute a public relations program aimed at influencing the public's opinion

What is not as readily apparent in this definition is that the administrator is really involved in a two-way communications process that is supposed to receive messages as well as send them. As Cutlip and Center have pointed out, public relations is empathetic listening as well as persuasive communication.

WHAT KINDS OF OBJECTIVES CAN ONE HOPE TO ACCOMPLISH THROUGH A PLANNED PUBLIC RELATIONS PROGRAM?

This question probably has as many answers as there are organizations practicing public relations. Every organization, however, has several basic objectives that it hopes to accomplish through a planned public relations program. Almost all organizations attempt to accomplish the following objectives.

Communicate Their Identity and Scope to the Public

Communicating an organization's identity and scope to the public is an extremely important endeavor. If you have any doubt about this, simply look around. Survey the community's attitude toward funding a physical education department when it considers the service offered by the department to be nothing more than a respite from the rigors of the school day. Find out what kind of public support a recreation department gets when its constituency thinks of it only as a scheduling agent for Little League sports. In each case you probably will discover that these departments are dying because of public ignorance.

If the public cannot identify the distinct characteristics and functions of an organization or the complete array of services the organization provides, it will more than likely consider the organization superficial and unimportant—a waste of the taxpayers' money. If this becomes the consensus of opinion the organization will be eliminated.

In short, if an organization intends to survive, its public relations program must do more than inform. It must educate the people about "who the organization is," "what it does," and "why it is important."

Keep the Public Informed About Available Resources and Facilities

Human service organizations exist to serve the people. Without public patronage these organizations quickly would become extinct. Recognizing this, a public relations-

---

1. Scott M. Cutlip and Allen H. Center, *Effective Public Relations* (Englewood Cliffs, N.J.: Prentice-Hall, Inc., 1958), p. 5.

oriented administrator uses every opportunity to keep the public informed about the resources and facilities that are available for their use. This practice should be used not only to advertise the available facilities, but also to educate the public about what they are receiving for their tax dollar. Remember, no quicker way exists to close the doors of a facility permanently than to close out the public, either by a lack of information or by a set of operating procedures that favor staff rather than clients.

Keep the Public Abreast of New Services and Expanded Capabilities

Some administrators may ask why the advertising of new services is a public relations objective. The answer is simple. In public relations parlance the organization that advertises new services and capabilities should do so not only to encourage public participation, but also to demonstrate to the people the organization's willingness and ability to adapt to changing needs in the community. This message should be sent in as many ways as possible each time an organization launches a new program. Doing so helps the organization build an image that portrays it as consumer oriented and responsive—two things that every human service organization should strive to be.

Communicate a Favorable Reputation to the Community

Everyone wants to be part of something good or outstanding. An organization that has a widely acknowledged and honorable reputation has several advantages over an organization that has a poor or nonexistent reputation. A good reputation will:

1. Attract talented personnel, and also interested, capable, and influential volunteers. This ensures that the organization will be well managed and well supported, and in turn raises the status of the organization.
2. Encourage participation, for the simple reason that individuals want to be associated or involved in an organization that has status, because they feel it will lend them status. Because an assumption of quality is often linked to high status, many individuals will avail themselves of the services provided by a particular high-status organization because they feel the services will be of a superior quality.
3. Stimulate support and growth, basically because an organization that has a superior reputation is a source of community pride. The community therefore will take care to nurture and stimulate the organization's growth and development.

In essence, then, a good reputation may be the best form of security an organization can have in the community.

Call Attention to Growth and Achievement

Growth and achievement in the marketplace usually stimulate public investment in business. These same phenomena easily could occur in the public sector if administrators in human service organizations took the time to communicate their organization's growth and achievement to the public. For instance, if a physical education department could demonstrate that the children in the community were healthier because of its programs, or if the local recreation department could prove to its clientele that its services reflected a better quality at a lower price than most commercial establishments, these departments would stimulate public investment, basically because people are inclined to support organizations that give them a return on their money.

Communicate Sincere Interest and Responsible Involvement in Community Affairs

It is alarming how many human service organizations become so immersed in their own little world that they completely isolate themselves from the greater community. One of the best ways for them to avoid this and to gain support from their constituency would be to become involved, where appropriate, in community affairs. A physical education department that becomes involved in a health fair or a substance abuse clinic that is outside its normal range of responsibility is likely to win more public support than it ever will by releasing a dozen stories on the "new physical education." The same thing holds true for recreation departments. Administrators who lend departmental assistance to a community project will gain greater recognition and support for their departments in that one act than they will through a superficial open house during National Parks and Recreation Month.

Communicate With Their Internal Publics

When we think of a public relations program we tend to focus on an organization's external publics, that is, those publics that are related to or serviced by the organization. In so doing, we often forget one of the organization's most important publics, the internal public. An organization's internal public consists of those persons who are directly involved in the organization's operation. They do the work of the organization. They also give the organization an identity in the community. If those who work for the organization feel they are treated fairly, the organization will acquire a reputation for being fair. If, on the other hand, the employees feel that the organization is using people, the organization will get a reputation for being insensitive and unscrupulous. In other words, the community will view an organization through the eyes of those who work there. Public relations activities for the organization's internal public should: (1) keep them informed so that they give out accurate information, (2) make them feel that they are an important part of the whole operation so that they will take pride in what they do, and (3) open up avenues for them to assist in the decision making so they will defend the organization's positions. These are just a few examples of what a public relations program aimed at an internal public should try to accomplish. What is most important in a discussion of internal publics, however, is that an organization must have a public relations program for their internal public if they hope to make a sizeable impact on their external publics.[2]

2. Adapted from John F. Budd, Jr., *An Executive's Primer on Public Relations* (New York: Chilton Book Co., 1969), p. 65.

WHERE DOES ONE BEGIN TO PLAN A PUBLIC RELATIONS PROGRAM?

Recreation and physical education were created by the will of the people to serve the people. This gives them a completely different perspective than the XYZ Company that came into existence simply to produce "widgets" for the ABC Company. XYZ Incorporated has to be concerned only with satisfying the needs and wants of ABC Limited, whereas a recreation or physical education department has to be concerned with satisfying a factionalized public whose needs and wants usually differ dramatically from one faction to the next.

For this reason the planning stage of any program, not just a public relations program, should begin with the questions: Who are the people we serve? What are their needs and wants? How does this organization fit into their lives?

THE PUBLIC: WHO ARE THEY, WHAT DO THEY WANT?

"Generally speaking, a public can be defined as a group of individuals who share common beliefs, have like interests, or possess common attributes."[3] Some are easily identifiable, some are not. Those groups that are centered on an organized and established institution such as a religion are easily targeted and zeroed in on, while those that result from a happenstance such as sex, age, or income are rather amorphous and therefore not as discernible. Make no mistake, however, that both types of groups can have a devastating effect on an organization if they are not dealt with in an appropriate manner.

Before attempting to define her organization's publics the administrator should realize that:

1. *A community is comprised of several hundred publics.* Just by filling in the categories listed in Table 10.1 you can see how easy it would be to name a hundred publics without much effort. This being the case, each public should be considered carefully before placing it on the list of populations with which one intends to work.

Table 10.1. Categories of Publics

Organization Clubs Recognized and Groups	Institutions	Attribute Groups
Civic clubs	Religious groups	Marital status
Athletic clubs	Political groups	Age groups
Social clubs	School groups	Sex
Business clubs	Political bodies	Socioeconomic groups
Interest groups	Social agencies	Race
Clubs based on national organizations	Business	Educational status
		Profession, career

3. Neil J. Dougherty and Diane Bonanno, *Contemporary Approaches to the Teaching of Physical Education* (Minneapolis: Burgess Publishing Co., 1979), p. 195.

2. *Publics exercise varying degrees of influence, depending on the situation.* For example, the Rotary Club may be quite influential in the community when it comes to zoning board matters or school board affairs, but not at all influential in matters concerning youth sports. Remember this when planning a public relations campaign.

3. *An individual can belong to several groups or publics simultaneously.* Take the case of John Clark, a white, Anglo-Saxon, Protestant male, age 35, father of two, who has been practicing law in town for the past seven years and who presently is a Republican serving on the recreation committee. A recreation director who is proposing a park in John's neighborhood is going to have to take into consideration the attitudes that are prevalent in each public John belongs to if she expects to have him vote yes on a bond referendum.

4. *Individual group membership may be either voluntary or involuntary.* Groups comprised of voluntary members are much easier to reach than are those whose membership occurs simply as a result of chance circumstance. In other words, organized groups tend to have a visible structure, a set code of behavior, and recognizable leaders that make them fairly predictable and accessible, whereas groups comprised of involuntary members tend to have no discernible structure or leadership to approach. Teenagers, for instance, belong to an amorphous group known as the youth culture, but their membership in this group is due to chronological circumstance rather than direct subscription. Although teenagers seemingly exhibit a set code of behavior that distinguishes them from the older or younger generations in a community, they are relatively impossible to communicate with as a group because they have no discernible leadership who speaks for them, nor do they have a structure that makes them in any way predictable.

Realizing these things, you must take time to begin defining your organization's publics. First, make a list of the publics in the community that appear to be directly related to your organization. Use the list of categories supplied earlier, as well as any other classifications that are deemed feasible. Be sure to remember internal publics such as employees or the advisory committees assigned to any related department. The initial list also should include any public that might be related even remotely to the circumstances, especially if that public has the potential of being influential in community politics. When the initial list is complete, circulate it to the staff. It is hoped that this will have two effects: (1) it may result in several additions to the list and (2) it will begin to make the staff aware—or more aware—of the publics they are serving.

Second, call a staff meeting to determine what each public that has been identified in the above process may want or need from the organization. Write a "need," "want," or "concern" statement next to the listing of each identified public; examples are given below:

> *Local taxpayers' association—Concern:* Tax dollars are being spent on recreation that individuals should be purchasing from commercial enterprises.

Senior citizens' club—Need: Transportation is vital to this program. Members must use an inexpensive, flexible service that they feel the recreation department should supply.

Little League baseball association—Want: The Little League would like to expand its program. This would mean obtaining use of the high school fields as well as additional maintenance service from the recreation department.

When this task is complete, cluster publics with similar concerns, wants, or needs. This provides a focus for future planning and helps the organization to determine the type of image it wishes to project.

Third, review the list to decide which of the identified publics are most important or influential to the operation, either because they are decision makers or primary users. Ask the following questions, as well as others designed to fit the particular situation:

Which of these publics are prime users?

When are the prime users most active?

Which publics represent powerful lobbying groups?

Which publics have powerful decision makers within their membership?

Which publics have a strong reputation?

Which publics directly influence or make decisions regarding organizational operation?

Which publics support opposite views from the organization's?

Which publics have the greatest influences on other publics?

Which publics can be most or least likely reached or persuaded?

Those publics earmarked as most influential or important become the definers. Channel information to them during the course of the public relations program. As a consequence of doing so, such publics also serve as a barometer to measure the organization's success or failure in carrying out its purpose and objectives.

THE ORGANIZATIONAL IMAGE: HOW DO WE FIT INTO THE COMMUNITY'S LIFE?

Remember, like it or not, the organization projects an image to everyone who comes in contact with it. If a secretary is careless about typing flyers or letters, the organization projects a careless and unprofessional image. If a staff person dresses poorly or fails to plan every detail of his program or lesson, the organization appears lazy and uncaring.

Proofreading a secretary's work or buying uniforms for the staff may help the overall impression the organization is making, but isolated efforts such as these probably will not produce the desired image. Only a planned and focused attack brings the organization closer to an image that is in keeping with its goals and objectives and in the long run guarantees the organization's growth and success.

Before deciding on an image, review organizational goals and objectives. Ask these questions. What does the organization hope to achieve? How does it hope to achieve it? Who does it hope to reach or serve? What role does it feel it fulfills in the community? What role does it feel it *should* fulfill in the community? What kind of community support does it want or need? What type of relationship does it want with the community and with other agencies in the community? These and other questions must be answered before an organization can decide on its image.

Decide on the parameters of the image. Ask what type of image could be portrayed by the organization at this point in time. The answer to this question relies on the position the organization holds in the social and political community, on the ability of the staff, on the facilities at the staff's disposal, on organizational authority, and on individual capabilities. While conducting this analysis you should try to determine the type of image to be projected one year from now, three years from now, and five years from now so as to have a positive impact on the future.

Decide on your image. Having gathered this information, the organization can decide who it wants to be and how it wants to be viewed; however, deciding what the image should be still requires a great deal of consideration. As one constructs an image statement, the following questions must be asked continually: Who are we? What is our special purpose? What is our philosophy? What do we want people to know about us? Keep the message simple and direct. It increases the likelihood of actually being able to project such an image.

An image statement does not have to be lengthy. It can be a simple, one-sentence statement like: "Sobos is a friendly neighborhood sporting goods store whose only interest is satisfying the customer." More complex statements, however, may be needed to represent all facets of a human service organization.

Here are two image statements, which have been constructed for a recreation department and a physical education department respectively, that illustrate this point.

I. The Shade Tree Township Parks and Recreation Department:
    A. Provides an important service to the citizens of Shade Tree Township.
    B. Is a service-oriented governmental agency that is deeply involved in community development and growth.
    C. Is responsive to changing needs and wants.
    D. Acts as a recreation facilitator by working to provide the people with the type of recreation they want, either by providing it directly or negotiating with others to provide it.
    E. Provides only high-quality service.
    F. Is a people-oriented agency.
    G. Is managed by professionals dedicated to their field.
    H. Believes that the people should be kept informed.
    I. Is a good place to work.
    J. Is a good agency to do business with.
II. The Hilton Heights Physical Education Department cares about the health, safety, and well-being of every child in town. We're in the business of making all of our children feel like champions.

The next step is to determine what the people think by assessing the status of the organizational image in the community. This step is often overlooked in the planning process because few people perceive public relations programs as anything more than vehicles for dispensing information. This unfortunate misconception can be costly.

Public relations planning is divided into two tasks:

1. Determining the organizational image from the public's point of view
2. Devising specific activities to maintain, improve, or alter that image

Of the two tasks, administrators spend most of their time planning activities they hope will influence public opinion. Little time is spent trying to determine what the public actually thinks. "The trouble sometimes seems to be that organizations are convinced that they know what people think about them, when actually their judgments may be based on old information, prejudices, and that most dangerous of all devices, the one-man opinion survey."[4] The chairman of a physical education department may feel that, because his son plays varsity football, he knows exactly what every varsity player in the school thinks about the athletic program. He is like the recreation director who, on hearing two complaints from a participant population of two thousand, thinks the program should be abolished because everyone is dissatisfied.

Projecting one person's opinion is a dangerous and sometimes costly affair. A sensible administrator avoids making generalities and adopts a more reliable, research-oriented approach that includes analysis of:

1. Opinion surveys conducted in the community
2   Comments (both complaints and praise) made to staff and advisory committees
3. Incoming mail
4. Advisory committee opinions
5. National surveys and polls
6. Election and legislative voting that reflects public opinion on certain issues
7. Speeches and writings of recognized opinion leaders
8. Press clippings and radio and TV monitorings of what has been said on a particular subject
9. User statistics[5]

Regardless of the method or methods used, to obtain the most accurate picture of its image in the community, an organization must make its efforts continuous and systematic for them to be of any benefit. These efforts also must yield information that can be used to determine a department's progress in regard to its objectives. If this purpose is to be accomplished, those who administrate public relations programs must be appraised of what they are expected to do, when they are expected to do it, and why it is expected. In other words, to be effective they need objectives that are written and approved by the organization's highest administrator. Without such direction a public relations program is apt to be little more than a flurry of meaningless publicity.

4. Edward Starr, *Public Relations* (Dobbs Ferry, N.Y.: Oceana Publishers, Inc., 1968), p. 17.
5. Cutlip and Center, *Effective Public Relations*, p. 119.

Following is a set of objectives that was prepared for an urban recreation department. Two things should be noted about these objectives: (1) they provide direction without eliminating the latitude and flexibility an administrator needs to create programs that are specific to a given situation and (2) they take into account not only the status and image the organization would like but the status and image it now has. Both of these points are extremely important. Without either emphasis, the public relations program lacks the potential to fulfill its purpose.

Oak City Parks and Recreation Department
Public Relations Program

Purpose

The purpose of the Oak City Parks and Recreation Department Public Relations Program is to help the department gain the public confidence and support it deems necessary to function successfully within the community.

Intent

To achieve this goal every operating unit within the department is expected to establish direct communications channels with the public, in whatever manner is considered appropriate for that unit, for the purpose of favorably influencing public opinion.

Objectives

In light of the image the Oak City Parks and Recreation Department hopes to project and mindful of the department's present status, the public relations program is expected to:

   I. Present the Oak City Parks and Recreation Department as a valuable asset in the community that will help attract both residents and business to the city.
  II. Reverse the generally held opinion that services provided by a community recreation department are of lesser quality than those offered by a commercial enterprise.
 III. Build increased confidence in services provided by the department.
 IV. Establish the department as a partner in community growth and development.
  V. Establish the department as the hub of recreation in the community—as responsible for coordinating, organizing, directing, and initiating all recreation planning.
 VI. Keep the public informed about the department's position on legislative matters that are directly related to department affairs.
 VII. Establish channels of communication during crisis situations.
VIII. Establish a rumor control mechanism.
 IX. Stimulate greater involvement by the department and its employees in community affairs.
  X. Develop an understanding in the community of the policies, goals, and procedures of the department.
 XI. Forward the department's image as:
    A. A service-oriented government agency
    B. A people-oriented programmer
    C. Responsive to changing needs and wants
    D. Purveyor of high-quality services at low cost
    E. A department that listens to the people
    F. A highly professional and innovative department

MECHANICS OF THE PUBLIC RELATIONS PROCESS

While an organizational image may be translated into a plan in many ways, the final product probably will be divided into four subsections: "Printed Material," "Verbal Contacts," "Assorted Image Builders," and "Special Events." The implications of each of these is discussed in the following text. One important point to remember is that no one area should be stressed to the neglect of another. Each plays an important role in the public relations program, and all must be present to provide a balanced attack.

Printed Material

These products may well constitute the greatest portion of the public relations program and the one area that is conducted on a continuing basis. These printed materials include letters and memoranda, house publications, handbooks, bulletin boards, information pieces, posters, news releases, or other forms. They are among the most versatile tools at the administrator's disposal.

"In industry and the professions writing is a means to an end, justifiable only if it is better than or as good as any other means available of accomplishing a desired purpose. The end may be political such as furthering one's personal interest; it may be social or organizational, such as creating better understanding among a group of employees who work together"[6] or it may be intended as a means for projecting an image. One thing should be understood, however; although the written word is extremely versatile, it is not always the most appropriate means of communicating your ideas. Before you consider writing, ask yourself the following questions, which are based on a set of guidelines devised by David W. Ewing.[7]

1. *Do you have a clear and practical purpose for writing?* The basic reason for writing any public relations piece is to influence someone in a particular manner with the intent being to achieve a specific attitude or outcome. Therefore, the administrator must be able to answer the questions, "Whom do I intend to influence?" and "What do I want them to think or do when I am finished communicating?" If an answer to either or both of these questions is lacking, no sufficient reason exists for writing, and the administrator should consider stopping the process before it begins in earnest. On the other hand, if a sufficiently clear and practical reason for writing exists, proceed to question number two.
2. *Is a written piece the best way to accomplish my objectives?* At times a written piece provides a permanent record when it is neither necessary nor advantageous. In some instances, a written agreement may even be detrimental. If an administrator, for example, finds it in the best interests of the community to append a particular policy he may not want the arrangement in writing for it may set a precedent or be construed as favoritism. Although not many situa-

---

6. David W. Ewing, *Writing for Results in Business, Government and the Professions* (New York: John Wiley and Sons, 1974), p. 19.

7. Adapted from Ewing, *Writing for Results in Business, Government and the Professions*, pp. 22-32.

tions require precautions of this magnitude, many are better left unwritten because of the situation or the public involved. If, after careful consideration, the written word is felt to be the best means of communication, proceed to question number three.

3. *Am I the best person to prepare and send the communications?* There are times when the best form of communication is the written word. Its effectiveness is lost, however, because the wrong person or group assumes the responsibility for producing the material. When this occurs, the impact of the written word may not be just negative, it may well be devastating. Remember that life is based on a set code of social behaviors and protocols that inevitably take precedence even over lofty goals such as justice and truth. In order to get a message across, it must come from a socially acceptable and appropriate source. The only other alternative is not to send the message.

4. *Is the time right?* Timing in communications is just as critical as the source. If a written piece is released at the right moment it will have a far greater effect than if it is released at random. Deciding when to release a written piece requires an understanding of the public, a careful analysis of the public's mood, an assessment of the climate, and an understanding of the effect your piece is supposed to have. If the timing is wrong, don't send the piece. Wait until the time is right, even if it means eventually having to discard the piece.

5. *Is the written word too risky?* Here the message is clear. If a written piece can have negative repercussions at a later time, don't write it.

6. *Is the written word too rigid an approach?* When you are speaking to someone face-to-face you have the opportunity to observe body language and modify your approach if the situation warrants it. You cannot do this if you are writing. You must operate from intuition or past experience and hope that what you have written creates the impression you desire. Written communication may be too inflexible when you are working with a particularly volatile situation or when you are not sure what direction should be taken in a certain action.

7. *Will writing sufficiently meet your needs?* The written word has many drawbacks: "It is impersonal, one-way, unidimensional, and often dull."[8] Before deciding to use it ask yourself if another form of communication would better serve your purposes.

If, after this careful review and screening, the written word appears to be the best choice, be aware that a number of variables control the effectiveness of the communications. Fortunately, all of them are relatively predictable and can be used to advantage. Ewing[9] suggests that one should consider the following points for the best results:

1. *"Consider how much background is necessary before you present ideas, directives, or recommendations for change."* If the individual or group is likely to be hostile to the message, start out slowly, ease the reader into the situation

8. Ewing, *Writing for Results in Business, Government and the Professions*, p. 30.
9. Ewing, *Writing for Results in Business, Government and the Professions*, p. 73.

point by point as if talking to him face to face. To do otherwise is to ask for trouble.

2. *"Your credibility with readers affects your strategy."* The greater your credibility is in the eyes of the persons you are communicating with the more likely it is that you will be able to influence or change their opinion. You can gain credibility either by position and credentials or by opinion. If credibility rests on opinion or acquired status, you can do one of several things to improve your credibility in the eyes of the reader: mention ideas or facts that support the reader's point of view, align yourself with the thoughts and perceptions of the reading audience, cite the work or opinions of experts who already have credibility with the readers, or underscore personal ideas with opinions from prestigious sources.

3. *"If your audience disagrees with your ideas or is uncertain about them, present both sides of the argument."* Introducing both or all sides of the argument to a hostile audience will set an atmosphere of objectivity. It also will help present the desired position relative to readers in a point-by-point fashion, thereby allowing them to form an opinion on each point rather than the whole. This, coupled with an attitude on the part of the writer that says, in essence, "I can see how you would take that position, it is only natural until you have heard what I have to say," should win several new advocates.

4. *"Put your strongest points last if the audience is very interested in the argument, first if it is not as interested."* When the audience is receptive the best approach is to lead readers point by point to the desired conclusion, making sure that each point is stronger than the preceding one. The reverse is true when the audience is hostile. Hit readers with the strongest point first in the hope that it will keep them reading until the end.

5. *"Do not hope to change attitudes by offering information alone."* The introduction of new information usually makes an impact only on those who already hold the same views as the writer. This occurs basically because it reinforces the readers' position and gives them something they can use to substantiate their argument.

6. *"'Testimonials' are most likely to be persuasive if they are drawn from groups with which readers associate."* Individuals usually hold the same opinions as members of the groups they belong to or the groups they admire; therefore, the simplest way to influence anyone is to use testimony from either of these sources.

7. *"Be wary of using extremes or 'sensational' claims, facts, or examples to support your message."* While the intent of any written piece is to make the reader "sit up" and take notice, be careful not to carry efforts in this direction too far. It may have the reverse effect. If the audience is shocked by certain statements it may become angry or defensive, thus drastically reducing the writer's ability to get the point across.

8. *"Tailor your presentation to the reasons for readers' attitudes, if you are pretty sure of them."* Giving readers the facts is not always the best approach for winning their approval, especially if their attitudes are based on individual

emotions. When analyzing the audience try to determine the cause that precipitated the prevailing attitude. The answer will help to tailor the approach.

9. *"Watch for the effect of third parties."* As pointed out previously, the opinions of third parties have a definite impact on the way an individual thinks. Third parties also can have a direct impact on an individual in another way. Casually referring to a person or group in writing will conjure up emotions almost automatically on the part of the reader, whether that response was intended or not. For example, a recreation department news release that mentions the sponsorship of a park project by a congressman who recently spoke against raising Social Security benefits will definitely make a negative impression on many of the senior citizens in the community. Their feelings about the park will be influenced by their feelings about the congressman. Recognizing this the recreation administrator either must divorce the issue from the congressman, and this is not always possible, or he must build an extremely strong case for the park and the benefits that will accrue because of the congressman's sponsorship. By vigorously demonstrating the positive worth of the park and supplying the reader with strong arguments for supporting its development, the recreation director may be able to overcome the negative influence that has been generated because of the congressman's stand on Social Security.

Again, before writing, analyze the audience. The information derived will be extremely helpful in planning an approach. Ask yourself:

1. *Are members of the audience interested in the topic about which I will be writing?* If so, to what degree does the topic affect them? Do they have a primary interest, such as parents of a Little League ball player might have if you were writing about an entrance fee increase, or would they have a passing interest, such as a 30-year-old man might have if he read about a new recreation building for senior citizens?

2. *Does the audience understand the perspective I represent?* If you are writing about replacing a competitive pee wee basketball league with a program that stresses instruction and cooperative activity, for instance, do they understand that you are not totally against competition but that you are in favor of teaching children group skills before you place them in a competitive situation in which such skills are needed?

3. *Does the audience know me or the person on my staff who is doing the writing?* Do they feel that you are competent professionals and that you have the experience and educational background to write an authoritative and accurate article? Do they understand that if you are a coach, you are an educator as well and that you understand the concepts associated with human development and pedagogy? Do they realize that as a recreation professional you are skilled at programming more than just sport skills?

4. *Is the audience committed to an opposing viewpoint?* If they are, how strong is their commitment? Would women in the city softball league, for example, feel discriminated against if you failed to give them equal time on all of the ball

fields in town (even if it were more convenient for them to play at one complex) just because the men's league used every field?

5. *Will the audience feel that my article is a veiled threat?* Will high school students, for instance, who read a statement by a representative of the local physical education department that decries the deplorable physical condition teenagers are in and that resolves to do something about it view this as a concern for student health or as another method for giving failing grades in physical education?

6. *Does the audience demonstrate an attitude that is the result of an identifiable belief or prejudice?* Can you trace, for instance, a group's reluctance to endorse long-distance running for women to the belief that women cannot handle the physiological stresses that occur in these events?

The News Release: A Special Printed Piece

Understanding when to write and how to be persuasive is important when dealing with any written piece, but no more so than when dealing with the news release. The news release is a valuable tool in public relations because it has the potential to reach so many people. Unfortunately most administrators are not familiar with how to prepare news releases properly, and this severely limits their ability to communicate with the public through mass media. The mechanics of preparing a news release are included in this section in the form of a series of questions.

I. *What is the organization doing that is newsworthy?* In essence the question is, "What is being done that will interest the reader?" This question is probably the most important one, given that a news release that does not appeal to the media's readership will not be published. It is also a question that should be asked daily. Too many organizations miss opportunities to get in print simply because they are not news conscious.

The key to finding a newsworthy topic is to make sure to focus on something that relates directly to the interests and experiences of the people. Farlow[10] points out that news is news when it contains certain elements of particular interest to the reading public, namely:

A. When it is something extraordinary or unusual. Is the building that is being dedicated on Saturday the biggest or the best in your region? Did the person who won the turkey trot this year set a new record or did four generations of one family register for the race?

B. When a well-known celebrity or an important person in town is involved in your program either as a sponsor or a participant.

C. When it involves the details of a well-kept secret or some facts about a mystery. Is the school really going to add an aquatics facility, or why have three hot air balloons been tethered in Johnson Park for the last three days?

D. When it is funny or has some universal appeal. Babies learning to swim, children learning to care for their puppies or kittens, a child waiting at the

---

10. Helen Farlow, *Publicizing and Promoting Programs* (New York: McGraw-Hill, 1979), p. 38.

finish line to embrace his grandmother as she completes a 10K race are all scenarios with wide audience appeal.

E.   When it makes an emotional statement or creates adversarial roles. The necessity to close a program for disadvantaged youth due to lack of funds or the decision to cancel the junior high school interscholastic athletic program often will be front page news in many towns.

II.   *How can something be made newsworthy?* There are times when the daily routine is not colorful enough for a news release. In this period news has to be manufactured. Below are several topics that fit the category of manufactured news.[11]

A.   Take advantage of the latest headlines. If juvenile delinquency is a growing concern in the community and it is receiving a lot of front page coverage, write a news release on what the organization is doing to keep youth off the streets and out of trouble.

B.   Conduct an opinion survey on the community's attitude toward recreation and physical education.

C.   Analyze a current situation (e.g., declining level of fitness) and make a prediction.

D.   Give additional material on a current topic, where appropriate. If a particular sport has become the latest fad in town, do a story on how to buy equipment, where to get instruction, or any other topic that may interest the audience.

E.   Apply national reports or surveys to what is happening in the community.

F.   Develop a calendar of events or write about the activities that are planned for the future.

III.   *How should a news release be written?* The first step in this process is to prepare a fact sheet and fill it in. This will help get the information organized. Finished fact sheets are a tremendous aid for preparing posters, brochures, flyers, and a number of other printed pieces. They can be used for answering questions on different programs your organization is offering. They also can accompany a news release so that the newspaper or magazine staff can elaborate on the piece, if they would like. Below is a sample outline for a program fact sheet.

A.   Title of program or project.

B.   Purpose.

C.   Goals or objectives.

D.   Cosponsors, endorsements.

E.   Location.

F.   Dates, times.

G.   Number of classes or sessions.

H.   Registration information, criteria, limits.

I.   Fee.

J.   Speakers, personnel, credentials.

K.   Special features, characteristics, items of interest.

11. Adapted from Farlow, *Publicizing and Promoting Programs,* p. 41.

L.   Target populations.

M. Possible media outlets.

     The second step is to write the copy. A general rule of thumb when writing copy for a news release is to put the most important facts up front. In other words answer the questions what, when, where, why, who, and how in the first paragraph. Succeeding paragraphs should follow with minor but interesting and pertinent points. This format is called an inverted pyramid. Its main advantage is that an editor can crop the release to fit a certain space and the most important facts will not be lost on the cutting room floor.

     When writing the news release be sure:

A.   The facts are accurate. Check them in every possible manner before release.

B.   Not to editorialize.

C.   The first paragraph is catchy and well written.

D.   What is said is pertinent and important.

E.   Sentence structure is short and crisp. Long, flowery sentences belong in novels, not news releases.

F.   It is written for the average reader. Avoid technical language and polysyllabic words.

G.   It is less than two pages.

H.   It is written in the appropriate style. Refer to stylebooks such as *The New York Times Guide to Style.*

I.   It follows a prescribed format:
1.   All copy should be typed double-spaced on 8½ in. by 11 in. quality white paper. Do not send carbons.
2.   Use only one side of the paper.
3.   Allow 1-in. margins on the sides.
4.   Leave a quarter page to a half page of white space between the contact information and the first sentence of copy for the editor to write a headline.
5.   Avoid breaking a paragraph at the end of a page.
6.   Number the pages. Write the word "more" on the bottom of a page if the copy continues to the next page.
7.   Include contact information.
8.   Indicate a release date in the right-hand corner of the first page.
9.   Signal the article has ended by placing a "30" or a "#" after the last word.

     Figure 10.1 is a sample news release that makes use of the guidelines listed above.

     Public service announcements for radio follow basically the same rules as other news releases with the following exceptions:

A.   All words should be in caps.

B.   Everything should be triple-spaced.

C.   Words should be counted.

D.   Copy should be timed.

E.   Copy should not exceed five typewritten lines (equals 15 to 20 seconds).

```
FOR:     The Daily Home News                    FOR IMMEDIATE RELEASE
         Women's Page Editor

FROM:    Dana Hade, A.D.
         Pine Tree High School
         East Glen Road
         Polar City, NJ

         (201) 765-4361—Office
         (201) 935-7763—Home

POLAR CITY—The Polar City Physical Education Department will sponsor a Learn to Swim
    and Sail Program for children of Polar City residents from July 1 to July 30. Courses are
    planned in Red Cross beginner, advanced beginner, and intermediate swimming, as well
    as in beginner and novice sailing. Registration deadline is June 1, 19XX.
        The program, under the direction of Mr. Craig Ritz, will be conducted in two-week blocks,
    Monday through Friday from 8:00 a.m. to Noon, at the Municipal Beach. Cost per session
    will be $21.00.
        For more information call the Physical Education Department at 932-7577 any weekday
    from 9:00 a.m. to 4:00 p.m. #
```

Figure 10.1 Sample news release

The following suggestions may prove helpful when writing radio spots:

A. Limit the number of points you wish to make. It is more likely that someone will remember what you have to say if you concentrate on one or two items.

B. Use words to describe what you want a person to recognize visually. If your park has brightly colored playground equipment, describe the colors and patterns to enhance listener interest.

C. Repeat anything you feel is important. If you are giving a phone number, an address, or some other vital piece of information, mention it at least twice.

D. Be sure to arouse interest in your message from the beginning. Use music, sound effects, or words that will make listeners stop what they are doing and concentrate on what you have to say.

E. Don't bomard the listener with sounds or facts. A constant pounding of any sort will create a negative effect.

F. Don't be trite. Avoid commonly used words or techniques. Use a fresh approach.

G. If you think a dialogue is the best approach be sure it is convincing. Listening to a dialogue that sounds contrived can make people believe just the opposite of what you want them to believe.

H. A strong ending is just as important as a strong beginning. Leave the listener with the most important point you want them to remember.

Figure 10.2 is a sample public service announcement.

IV. *Who would be interested in the release?* When the release is finished determine the exact news outlet that would be most interested in what has been said. Be selective. A few well-placed releases reap far greater returns than several hundred

---

NORTH GANGSTON DEPARTMENT OF PARKS AND RECREATION, 4 LINWOOD PLACE, NORTH GANGSTON, NJ 08769, (201) 697-1442

Contact: Ernie Oppenheimer   March 20
             Program Coordinator   FOR IMMEDIATE RELEASE
             Home: (201) 972-6072
             Office: (201) 697-1443   Expires: June 1

PUBLIC SERVICE ANNOUNCEMENT
TIME: 20 seconds
WORDS: 50

THE POLAR CITY PHYSICAL EDUCATION DEPARTMENT WILL SPONSOR A LEARN TO SWIM AND SAIL PROGRAM FOR CHILDREN OF POLAR CITY RESIDENTS, FROM JULY 1 TO JULY 30. REGISTRATION DEADLINE IS JUNE 1, 19XX.

FOR MORE INFORMATION CALL THE PHYSICAL EDUCATION DEPARTMENT AT 932-7577 ANY WEEKDAY FROM 9:00 A.M. TO 4:00 P.M.

Figure 10.2. Sample public service announcement

sent out at random. Having made the selection, decide which person at the news outlet is most likely to use the story and send it to her by name, if possible. Sending the release to a specific person increases the chances of it being published.

As the public relations program progresses, seriously consider developing a media list that would include the names, addresses, and telephone numbers of contact people in each of the media outlets.

Below is a listing of possible media sources:

A. Newspapers including daily, weekly, and biweekly.

B. Subscription publications or those targeted to specific groups of people. These would include materials printed by groups representing various political parties, religious denominations, labor unions, clubs (fraternal, athletic, business, and so forth), colleges, and interest groups.

C. Professional association publications at the state, regional, and national levels including journals, magazines, and newsletters. A complete listing of associations can be found in the reference book entitled *The Encyclopedia of Associations.*

D. Other general-interest (unrestricted readership) print outlets: general magazines, wire services, news and feature syndicates, regional bureaus of national publications.

E. Local, immediate-area, and statewide print outlets with their own targets: house organs, newsletters (in-house, agency, vocational, organizational club, associational, industrial, business, church . . . avocational), city guides and calendars.

F. Community radio.

G. Special-audience radio.

H. Metropolitan radio.

Verbal Contacts

Verbal contacts with the public usually occur via meetings, speeches, phone calls, and face-to-face encounters. Although it is more difficult to control verbal contacts in a prescribed manner than it is to control the written word, verbal contacts nevertheless can be made manageable through policies and procedures. Policy in public relations is simply an extension of the program goals and objectives that sets the tone or climate for a particular situation. The procedure is an extension of the policy that directs the actions of an employee in specific instances.

Policies and procedures should be designed to cover as many commonplace situations as possible to ensure the continuous projection of the desired image. How to answer and screen phone calls, how to handle complaints or inquiries, or suggestions for making speeches or conducting public meetings are just a few of the topics that might be covered in a set of procedures governing verbal contacts.

Image Builders

Peter Schladermundt has pointed out that "in today's competitive market, where every advertising dollar must be used widely and with the greatest impact, more and more business leaders seem to be waking up to the fact that it can be of great value for each public appearance of a company—its buildings and billheads, its trucks and packages, its signs and television commercials, its business cards and letterheads—to be presented in an integrated manner which is immediately recognized as the family emblem or hallmark of that particular company. The successful corporate image will say immediately to the public: 'This is a company . . . I have heard about; its policies are sound and its advertising claims are honest; I feel safe in buying its products or using its services.'"[12] What is true of a business is no less true of a human service organization involved in physical education or recreation. These agencies, like businesses, also must portray an "honest" image so that people feel safe and secure when using their services.

An organization's design image, such as its insignia, symbol, or trademark, symbolizes the organization's personality and capability. This sort of visual device permits a series of impressions to evolve in the mind of the consumer. If it is to be effective it must:

1. Be in keeping with the organization's image. If the organization wishes to portray a conservative image, for instance, its design image must be conservative rather than flamboyant or folksy.
2. Be distinctive so that it is not confused with a symbol that belongs to another organization.
3. Be done in a professional manner so that it does not detract from the professionalism of the organization. There is nothing more distracting than a logo that does not have professional polish.

---

12. Peter Schladermundt, "The Image and Design," in *A Management Guide to Public Relations*, ed. Lee H. Bristol, Jr. (New York: Charles Scribner's Sons, 1960), p. 238.

4. Be up to date. If an organization has used the same symbol for many years it should consider updating it to reflect its present position in the community and to communicate that it has changed with the times.

Symbols are extremely important. A strong design can be an organization's best promoter or salesperson. As an invaluable asset in a public relations program, this symbol should not be left to chance. Every aspect of its design, including color and texture, lithography, and any slogan used, should be planned in careful detail to ensure the appropriate image. Avoid at all costs the amateur artist's inspiration, the boss's wife's rendition, or the well-meaning citizen's idea. Take the time that is necessary to design a symbol that portrays the organization's true identity.

Schladermundt[13] offers the following guidelines when designing a symbol:

An identification mark is a distinctive word, emblem, symbol, or device used to indicate or identify a particular company.

The optimum mark must have:
1. Impact—Single impact with immediate appeal
2. Legibility—Instant recognition and impression
3. Simplicity—Ease of understanding
4. Distinction—Recall and remembrance
5. Adaptability—Reproducible in any size or medium

In addition, because a particular function is required of this identification symbol, it should:
1. Emphasize the high quality of your service
2. Indicate that your organization is people-oriented
3. Emphasize that the organization is adaptable and future-oriented

Special Events

Special events mean visitors, and visitors mean an opportunity to influence favorably the public's opinion of the organization. How visitors are treated when they enter the facility probably has a greater impact on their impressions of the organization than does the program. Be careful to plan every detail of the program arrangements from the visitors' perspective. This keeps their convenience and pleasure first and foremost. Here are some suggestions from a public relations point of view for dealing with the public during a special event:

1. Arrange to greet all guests
2. Designate organizational personnel to act as hosts
3. Study traffic patterns to avoid bottlenecks
4. Place explanatory signs where they would be helpful, placing them at eye level.
5. Assign employees to specific duties, and if possible, rotate tedious jobs
6. Make registration quick and efficient; avoid lines, if possible
7. Have employees briefed to explain their work in lay terms
8. Have employees briefed on all aspects of the event so they can answer questions

13. Schladermundt, in Bristol, *A Management Guide to Public Relations*, p. 247.

9   Arrange good, professional-looking exhibits
10.   Make it easy for guests to locate the site of the event
11.   Have employees available to help with seating and directions
12.   Remove or cover any eyesores
13.   Hire professionals to handle automobile traffic, if necessary
14.   Save closest parking for guests
15.   Have someone stationed to thank departing guests
16.   Make sure that there is more than enough of everything, including refreshments, literature, and seating

PREPARING THE PUBLIC RELATIONS CALENDAR

A public relations calendar is essential if you intend to conduct a program in an orderly and organized fashion. Without such a device you may communicate more than necessary with a public that has little influence over the program, or worse yet, you may fail to communicate with a public that is important to the operation. A calendar also is a good way to avoid over-extending the capabilities and resources of the department.

A good public relations calendar should indicate the time needed to prepare the program, and whatever is needed to implement and evaluate the program. Calendars that simply show the date of an event or anticipated news release are not as useful. Calendars that show the length of a campaign from the first day of preparation allow the administrator to design worksheets and deadlines for those who are directly assigned to the program. They also solidify the entire operation along a time line so that everyone knows what is happening.

Figure 10.3 is a sample two-week section of a yearly calendar. Note the detail that is necessary.

The final step in any public relations effort should be evaluation. The feedback on the program not only tells how effective it has been, it also helps in planning for the future as well.

A public relations program can be measured from four different perspectives: audience coverage, audience response, communications impact, and process of influence. Gaining information on each of these areas is essential, as Wright[14] points out in the following commentary:

1.   Audience Coverage: to produce results you first must reach the audience. How large an audience is reached? What are its members like? What proportion of the desired audience is represented?
2.   Audience Response: How do members of the audience respond? Does the content of the message strike them favorably or unfavorably? Does it arouse their interest? Does it bore them? Do they understand it?
3.   Communications Impact: After an appraisal of these immediate reactions, you must consider the impact that a message has on its audi-

14. Charles Wright, *Evaluation of Mass Media Effectiveness*, UNESCO International Social Science Bulletin, vol. 7, no. 3, as cited in Cutlip and Center, *Effective Public Relations*, p. 147.

Date	Task	Personnel
March 16	Hold a meeting to begin planning for National Parks and Recreation Month in July Decide which publics we should communicate with Define the terms in which we will communicate	
March 17	Circulate results of March 16 meeting to entire staff Request feedback by March 20	
March 20	Review feedback from personnel Interpret results, design preliminary plans	
March 21	Present preliminary plans to program committee Refine plan Allocate basic resources Divide into subcommittees Set committee objectives Distribute deadline dates	
March 23	Release article on volunteer project Prepare for press conference on fitness trail opening 1. Arrange room 2. Package written material for distribution 3. Review slide show 4. Confirm refreshments 5. Review work responsibilities with project crew	
March 26	Meeting: planning committee for National Parks and Recreation Month Report on progress Determine media contacts for each target group	
March 27	Meeting: recreation advisory board subcommittee on program development	
March 28	Release information to newspaper on future plans for program development	
March 29 April 2	Interview with Bob Dunn, WMJJ, on program development All summer program fact sheets due	
April 4	Prepare news releases on summer program Distribute preliminary releases to newspapers	

Figure 10.3 Sample two-week section of a yearly calendar

ence. What are the lasting, discernible effects upon people exposed to the message?

4. Process of Influence: What is the process by which a communication operates to influence its target audience? Through what channels of influence and mechanisms of persuasion does the message finally affect the individual? How effective is the program in setting into motion the social processes necessary to influence the opinions and behavior of its target audience?

Probably the simplest way to evaluate the effects of a public relations program is to survey the different publics that were targeted in each activity. In this way you will have constant and continuous feedback.

Why does there
never seem to
be enough time?

How can the
administrator
derive the maximum
benefits from the
time available?

What are the time
traps in an
administrator's
professional life?

How can time
traps be avoided?

What are the elements
of an effective
time management
program?

Chapter 11

Time Management

Life used to be simpler and more predictable. If a person knew the role he was expected to play, he knew exactly what to do every hour of the day, every day of the week. Barring catastrophes the routine remained the same, day in and day out. Every moment of the person's life was regulated and accounted for. The individual had a prescribed time to rise, a prescribed time to work and recreate, and a prescribed time to retire. Little, if anything, interfered with the daily course of action in his life. Having time at his disposal to do with as he saw fit was unheard of. Bound by a rigid set of time expectations, the person wasted few of the precious moments in his lifetime.

As society became more complex, roles began to differentiate and time was no longer accounted for so explicitly. Consequently, vast numbers of persons acquired discretionary time, that time a person could use according to his own judgment. Discretionary time has been a great boon to mankind, and has permitted individuals the personal freedom to accomplish goals and aspirations. Regrettably, having discretionary time also has permitted mankind to squander the precious resource involved —time.

Discretionary time provides a person with a greater opportunity to control, and thus make an impact on, what is being done. Unfortunately, because most persons lack the self-control and self-discipline to restrict the influence of external forces, they have drastically limited their ability to use time to their advantage. The end result is that individuals no longer have control over their time, not because they are bound by a rigid set of time expectations, as they were before, but because of their inability to control themselves.

Most would agree that it is sometimes impossible to complete everything that one is supposed to do in the course of a single day. The common complaint heard over and over again is that there just is not enough time. "This is an alarming, indeed a critical situation when we realize a startling fact about time—there isn't any more of it. Each of us already has all there is."[1] Unlike other resources it cannot even be used conservatively. Time is the one constant in life. No matter how it is used or abused, once it has ticked by it is lost forever. Successful administrators realize this. They also realize that the limits of their success often are set, not by their ability to control and manage time (because it is impossible to do so), but by their ability to control and manage themselves.

THE ADMINISTRATOR AND THE TIME TRAP

Every administrator is a prime target for time traps, those insidious pressures that allow her to abuse time and use it unproductively. They may stem from a loyal supporter who wants to kibbitz about an upcoming bond issue for new facilities, or from a subordinate who walks in unannounced and disturbs her deepest thoughts, but time traps abound in an administrator's life.

Time traps are not always the result of external forces, however. As MacKenzie points out, many are internally generated and generally linked to a lack of self-control.

> When asked to identify their major time wasters, managers invariably list external causes first, such as the telephone, meetings, visitors, paperwork, and delays. After time management problems and principles have been discussed, a new source is invariably identified—the man within, generating such time wasters as a lack of delegation, fire fighting, lack of plans and priorities, the open door policy, and procrastination.[2]

No matter what the source of a time trap, one fact is clear. Time traps can be devastating and costly to an organization. They hamstring an administrator's effectiveness and in so doing cripple an organization's efforts by severely limiting the already scarce resource of time. If administrators are to maximize their potential, they have to maximize their use of time by consciously avoiding the time traps in their daily routines.

One way to do this is to equip oneself with an early warning system. The old saying "forewarned is forearmed" is particularly appropriate in this effort. If an administrator knows what constitutes a time trap and what to look for, she should be able to stop this trap before it begins.

Below is a list of externally and internally generated time traps that most administrators have encountered on more than one occasion. Try to visualize specific instances in which they could occur in the course of an administrator's daily routine. This makes them more easily recognizable when they occur again. Remember, the key to dispelling the notion that time traps are legitimate patterns in your life is to recognize them for what they are, insidious pressures that allow you to abuse time and use it unproductively.

---

1. R. Alec MacKenzie, *The Time Trap* (New York: McGraw-Hill Book Co., 1972), p. 1.
2. MacKenzie, *The Time Trap*, p. 1.

External Time Traps

Ask yourself, "Do I waste time because of":

1. Telephone calls that could be handled by someone else if they were screened properly?
2. Meetings that are too numerous and often poorly conducted?
3. Paperwork that could be eliminated or handled by a subordinate?
4. Memo writing that could be handled better by a telephone call or a standard form letter?
5. The organization's inconsistency in policy or procedure?
6. The inaccessibility of information I need to do my job?
7. My lack of understanding of what it is I am supposed to do?
8. Poor support staff (e.g., secretaries, clerks)?
9. The bureaucratic red tape?
10. Poor lines of internal communication?

Internally Generated Time Traps

Ask yourself, "Do I waste time because I":

1. Try to accomplish more than is humanly possible in the time allotted?
2. Procrastinate over even minor matters?
3. Organize my affairs in a haphazard manner so that I can never find anything or get my hands on it quickly when I need to?
4. Insist on perfection even when it is not necessary or desirable?
5. Refuse to delegate authority or to let others help me?
6. Do not allow myself enough time to do something well?
7. Fail to learn or use accepted policies and procedures?
8. Attempt to implement projects without fully planning every detail?
9. Make snap decisions without all the information just so it can be checked off my list of things to do?
10. Find my job too routine and boring or too demanding and impossible?

Knowing that these time traps exist is half the battle in avoiding them. Be alert to recognize them whenever they occur.

THE TIME MANAGEMENT PROCESS

Being able to recognize and avoid those situations that have the potential of reducing administrative effectiveness, although extremely helpful, is at best only a superficial method of attacking the problems associated with time abuse. In essence it is like trying to cure an illness by treating the symptoms rather than the disease.

An effective time management program is really a five-stage process that will help get at the heart of the time management problem, that is, the administrator and his behavior. The process is actually quite simple.

Stage one: Analyze your own goals and aspirations

Stage two: Analyze the organization's goals and objectives in relationship to your own

Stage three: Determine the kind of administrator you are

Stage four: Create an environment in which you can work

Stage five: Plan your work

Notice that planning is the last stage in the process, not the first. A series of stages precede it that allow the manager ample opportunity to collect data from every perspective. This keeps managers from making plans in a vacuum, based only on partial truths that would make the plans essentially useless. Conducting planning in the last stage of the process ensures that managers base their plans on who they are rather than the mythical person they think they are, and in so doing tailor their plans for their specific needs.

Know Thyself—The First Step in Positive Time Management

Time management is not time control, it is self-control. Consequently, the most important information administrators can gather concerns themselves. Discovering who they are and where their priorities lie is exceedingly important. This information eventually becomes the basis for all decision making in regard to time. Managing time is like managing money. If the administrator knows what is important to her and what she wants, she knows where to cut back and where to indulge. It only makes sense, then, to start her time management program with a critical analysis of herself and her time.

Begin the Self-Study by Asking the Question, "What Are My Personal Goals?"

Asking yourself "What are my personal goals?" will:

1. Help you discover what you really want from life.
2. Help you become highly self-motivated at work and at play.
3. Help you use your time in a way that is meaningful to you.
4. Help you focus your energies in a direction that is rewarding to you.
5. Help you reduce conflict on how to spend your time productively.
6. Help you determine a basis for choosing what you will do with your time.[3]

Although a person's understanding of what he wants to do with his life does not help him directly to manage time more effectively, it does help him to recognize those activities that move him closer to achieving his goals, and in so doing motivates him to make plans to his advantage with a minimum of wasted time and effort. If he determines that one of his goals is to achieve national prominence in his area of expertise, for example, he might decide that giving workshops and publishing his ideas are critical to the advancement of this goal. Given a choice, then, between taking time to chair the local Memorial Day Parade Committee and using his time to write an article, the choice would be obvious. The time would be far better spent writing the article.

---

3. Alan Lakein, *How to Get Control of Your Time and Your Life* (New York: A Signet Book, 1974), p. 30.

Although all decisions are not as obvious nor quite as simple to make as the one in the illustration, two things are certain: (1) it is far easier to choose between two alternatives when a person has a particular goal in mind and (2) time is rarely wasted or squandered when a person makes a decision that is aligned basically with personal goals.

Determining goals is a relatively simple task. To do it effectively, however, you must be prepared to invest time and energy until the task is complete. Take the time to sit down on more than one occasion to commit goals to writing. Do not be afraid to use words like happiness or success, but eventually you should define them in concrete terms so that their personal meaning is exact. Do not be limited to conventional middle-class goals like owning a house or becoming the head of a department. Dig deep and find out what you really desire in life. Regardless of whether it involves breaking a record or marketing a game or writing a short story, commit the ideas to paper. There is nothing to lose, and everything to gain. Further, no restrictions should be placed on the imagination. Goals should be written as fast and as furiously as the hand allows. Value judgments can be made after the writing is done.

When the list is complete, review each goal in detail. Similar or like goals should be paired, and a direction established. Frivolous goals or those not in consonance with the rest of the group should be eliminated. Finally, determine the subtle characteristics of each goal, then assign priorities to all of the goals according to the following rating scheme:

1. Give a five-star rating to those goals about which you feel strongly. Be frugal with this rating. Award it only after careful consideration. Ask yourself, "Would I be willing to sacrifice practically everything to accomplish this goal?" If the answer is a definite "yes," you have identified one of your highest priorities.
2. Give a four-star rating to those goals you sincerely would like to accomplish to any degree that is possible. If, for instance, you would be satisfied with being financially comfortable even though your goal was to be a millionaire, you have identified a four-star rather than a five-star priority.
3. Give a three-star rating to those goals that could be accomplished only as a result of accomplishing a goal of a higher priority. If, for example, you would like to return to school to study law but you only would consider doing so after you had achieved prominence in your present field, you would have established a three-star goal.
4. Give a two-star rating to those goals you would like to accomplish if and when the opportunity presented itself. Two-star goals can be equated to your Walter Mitty-like desires. If you always wanted to climb the Matterhorn but you wouldn't even bother to try unless circumstances brought you to the base of the mountain (e.g., you won a trip), you have identified a two-star goal.
5. Give a one-star rating to those goals you think you should accomplish because of outside pressure or influence rather than your own desire.

Determine the Goals Set by the Organization

Having determined personal priorities it is time to determine the priorities that have been set by the organization. This task is an important one because, more often than not, organizational goals rather than the administrator's own are consuming and directing her time. Determining organizational goals will provide her with two important pieces of information:

1. It will help her to ascertain whether her goals are compatible with those established by the organization.
2. It will help her to determine whether she will be able to forward her goals within the organizational structure.

This kind of information is of great value. It can help an administrator decide whether her time is being used to her best advantage or whether it is being exploited with little promise of a return for her investment. Take the individual in the last illustration who aspired to national prominence. If she worked for an organization that wished to make an impact on a national audience, it would be a relatively simple matter to forward her own goals while satisfying the objectives set by the organization. If, on the other hand, the organization took the position that all efforts should be directed at local affairs and that all personnel should maintain a low profile, her goals not only would be incompatible with those of the organization, they would be diametrically opposed to them. In this second instance her interests would be best served by modifying her goals or moving to a setting that was more conducive to satisfying her needs. To do otherwise would be to waste her time.

Organizational goals can be determined in three ways:

I. *Review the formal goal statement of the organization.* Most school systems and recreation departments have a prepared goal statement that outlines the purpose of the organization and what it intends to accomplish. Reading this statement will make a person aware of the parameters that the organization has set for its activities and the measure it will use to verify its success or worth or both.
II. *Review the organizational policy manual.* Most organizations also maintain a set of written rules, which are known formally as the policy manual. These rules or policies prescribe a particular course of action that the organization feels is the most expedient method for handling a situation in accordance with its goals. Reviewing these rules or policies provides a better understanding of how the organization intends to accomplish its goals.
III. *Determine the ideology of the organization.* Every organization has a rationale that prescribes or prohibits its actions. This rationale is known as an organizational ideology. Understanding an organization's ideology aids in understanding the behavior of an organization's members, because an ideology:
   A. Specifies the goals and values toward which the organization should be directed and by which its success and worth should be measured.
   B. Prescribes the appropriate relationship between individuals and the organization (i.e., the "social contract" that legislates what the organization should be able to expect from its people and vice versa).
   C. Indicates how behavior should be controlled in the organization and what kinds of control are legitimate and illegitimate.
   D. Depicts which qualities and characteristics of organization members should be valued or vilified, as well as how these should be rewarded or punished.

E. Shows members how they should treat one another—competitively or colla-boratively, honestly or dishonestly, closely or distantly.

F. Establishes appropriate methods of dealing with the external environment—aggressive exploitation, responsible negotiation, proactive exploration.[4]

In an article entitled "Understanding Your Organization's Character" Harrison identified four organizational ideologies: (1) power orientation, (2) role orientation, (3) task orientation, and (4) personal orientation. Table 11.1 outlines the characteristics of each and how they relate to what Harrison calls the primary interests of people. These are: "(1) security against economic, political, or psychological deprivation, (2) opportunities to voluntarily commit one's efforts to goals that are personally meaningful, and (3) the pursuit of one's own growth and development even when this may conflict with the immediate needs of the organization."[5]

Although organizations rarely espouse one ideology to the total exclusion of all others, they do tend toward a specific direction and exhibit most of the qualities associated with an ideology. Knowing this, one should be able to determine whether the organization is permissive or prohibitive in terms of advancing individual goals.

4. Roger Harrison, "Understanding Your Organization's Character," *Harvard Business Review on Management* (New York: Harper and Row, 1975), p. 40.

5. Ibid., p. 51.

Table 11.1. Organizational Ideologies Related to Primary Interests

Ideology and Characteristics		Personal Security	Meaningful Goals	Personal Growth and Development
I.	*Power Orientation*	Poor	Poor	Poor
	A. Attempts to dominate environment	Organization's	Must subscribe	Little
	B. Highly competitive, protective of its territory	security is paramount,	to organiza-tion's goals	opportunity for personal
	C. Will not submit to external law or power	personal security in-	regardless of one's own	growth
	D. Expands its control at the expense of others	consequential	orientation	
	E. Takes satisfaction in dominating weaker opponents			
II.	*Role Orientation*	Excellent	Poor	Poor
	A. Extremely rational and orderly	Personal rights	Not at all	Allows
	B. Attempts to conduct itself legally and responsibly	secure because	flexible. Can-not accommo-	little devia-tion from
	C. Operates within the confines of agreements, rules, and procedures	rights are well defined	date personal goals	prescribed roles
	D. Carefully defines rights and privileges			

continued

Table 11.1/ continued

Ideology and Characteristics	Personal Security	Meaningful Goals	Personal Growth and Development
E. Values stability and respectability F. Slow to adapt to change			
III. *Task Orientation*	Good	Excellent	Poor
A. Energies directed solely toward the achievement of one goal	Person secure only if they	Person is in organization	Only achievement of supreme
B. Worthiness and success of all activities evaluated only in regard to accomplishing the supreme goal	add substantially to achievement of supreme goal	because they subscribe to supreme goal	goal matters, personal growth not important
C. Anything or anyone that impedes progress toward achieving the goal is retooled or replaced			
D. Organization extremely flexible, able to adapt to change almost immediately			
E. Not competitive with other organization, seeks alliances to forward goal rather than to gain an advantage over the ally			
F. Usually a conglomeration of zealots with a specific interest			
IV. *Person Orientation*	Excellent	Excellent	Excellent
A. Exists to serve its members, members use organization to meet own needs	Individual security	Goals are meaningful	Growth and development
B. Positions of authority exist only when necessary and then are assigned according to expertise	paramount interest of organization	because they are one's own organization	possible because
C. Group decision making preferred		exists for individual	
D. Undesirable tasks shared equally by membership			
E. Roles are chosen, not assigned			
F. Members depend on each other for inspiration, assistance, and instruction			

Adapted from "Understanding Your Organization's Character" by Roger Harrison, *Harvard Business Review on Management* (New York: Harper and Row, 1975), p. 52.

Determining personal priorities provides an administrator with an individualized perspective for evaluating the appropriateness and value of each project he is asked to undertake. In short, it can help him to decide whether he should invest his time. However, it does not help him to predict how effectively he will manage time once he invests it. To decide this, he has to analyze the type of administrator he is.

Analyzing Administrative Style

An individual's administrative style has a definite effect on his ability to manage time. In most instances it represents an administrator's approach to life. As such it represents not only his use of time at work, but also his use of time in general.

The relationship of administrative style to time management as it affects administrative performance is illustrated in Table 11.2. After reading each of the styles, the administrator should try to determine which characteristics apply directly to his style. He then should evaluate the effects of these characteristics on his ability to manage time.

Knowing the weaknesses in your administrative style is half the battle in correcting them; however, knowing these weaknesses will not explain to what extent they are controlling and directing your time use patterns nor how you could go about correcting them. Only a careful study of your daily routine will help to determine the extent to which it is being controlled by your own bad habits or by external forces, and the form these time traps take.

Conducting a Time Study

Before you can begin a time management program one last bit of information is needed. This can be gained from a time study log. A time study log is simply a detailed record of how an individual spends every moment of the day. Figure 11.1 is a sample of a time study log, and the following are rules for using a time study:

Table 11.2. Relationship of Administrative Styles to Time Management

Administrative Styles Developed by Pearse[a]	Possible Effect on Ability to Manage Time
I. The task and achievement-oriented manager	
A. Demonstrates a strong need to finish all projects personally	Inability to delegate authority or responsibility forces him or her to invest large amounts of time in all projects regardless of their importance.
B. Derives great satisfaction from completing tasks personally	
C. Does not delegate authority	
D. Tends to be an overachiever	
II. The leadership dominant, decision maker-oriented manager	

[9] R. Alec MacKenzie, *The Time Trap* (New York: McGraw-Hill Book Co., 1972), p. 18.

continued

Table 11.2/continued

Administrative Styles Developed by Pearse	Possible Effect on Ability to Manage Time
A. The "take charge" type B. Needs to dominate subordinates C. Needs to be in control at all times D. Values ability to make quick decisions E. Has difficulty delegating authority	Making quick decisions without all the facts often creates more work (1) to undo what was done and (2) to do it right the second time. If taking charge means having to do tasks that others can do, individual is wasting time.
III. The impulsive, physically energetic manager A. Action oriented, has to be on the move constantly B. Known for making impulsive decisions C. Gets things done witha great deal of activity and commotion	Impulsive decisions often have to be compensated for, thus creating much more work. Failure to plan makes implementation much more difficult and time consuming.
IV. The colorful, personable manager A. Enjoys close personal contacts B. Feels a need to be noticed C. Spends large amounts of time on interpersonal communication D. Likes to be emotionally close to those around	Nurturing personal contacts often requires time that would be spent more profitably doing work.
V. The theoretical, detailed, structured manager A. Spends a great deal of time analyzing every detail of a project B. Relates best to abstractions and conceptual thinking C. Likes to attend to detail personally D. Feels most comfortable in highly structured environment E. Institutes rigid organizational patterns	Wastes time on minor and insignificant detail. Often fails to be pragmatic or to implement work. Rigid organizational patterns and procedures waste time.
VI. The change-oriented manager A. Finds routine oppressive and boring B. Likes changes C. Resents doing repetitive-type work D. Uses time to avoid emergencies	Initiating change requires energy. Energy requires time. If the change is not necessary the individual has wasted time.
VII. The fellowship-oriented manager A. Feels a need to defer to authority B. Has difficulty working independently C. Needs praise and reassurance from superiors D. Needs highly structured environment to operate effectively E. Likes the entanglements of a bureaucracy	Having to get approval every step of the way slows down the work process not only because of the constant interruptions, but because it breaks the continuity of thought. Starting the process after an interruption requires a renewed vigor that is costly in terms of time and energy.

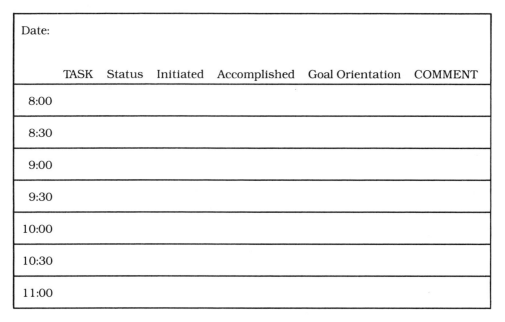

Figure 11.1. Sample time study log

I. Write down a task when you begin. Don't trust your memory at the end of the day, because if you do you are likely to miss important time use patterns. Also be sure to write down everything. Don't forget phone calls or chatting over coffee.

II. Keep the log for at least two weeks so that you have time to let your time use patterns develop on paper.

III. At the end of the day:
   A. Indicate the status of the task. Was it of high priority (HP), medium priority (MP), or low priority (LP)?
   B. Indicate who or what initiated the task (for example: your superior, a crisis, a subordinate).
   C. Indicate whether you accomplished the goal or not by writing a YES or NO in the column headed "Accomplished." Do not cheat. Make sure the task is absolutely complete (no loose ends) before you write YES.
   D. Indicate how the task relates to your own priorities. Establish whether it was directly related (DIR), indirectly related (IND), or not at all related (NR).
   E. Ask yourself the following questions and then comment on what you can do:
      1. What am I doing that really does not need to be done at all by me or anyone else?
      2. Which of the activities on my time log could be handled by somebody else just as well, if not better?[7]

6. Peter F. Drucker, *The Effective Executive* (New York: Harper and Row, 1967), pp. 36-39.
7. Ibid.

3. What do I do that wastes the time of others?[8]
4. Is any one person or thing controlling my time more than they have a right to do?
5. Are most of my interruptions external or internal?
6. How long do I really work before I get bored or distracted easily?
7. Do the majority of tasks I perform during the day relate to my goals?
8. How much time do I spend (1) on the telephone, (2) at meetings, (3) in formal and informal conversation or appointments?
   a. Could any be eliminated?
   b. Could the time be shortened on each?
9. Devise your own question here.

The information gained from a time study log can be useful in helping administrators to control themselves and their time, particularly if they are diligent in recording information each time they conduct a study and if they make it a habit to conduct a study approximately every six months.

Devising a Time Management Program

Equipped with the data collected thus far, the administrator is ready to design a time management program expressly for herself. The first step in the process is to create a working environment that is time efficient. The comments made on the time study log will give direction and focus to this effort. Thus, the log should be studied carefully before beginning.

Creating a time-efficient working environment results in two things: (1) you will create large blocks of uninterrupted time and (2) you will form efficient time use habits.

Creating Uninterrupted Time

In order to complete a task one needs large blocks of uninterrupted time. Without them one is doomed to frustration and quite often second-rate performance. Below are several suggestions that may help to create the kind of time blocks needed to complete one's daily workload.

I. *Decide when you work best.* Are you a morning, afternoon, or evening person? When do you feel your attention span is longest? When do you have the most energy and desire to do work? Whenever it is, create your large blocks of time during that period.

II. *Declare your work time to be "Private Office Hours" for your use only.* Make sure everyone on your staff knows that between 8:00 a.m. and 10:00 a.m., for instance, you are not available unless there is an emergency. Decide what constitutes an emergency and inform your secretary what the criteria are. It will be his or her job to enforce this rule.

8. Ibid.

III. *Save the trivial matters for your down time.* Each of us gets sidetracked daily on tasks that could have been tackled much later. If you really are interested in preserving your uninterrupted time have your secretary:
   A. Hold your mail until your office hours officially begin.
   B. Hold your telephone calls until your office hours officially begin. When office personnel receive calls during this period they should:
      1. Screen the calls to ascertain whether there is someone else in your office who could handle the matter.
      2. Screen the calls to ascertain the exact matter the person is calling about so that you have that information when you call back and they can gather whatever materials you will need when you do call back.
      3. Determine when the person will be available to receive your call-back so that you do not waste time making several useless attempts.
IV. *Find a secondary office.* Sometimes no matter how hard you and your secretary try, there still are too many distractions in your environment. Exactly for these times you should have another space to which you can retire; only you and your secretary can know the location, otherwise your plan will be defeated.
V. *Establish "availability" hours.* Set specific times in the day when you can be reached easily. This takes a great deal of pressure off your "private" hours.

Form Good Working Habits

Having large blocks of uninterrupted time at one's disposal is meaningless if one's work habits are poor. The following are a few suggestions that increase the efficiency of one's efforts:

1. *Get everything you need before you sit down to work.* Nothing is more frustrating than not having at your disposal what you need to complete a project. Every time you get up to get something you are wasting time. Before you begin a project make a list of what you need (include even your pencils) and do not sit down to work until you have every item on your list in front of you.
2. *Clear your work area of extraneous material.* When you sit down to work make sure your work space is clear of all distractions or temptations. A pile of unanswered memos, a new sports equipment catalog, or even a telephone message to be answered can sidetrack you when you are deep in thought.
3. *Determine how long your attention span is.* Most of us can work on a project only for a specific amount of time before we get bored or tired. Determine how long your attention span is and limit yourself to this amount of time each time you undertake an assignment.
4. *Handle a piece of work only once.* Do not tackle a project or even a routine matter until you have all the information you need or until you are really in the mood to start and finish it in one sitting. To do otherwise is to waste time.
5. *Make your telephone calls short and to the point.* Before you place a call write down all the points or questions you have, placing them in the form of a mini-agenda. When you make your phone call, keep your agenda and you will accomplish more in less time.

6. *Limit your socializing.* Kibbitzing uses a great deal of time. Try to limit it to specific times of the day (e.g., lunch time, after work, Friday afternoons).

7. *Learn to say no.* When someone asks you to do something, quickly determine whether it will forward your priorities. If it will not, say no. If you say yes when you would prefer to say no, the chances are that you will perform the task half-heartedly anyway, and that would not serve your purpose or theirs.

Once the most efficient environment has been created, a work plan can be developed to ensure time efficiency.

I. *Review your priorities and your department's goals.* Decisions are difficult to make in a vacuum. Your goals and those of the department should serve as the basis for your decision making. If a project substantially forwards any or all of the goals you would like to achieve, you are faced with a project of high priority. All other projects are secondary and should receive less of your time and energy.

II. *Devise a priority rating system.* Set down a priority system for a "To Do" list that has distinct criteria for each rating, similar to what we did to attach priorities to your goals. Limit yourself to three or four categories; perhaps they may range from "urgent" to "may not have to be done."

III. *Make a list of things to do.* Write down everything you have to do. Keep professional and personal items on separate lists.

IV. *Attach priorities to each item.* Using your priority system, classify each item, then go back and number each in the order that it should be completed. Below is an example of a priority system that classifies an item on a scale from high to low. Using such a rating scale, the administrator first would review the list and give each item a high, medium, or low rating. Having done this, she then would proceed to number each item in the category from the most important to the least important, and would give the most important item the number one. Once each item is classified (i.e., high = 1, low = 3) the administrator would systematically work her way from high = 1 to the last number assigned in the low category.

A.	Order equipment	low = 2
B.	Write evaluation	medium = 3
C.	Call John Katz	medium = 1
D.	Write employee recommendation	low = 1
E.	Do safety check of gymnastic equipment	high = 3
F.	Check on police security for Friday	high = 1
G.	Order refreshments	high = 2
H.	Place personnel recruitment ad in paper	medium = 2

V. *Plan your day.* Using your priority-ranked "To Do" list, plan your day. Try to determine the amount of time each project will take, then assign the project to a time slot.

VI. *Keep to your deadlines.* Remember you only want to handle an item once, if possible, and you want to make the most of your time. Schedule a deadline that is reasonable, then meet it.

VII. *Divide large projects into manageable pieces.* Sometimes a project cannot possibly be finished in one sitting. Having that whole project appear on your list of things to do everyday can be frustrating, because it appears as if you are not making any progress. To avoid this frustration and also to handle the situation more efficiently, you should divide the project into more manageable components and set deadlines for each. In this way you can see your progress toward completion.

VIII. *Reevaluate your priorities each day.* The status of an item changes with time. Some could become pressing overnight. Be sure you are evaluating each item constantly as it relates to your priorities.

IX. *Make your plan before you leave each evening.* At the end of each day, take time to plan for the next day. You gain several advantages this way:
   A. You will have time to evaluate the plan.
   B. Your secretary will have time to gather what you need.
   C. You can start to work the next morning when you are fresh and energetic without wasting time to prepare.

Time management can make a difference in administrative effectiveness. It is worth the time to plan.

Chapter 12

Summary Project

North Chelten is a community that has undergone tremendous growth during the past five years. In this relatively short period the township's population has risen from 10,480 to 16,691. A well-executed public relations program on the part of the township planning committee has led to a significant increase in the amount of light industry located within the township and has attracted the corporate headquarters of several large businesses as well. Figure 12.1 and Tables 12.1–12.7 provide information about North Chelten.

Although it previously was a sending district to the nearby city of Selwin, the township of North Chelten has given conceptual approval to a new high school. The school will be a community education center serving the academic, extracurricular, and recreational needs of the students and the community.

I. Assume one of the following roles:
    A. North Chelten Township Director of Recreation and Parks.
    B. North Chelten Township Director of Health and Physical Education.
    C. North Chelten Township Director of Athletics.
II. Develop a mission statement for your organization. Develop the goals and objectives necessary to accomplish the stated mission.
III. Work with your counterparts from recreation, athletics, or physical education to plan the appropriate portions of the physical plant and grounds for the North Chelten Community Education Center.
    A. Plan the facilities and the initial equipment package. Be sure to consult appropriate federal and state regulations and standards.
    B. Determine the computer needs for your unit. Select the type of computer and the software packages that will be purchased, and specify the applications of each to the mission of your unit.

Figure 12.1. Recreational space fact sheet for North Chelton

The township of North Chelton maintains approximately 200 acres of public land for recreational purposes. At present there are 13 areas in use representing approximately 81 acres of park space or 40 percent of the total land set aside for recreation. Following is an overview of recreational space planning and development.

Recreational Space Philosophy

North Chelton is divided into four sectors by two superhighways. These artificial, but imposing, barriers make travel between sectors virtually impossible except by car. Those without vehicular transportation are isolated within their neighborhoods. This situation is particularly difficult for children. In view of this situation the North Chelton Parks and Recreation Department has adopted a decentralized policy in regard to land use that dictates that:

I. All sectors must have recreational space in proportion to the percentage of the total population living in that area.
II. Recreational space should be within walking distance for any resident.
III. Recreational space should be developed:
    A. Equally—all parks having the same basic format.
    B. According to natural features.
IV. A large indoor-outdoor complex should be developed within each sector, preferably at a central location.
V. Neighborhood satellite facilities should surround the complex

Table 12.1. Age and Sex Distribution of Population in North Chelten in 1980

Age Group	Total		Males		Females	
	Number	Percent	Number	Percent	Number	Percent
Under 5	1,376	8.2	733	8.9	643	7.6
5-14	3,422	20.5	1,762	21.3	1,660	19.7
15-24	2,380	14.3	1,141	13.8	1,239	14.7
25-34	2,407	14.4	1,135	13.7	1,272	15.1
35-44	2,307	13.8	1,190	14.4	1,117	13.3
45-54	2,164	13.0	1,083	13.1	1,081	12.8
55-64	1,466	8.8	719	8.7	747	8.9
65 & Over	1,169	7.0	506	6.1	663	7.9
Total	16,691	100.0	8,269	100.0	8,422	100.0

Table 12.2.
Population Growth and
Projections for North Chelton

Year	Total Population
1975	10,480
1980	16,691
1985	23,146
1995	31,738
2010	43,351

Table 12.3. Projections of Age and Sex Distribution of Population for North Chelten in 1995

Age Group	Total		Male		Female	
	Number	Percent	Number	Percent	Number	Percent
Under 5	2,856	9.0	1,463	9.3	1,393	8.7
5-14	5,486	17.3	2,814	18.0	2,672	16.6
15-24	3,838	12.1	1,973	12.6	1,865	11.6
25-34	5,037	15.9	2,458	15.7	2,579	16.0
35-44	4,584	14.4	2,163	13.8	2,421	15.1
45-54	3,873	12.2	1,808	11.6	2,065	12.8
55-64	3,578	11.3	1,849	11.8	1,729	10.7
65 & Over	2,484	7.8	1,123	7.2	1,361	8.5
Total	31,736	100.0	15,651	100.0	16,085	100.0

Table 12.4. Employment of Population by Work Type for North Chelton in 1980

Work Type	Number	Percent
Professional, technical, and kindred workers	1,445	20.0
Managers and Administrators	674	9.3
Clerical and kindred workers	1,382	19.1
Sales workers	498	6.9
Craftsmen, foremen, and kindred workers	1,018	14.1
Operatives and kindred workers	1,365	18.8
Private household workers	10	.1
Service workers	558	7.7
Laborers	290	4.0
TOTAL EMPLOYED	7,240	100.0
Private wage and salary workers	5,752	79.5
Government workers	1,075	14.8
Self-employed	407	5.6
Unpaid family workers	6	.1
TOTAL EMPLOYED	7,240	100.0

Table 12.5. Existing Public School Facilities for Township of North Chelton

Name of School	Grade Level	Year Built	Year Addition Built	School Enrollment Feb. 1982	Regular Classrooms		Special Instruction Classrooms				Total Class-rooms	Special Rooms					
					Standard	Sub-Standard	Shops	Domestic Science	Science Labs	Others		Library	Auditorium	Cafeteria	Gymnasium	Multi-Purpose	Total Special Rooms
Lincoln	K-3	1927		187	8	3					11	1	1				2
Washington	K-6	1930	1961 1964	485	22						22	1				1	2
Jefferson	7-9	1951	1955 1964	868	26		2	1	4	4	37	1		1		1	3
Monroe	K-4	1961	1964	430	20						20	1				1	2
Kennedy	K-6	1965		413	19						19	1				1	2
Roosevelt	K-6	1967		700	30						30	1		1		1	3
ALL SCHOOLS				3,083	125	3	2	1	4	4	139	6	1	2	0	5	14

Table 12.6. Total Public School Enrollment Trends by Grade for Township of North Chelten

Grade	1978-1979	1979-1980	1980-1981	1981-1982
K	351	370	303	285
1	328	333	350	300
2	333	314	309	338
3	322	325	318	304
4	316	320	332	315
5	308	316	331	322
6	284	308	304	328
Subtotal K-6	2,242	2,286	2,247	2,192
7	265	277	329	296
8	283	260	276	314
9	265	278	237	258
Subtotal 7-9	813	815	842	868
10	218	248	245	218
11	200	224	223	232
12	169	205	206	207
Subtotal 10-12	587	677	674	657
Total	3,642	3,778	3,763	3,717

Table 12.7. Present Facilities in North Chelten

Name	Location	Size	Type	Comment
Oak Leaf	Sector 3	1.75 acres	Playground	Located in a large housing development two blocks from a large elementary school.
Titon	Sector 3	0.27 acres	Tot lot	Located in an isolated neighborhood. Contains playground equipment and basketball backboard.
Blakely	Sector 3	21.66 acres	Park	Located in far corner of Sector 3 in sparsely populated area. Approximately 1/2 acre is developed.
Springer	Sector 3	14.0 acres	Park	Located centrally in Sector 3. Contains playground equipment, small ice rink, picnic facilities, and two ball fields.
Sendry	Sector 4	1.32 acres	Playground	Located within a small development. Contains playground equipment, basketball court, and small ball field. No parking available.
Cantor	Sector 4	2.31 acres	Playground	Services a large apartment complex and a small housing development. Contains playground equipment, basketball court, and two tennis courts. Located two blocks from a junior high school with excellent athletic facilities.

continued

Table 12.7/continued

Name	Location	Size	Type	Comment
Stockton	Sector 4	16.26 acres	Park	Centrally located within Sector 4. Contains a ball field, playground equipment, two tennis courts, an ice rink, above-ground pool, and picnic facilities. Situated adjacent to an elementary school.
Packer	Sector 2	2.23 acres	Playground	Located within a large residential area directly off the highway. Predominantly a passive area located around three ponds. Playground equipment available.
Green Tree	Sector 2	17.81 acres	Park	Located centrally in Sector 2. Services large housing development. Situated on a plot of land midway between the proposed high school and an elementary school. The boundaries of all three pieces of property abut each other. Contains two ball fields, basketball court, four tennis courts, picnic area, above-ground pool, and a redwood structure with kitchen facilities, concession stand, and large multi-purpose room.
Houtman	Sector 1	21.82 acres	Park	Only one acre of this park is developed. Contains playground equipment. Located in an area that is expected to expand rapidly. Centrally located in Sector 1. Poor access.
Duncan	Sector 1	101.00 acres	Park	Totally undeveloped. Heavily wooded. Pine forest at one end. Situated on a man-made lake. Large grassed area in the middle. Approximately 3/4 mile from proposed high school.
Sorbon	Sector 1	0.56 acres	Tot lot	Located at far end of Sector 1. Playground equipment available. Situated between three homes.
Metlar	Sector 1	30.00 acres	Park	Totally undeveloped. Sits adjacent to Duncan Park. Old footpath runs through the middle. Remnants of old dwellings and a bridge on site. Poor access from road. Easy access from Duncan Park.

C. Determine reasonable sources of financial assistance and prepare proposals.

D. Develop policies for the shared use of the facilities. Delineate unit responsibilities with regard to all facets of operation, including maintenance, safety, and insurance.

E. Develop a public relations program for the community regarding the impact of the Community Education Center on taxes and bond issues.

IV. Within the framework of the facility's use policies, develop the program for your administrative unit during the first two years of operation.
  A. Project budgets for personnel, equipment, and supplies.
  B. Prepare job descriptions for all personnel.
  C. Establish policies for personnel search and recruitment.
  D. Develop specific policies regarding programming, user access, and additional program charges.
  E. Develop policies and procedures for the ongoing evaluation of personnel and programs.
  F. Develop a public information program for your unit.
V. Plan special summer programs that can be conducted by your unit or jointly with others that will:
  A. Make better use of the facilities and personnel on a year-round basis.
  B. Enhance the ongoing mission of the unit.
  C. Provide enrichment opportunities for the community at large.
These programs may be designed to generate additional funds, where appropriate. Repeat the steps followed in IV-A through IV-F above.

Appendix 1

A Sample Guide for Preparing a Policy Manual

The following sample guide has been separated into seven basic parts. Each basic part or heading has a number that carries throughout that part. For example, "Administration" is designated by the number "1000," and each policy matter that falls under Administration has a number prefix with 1000. Major subclassifications have a number prefix beginning with 100 and other subsequent classifications begin with 10. Seven basic parts of this sample policy manual include:

1000	Administration
2000	Public Relations
3000	Finances and Fiscal Policy
4000	Personal and Personnel Practices
5000	Citizen Participation
6000	Program Delivery
7000	Maintenance Practices

We recognize that not all municipal recreation departments will utilize all of these categories, while other departments will use even more. Therefore, each department will have to judge which categories are most adaptable to their operations.

1000 Administration

1100   PURPOSE AND OBJECTIVE OF THE MUNICIPAL RECREATION DEPARTMENT
      1. General policy statement for the entire department
        a. Preamble to the statement.
        b. General statement of objectives of department
1110   Authority
      1. Cite municipal resolution, ordinance, and state enabling legislation.

1200   BOARD
1210   1. Function and duties—the responsibility of the policy-making body.

a.   Legal authority to operate (State Statute—Title 40:12 Chapter 12 of New Jersey State Statutes and local ordinance)

b.   Duties of officers—President, Vice-President, Secretary, Treasurer

2.   Office of the board

a.   Specify location

b.   Hours of operation if applicable

1220   Board Meetings

1.   When they are held, who must attend, and how many members comprise a quorum

2.   Public attendance and participation

a.   Regular or special meetings

b.   Individual or groups wishing to petition the board for specific action

3.   Statement of how board minutes are kept and how they are available

1230   Board Compensation

1.   If board members are to receive compensation, how much, and for what purposes

1300   AGREEMENT WITH OTHER MUNICIPAL DPEARTMENTS

1310   Planning Department—how they are to cooperate

1320   Legal Department—who supplies legal counsel and when

1330   Accounting and Budget Department

1340   Engineering Department

1.   Whether they will lay out site

2.   Whether they will draw plans

3.   Whether they will supervise construction

1350   Public Works Department

1.   Whether they will maintain areas

2.   Whether they will do minor or major repairs or both

1360   Public Schools (Board of Education)

1.   Who plans playground sites on school properties

2.   Who plans indoor recreation facilities within schools

3.   When can you use school facilities and what are the costs involved regarding overhead charges for such use

1370   Central Motor Pool

1.   What equipment you may use

2.   Who must do the driving

3.   How the cost will be shared

1380   Police Department

1.   When you call them

2.   What you may expect of them

1400   CONFERENCE ATTENDANCE

1.   Who may go

2.   What conferences, meetings, and schools may be attended

3.   What receipts must be turned in

4.   How much money is provided and what mileage allowance is allowed

5.   Who must be notified or give approval

6.   Who must submit written or oral reports on meetings attended and to whom must they be submitted

1500   RECORDS AND REPORTS
       1.   What records and reports must be kept and when or how they are to be submitted
       2.   How long they are to be kept before being destroyed

1600   AUTOMOBILE USE
1610   Whether a municipal car is to be furnished
       1.   For what purposes it may be used
       2.   If it may or may not be driven to conferences out of town
1620   Employees' Own Car
       1.   Whether there will be a car allowance
          a.   Amount to be paid per mile traveled
          b.   How often mileage allowance will be paid
       2.   Whether employees are permitted to transport participants to activities in their own vehicles
       3.   Employees driving own vehicle provide own insurance
          a.   Types of insurance required
          b.   Minimum amount of insurance required

1700   PLANNING
1710   Master Planning
1720   Who plans for the long-range physical development of the department
       1.   With whom the planner should consult
       2.   How far in advance the long-range physical plan is projected
1730   Who plans for the long-range economic development of the department
       1.   How far in advance the economic planning is projected
       2.   With whom the economic planners should consult
1740   Who plans the long-range recreation programs of the department
       1.   How far in advance the recreation plans are projected
1750   Facility Planning
       1.   Long-range plans that must be submitted for facility
       2.   Development, purchase, or improvement
       3.   Priority of work
1760   Program Planning
       1.   Activities authorized to sponsor or conduct
       2.   Activities planned for the future
1770   Land Acquisitions
       1.   Need to acquire more land for parks and recreation
       2.   Legal authority to acquire and hold lands
1780   Methods of Acquiring Land
       1.   Direct purchase
       2.   Gift
       3.   Lease
       4.   Condemnation proceedings

2000 Public Relations

2100   PURPOSE AND OBJECTIVES OF THE DEPARTMENT
       1.   Statement and philosophy of recreation
       2.   Objectives
          a.   Of the department as a whole
          b.   Of the separate divisions of the department
2110   Important dates in the department's history
       1.   When established

	2.	Adoption of local and state statutes affecting department
	3.	Major changes in policy
2120	Purpose of Public Relations	
	1.	Statement of objective of public relations

2200 **RESPONSIBILITY**
1. Responsibility of policy-making authority (governing body of recreation board)
2. Responsibility of the department administrator
3. Responsibility of staff members
4. Responsibility of volunteers

2300 **DIRECT COMMUNICATION WITH THE PUBLIC**
2310 General Policies
1. Authorized by whom—method of authorization
2. Responsibility for performance
3. Method of recording
4. Method of evaluation
2320 Communication Media
1. List all media authorized for use
2. Specify authorized contact person or office in each medium
2330 Mass Media
1. Who prepares releases
2. Time of releases
3. Who approves and authorizes releases
4. How releases are made
5. To whom releases are recorded
6. How releases are recorded
7. Policy of verbally giving information to reporters who contact staff members personally
2340 Speeches
1. Who is authorized to give speeches
2. When and where speeches can be delivered
3. Who approves speeches
4. On what subjects speeches can be delivered
5. Whether speeches are recorded and how
6. Whether speeches are evaluated
2350 Personal Contacts
1. Policy of disclosing information about staff members
2. Policy of disclosing information about programs
3. Policy of disclosing information about departmental policies
2360 Pamphlets and Brochures
1. What department personnel are authorized to disseminate these publications
2. Who approves and authorizes format, production, and distribution of these publications
3. How and where these publications are distributed
2370 Annual Reports
1. Responsibility
2. Purpose
3. Format
4. Contents
5. When published
6. Distribution

2380   Board Meetings
      1.   Table of organization
      2.   Bylaws and purpose
      3.   How, when, and by whom meetings are announced
      4.   Who releases report of board action to governing body and public
      5.   Policies regarding fiscal matters
      6.   Policies regarding public meetings

2390   Complaints
      1.   Policy for handling complaints—those received in writing, those made in person, and those that reach the department indirectly
      2.   How complaints are recorded
      3.   Who is responsible for taking action
      4.   Who is informed about action taken on complaints

2400   USE OF FACILITIES AND EQUIPMENT
      1.   Facilities available
      2.   Equipment available

2410   Responsibility
      1.   Who authorizes the use of facilities and equipment
      2.   Who assumes responsibility when facilities and equipment are used
      3.   Supervision by department personnel required when facilities are used
      4.   Who is responsible for condition of facilities and equipment after use

2420   Eligible Organizations
      1.   Organizations that qualify for use of facilities
      2.   Order of priority for use of facilities
      3.   Who qualifies for use of equipment

2430   Requirements
      1.   Procedures for application and approval
      2.   Nature of supervision required
      3.   Regulations regarding condition in which facilities and equipment are left
      4.   Policy regarding use of facilities and equipment for profit

2440   Fees and Charges
      1.   Policy regarding fees and charges for use of facilities or equipment

2500   GIFTS
Policy regarding acceptance of gifts by Department
      1.   Whether department will accept gifts
      2.   What kind of gifts department will accept—funds, lands, equipment
      3.   Policy for disposal of unwanted or unusable gifts

3000 Finances and Fiscal Policy

3100   BUDGET
3110   Planning the Budget
      1.   When it is to be done
      2.   How often
      3.   Who is responsible

3120   Preparation of the Budget
      1.   What form and format are to be used
      2.   To whom it is to be presented

3130   Adoption of Budget
      1.   Who will adopt budget
      2.   Dates of adoption

3140   Publication of the Budget
        1.   When and how it is to be published
        2.   To whom the published budget will be distributed
3150   Transfer of Funds
        1.   When and how funds will be transferred in conformance with state statutes
        2.   Who has the authority to transfer funds from one account to another

3200   INCOME
3210   General Revenues (what they will include)
        1.   Municipal levies
        2.   Other sources
3220   Fees and Charges
        1.   Position statement by department regarding fees and charges
        2.   Fee and charge schedule
            a.   Time that fees and charges are to be in effect for specific activities or facilities
            b.   Method of collection and subsequent accounting procedures.
3230   Concessions
        1.   Under what conditions they are leased out or operated by the department
        2.   Contract arrangements with concessionaire
            a.   Standards for operation of concession
            b.   Health standards
            c.   Responsibility for overhead items
            d.   Responsibility for maintenance
            e.   Percentage the concessionaire must pay

3300   EXPENDITURES
3310   Requisitions
        1.   Whose responsibility it is
        2.   What it consists of
        3.   Who keeps what
        4.   Who approves purchases when requisitions are not necessary
3320   Bids and Quotations
        1.   How bids are to be let (in conformance with state statute)
        2.   Who sets up specifications
        3.   How much may be purchased without bid
        4.   Whether bids are to be sealed and opened in public at a prescribed time and place
        5.   What is to happen in case of a tie bid
3330   Purchasing Procedures
        1.   Who is authorized to make purchases
        2.   Who is to award contracts
        3.   Whether performance guarantees will be necessary
        4.   Whether purchase orders are needed, and if so, of what do they consist
3340   Payment of Purchases
        1.   Method of payment (voucher or other)
        2.   Who authorizes voucher
        3.   Who endorses voucher
        4.   Who issues check for payment
3350   Payroll and Services
        1.   When employees of department will be paid and how often
        2.   Define the basis on which employees shall be paid

3400   HANDLING OF FUNDS
        Disposal of monies collected by department
                1.   How they are to be deposited
                2.   Under what accounts

3500   AUDITING
                1.   How it is to be done
                2.   When it is to be done
                3.   By whom it is to be done
                4.   What phase of the operation of the department is to be audited
3510   Who is to receive the auditors' reports
                1.   Mayor and governing body
                2.   Recreation board
                3.   Recreation administrator
                4.   Others

4000 Personal and Personnel Practices

4100   PERSONNEL ORGANIZATION CHART FOR THE DEPARTMENT

4200   EMPLOYMENT
        Recruitment and Selection
                1.   Whose services are to be engaged
                2.   Whether professional or nonprofessional status affects appointment
                3.   Residency requirements
4210   Appointment for Employment
                1.   Made by whom
                2.   Upon whose recommendation
                3.   Term of appointment
                4.   Effect of Civil Service regulations
                      a.   Temporary employee
                      b.   Permanent employee
                5.   Probation policies
                6.   Permanent employment practices
4220   Certification for Employment
                1.   Whether there is a state statute or local ordinance that must be met
                      (e.g., New Jersey has only permissive certification for recreation admin-
                      istrators and recreation supervisors. Chapter 291, Laws of 1966)
4230   Evaluation of Employees
                1.   The purpose
                2.   When it is done and by whom
                3.   Disposition of an evaluation
4240   Advancement and Merit Ratings
                1.   How advancement may be made and by whom
                2.   On what it is based
4250   Disciplinary Action—When and How
                1.   Appeals and separations
                      a.   Whether an appeal will be allowed
                      b.   Before whom and how
                      c.   How much notice is required if relieved
                      d.   Separation policy in conformance with Civil Service standards
                      e.   Compensation the employee will receive on separation

2.   What expenses they may charge to the department
4620   Receipts and Vouchers
1.   What must be turned in for expense
2.   How they must be turned in
3.   To whom must they be turned in
4.   Whether they must be approved by department head prior to payment
4630   Mileage and Expenses
1.   How much mileage will be allowed and for what
2.   Other expenses and under what circumstances allowed

4700   COMPENSATION AND RELATED BENEFITS
4710   Salary Classification and Guides
1.   How the jobs are classed
2.   Starting and maximum salaries
3.   Longevity
4.   Increment anniversary dates
4720   Accident and Liability
1.   How much is covered
2.   What will it cover
3.   How reports must be filed
4730   Sick Leave
1.   How it is accumulated
2.   How many days per year
3.   How many total days may be accumulated
4.   Whether a doctor must be seen and a report given to the department
4740   Holidays
1.   What days the employee is entitled to
2.   If the employee is required to work on some holidays, whether he is paid extra or given compensatory time off
4750   Vacation
1.   How many days per month or year are allowed
2.   When it must be taken
3.   Whether it can be built up
4.   Whether it can be carried over to the succeeding year
4760   Retirement
1.   How much must be paid in
2.   What is the retirement age
3.   Under what circumstances is a person permitted to retire
4.   Whether unusual circumstances permit early retirement
4770   Maternity Leave
1.   Who has authority to grant it
2.   How long
3.   Whether employee has the right to return to the same job

5000 Citizen Participation

5100   MEMBERSHIP ON BOARDS OR ADVISORY COMMITTEES
1.   Who appoints citizens to these boards or committees
2.   Term of office
3.   Duties
4.   Powers

5200   USE OF CITIZEN VOLUNTEERS
1.   Whether they will be allowed

  2. Whether they must be given training
  3. What activities they will be allowed to conduct and under what circumstances
  4. Whether they are covered by workers' compensation and other insurance
  5. Who supervises citizen volunteers

6000 Program Delivery

6100 STATEMENT OF OBJECTIVES OF THE RECREATION PROGRAM
6110 Planning the Program
  1. Who plans the program
  2. Who approves the overall program
  3. Who plans the detailed program and schedules the activities
6120 Program Practices for Playground Program
6130 Program Practices for Community Center Program
6140 Program Practices for Swimming Pools or Beach Programs
6150 Program Practices for Senior Citizen Programs
6160 Program Practices for Athletic Programs
6170 Program Practices for Teen Programs
6180 Program Practices for Special Recreation Programs

7000 Maintenance Practices

7100 ORGANIZATION CHART OF THE MAINTENANCE SECTION OF THE DEPARTMENT

7200 CLEANING AND SANITATION
7210 Policing of Grounds and Facilities
  1. How often
  2. By whom
  3. Who supervises work
  4. Who allocates work schedule
7220 Roster of Facilities and Grounds to be Maintained
  1. Department facilities and grounds
  2. School facilities and grounds
  3. Leased facilities and grounds
7230 Duties and Responsibilities of Maintenance Personnel
7231 Supervisor of Maintenance
7232 Maintenance Foreman
7233 Maintenance Specialist (Carpenter, Plumber, Truck Driver)
7234 Recreation Maintenance
7235 Laborer

7300 OTHER SPECIALIZED MAINTENANCE
  1. Marinas
  2. Vehicle maintenance
  3. Others

Appendix 2

General Plan for a Multipurpose Recreational Facility

The committee feels it is essential during all phases of the planning of this facility to remember that the population to be served by this center is unique within New Brunswick, as well as the university. The site currently under consideration places the center in close proximity to married student housing, the Silvers Apartments, the new Rutgers College dormitories, and the academic facilities for Engineering, Chemistry, and Mathematics. Thus, one must keep in mind the needs of a population ranging from the infant children of married students to the academic personnel in the adjacent area.

An important consideration in the planning of this facility is that additional monies to support its staffing probably are not available. Therefore, considerable emphasis must be given to the inclusion of services that provide sufficient revenue to cover not only their own expenses, but also the salaries of the professional and support staff necessary to ensure smooth and efficient operation of the building. It is important, then, that the key revenue-producing areas (the pub and snack bar and the recreation room) be located in such a way as to be easily accessible to main entrances or the activity areas of the building, and that these facilities not be abandoned at some point as a "cost-saving" measure.

Because construction of this building is being financed by yet another increase in student fees, the committee feels the building should be designed to be a utilitarian, modular structure, and should not be designed as an expensive architectural monument. A utilitarian emphasis should provide the maximum usable square footage at a minimum expenditure, and modular construction allows for expansion at a future date, should the population continue to grow on this campus. Functionality and aesthetics are extremely important considerations under this concept, as use of the building is tantamount to its survival. The committee also feels that the possibility of developing an air-conditioning system that services both the dining hall and the student center might result in a cost savings for both projects, and therefore should be investigated. Utilization of operable windows throughout the building allows for operational cost savings because these windows can provide ventilation of the building in lieu of air conditioning on all but the hottest summer days. Maximizing the amount of natural lighting in the building via windows and skylights also reduces utility costs during the day.

In conclusion, the committee feels that the architect should give considerable attention to the interior treatment of the center through the use of color, texture, dimmable lighting, and natural lighting, as a student center is somewhat different than other buildings on a college campus. In a classroom building or dining hall, for example, students spend no more than an hour and a half in a given space, but it is conceivable that students might spend 4 to 5 hours in student center spaces such as the recreation room, main lobby, quiet lounge, or the pub and snack bar. Therefore, considerable emphasis must be given to developing an interior decor that is comfortable, warm, and inviting for extended periods of time.

The committee indicated that serious consideration be given to the inclusion of outdoor recreational facilities (specifically, basketball nets and tennis courts) in the site development plans for the center. Should this not be possible, development of these facilities in an adjacent area should be given a high priority.

As the various priorities were developed into spaces, three functional areas developed. It was felt that the spaces within each area would have considerable interrelationship, although the three areas need not.

AREA I
    Recreation Room
    Main Lounge
    Multi-purpose Room
    Administrative Offices
    Main Entrance

AREA II
    Snack Bar
    Pub
    Kitchen
    Food-service Storage Area

AREA III
    Arts and Crafts Workshop
    Quiet Lounge
    TV Room
    Organizational Workroom
    Meeting Rooms

Appendix 3

Checklist for
Facility Planners Relating to
General Indoor Facility Features[1]

As an aid to those responsible for planning facilities for athletics, physical education, and recreation, a checklist has been prepared. The application of this checklist may prevent unfortunate and costly errors.

General

1. A clear-cut statement has been prepared on the nature and scope of the program, and the special requirements for space, equipment, fixtures, and facilities have been dictated by the activities to be conducted. _____

2. The facility has been planned to meet the total requirements of the porgram as weel as the special needs of those who are to be served. _____

3. The plans and specifications have been checked by all governmental agencies (city, county and state) whose approval is required by law._____

4. Plans for areas and facilities conform to state and local regulations and to accepted standards and practices. _____

5. The areas and facilities planned make possible the programs that serve the interests and needs of all the people. _____

6. Every available source of property or funds has been explored, evaluated, and utilized whenever appropriate. _____

1. *Planning Facilities for Athletics, Physical Education and Recreation.* Rev. ed. (North Palm Beach, Fla.; Athletic Institute, and Reston, Va: American Alliance for Health, Physical Education, Recreation, and Dance, 1979). pp. 49-51. Reprinted with persmission.

7. All interested persons and organizations concerned with the facility have had an opportunity to share in its planning (professional educators, users, consultants, administrators, engineers, architects, program specialists, building managers, and builder—a team approach. _____

8. The facility will fulfill the maximum demands of the program. The program has not been curtailed to fit the facility. _____

9. The facility has been functionally planned to meet the present and anticipated needs of specific programs, situations, and publics. _____

10. Future additions are included in present plans to permit economy of construction. _____

11. Lecture classrooms are isolated from distracting noises. _____

12. Storage areas for indoor and outdoor equipment are of adequate size. They are located adjacent to the gymnasiums. _____

13. Shelves in storage rooms are slanted toward the wall. _____

14. All passageways are free of obstructions; fixtures are recessed. _____

15. Facilities for health services and the first-aid and emergency-isolation rooms are suitably interrelated. _____

16. Buildings, specific areas, and facilities are clearly identified. _____

17. Locker rooms are arranged for ease of supervision. _____

18. Offices, teaching stations, and service facilities are properly interrelated. _____

19. Special needs of the physically handicapped are met, including a ramp into the building at a major entrance. _____

20. All "dead space" is used. _____

21. The building is compatible in design and comparable in quality and accommodation to other campus structures. _____

22. Storage rooms are accessible to the play area. _____

23. Workrooms, conference rooms, and staff and administrative offices are interrelated. _____

24. Shower and dressing facilities are provided for professional staff members and are conveniently located. _____

25. Thought and attention have been given to making facilities and equipment as durable and vandalproof as possible. _____

26. Low-cost maintenance features have been considered. _____

27. This facility is a part of a well-integrated master plan. _____

28. All areas, courts, facilities, equipment, climate control, and security conform rigidly to detailed standards and specifications. _____

29. Shelves are recessed and mirrors are supplied in appropriate places in rest rooms and dressing rooms. _____

30. Dressing space between locker rows is adjusted to the size and age of students. _____

31. Drinking fountains are conveniently placed in locker room areas or immediately adjacent thereto. _____

32. Special attention is given to provision for locking service windows and counters, supply bins, carts, shelves, and racks. _____

33. Provision is made for repair, maintenance, replacement, and off-season storage of equipment and uniforms. _____

34. A well-defined program for laundering and cleaning towels, uniforms, and equipment is included in the plan. _____

35. Noncorrosive metal is used in dressing, drying, and shower areas except for enameled lockers. _____

36. Antipanic hardware is used where required by fire regulations. _____

37. Properly placed hose bibbs and drains are sufficient in size and quantity to permit flushing the entire area with a water hose. _____

38. A water-resistant, covered base is used under the locker base and

floor mat and where floor and wall join. _____

39. Chalkboards and tackboards with map tracks are located in appropriate places in dressing rooms, hallways, and classrooms. _____

40. Book shelves are provided in toilet areas. _____

41. Space and equipment are planned in accordance with the types and number of enrollees. _____

42. Basement rooms, undesirable for dressing, drying, and showering, are not planned for those purposes. _____

43. Spectator seating (permanent) in areas that are basically instructional is kept at a minimum. Roll away bleachers are used primarily. Balcony seating is considered as a possibility. _____

44. Well-lighted and effectively displayed trophy cases enhance the interest and beauty of the lobby. _____

45. The space under the stairs is used for storage. _____

46. Department heads' offices are located near the central administrative office, which includes a well-planned conference room. _____

47. Workrooms are located near the central office and serve as a repository for departmental materials and records. _____

48. Conference area includes a cloak room, lavatory, and toilet. _____

49. In addition to regular secretarial offices established in the central and department chairmen's offices, a special room to house a secretarial pool for staff members is provided. _____

50. Staff dressing facilities are provided. These facilities may also serve game officials. _____

51. The community or neighborhood has a "round table" for planning. _____

52. All those (persons and agencies) who should be a party to planning and development are invited and actively engaged in the planning process. _____

53. Space and area relationships are important. They have been carefully considered. _____

54. Both long-range and immediate plans have been made. _____

55. The body comfort of the child, a major factor in securing maximum learning, has been considered in the plans. _____

56. Plans for quiet areas have been made. _____

57. In the planning, consideration has been given to the need for adequate recreational areas and facilities, both near and distant from the homes of people. _____

58. Plans recognize the primary function of recreation as being enrichment of learning through creative self-expression, self-enhancement, and the achievement of self-potential. _____

59. Every effort has been exercised to eliminate hazards. _____

60. The installation of low-hanging door closers, light fixtures, signs, and other objects in traffic areas has been avoided. _____

61. Warning signals—both visible and audible—are included in the plans. _____

62. Ramps have a slope equal to or greater than a 1-ft rise in 12 ft. _____

63. Minimum landings for ramps are 5 by 5 ft, they extend at least 1 ft beyond the swinging arc of a door, have at least a 6 ft clearance at the bottom, and have level platforms at 30 ft intervals on every turn. _____

64. Adequate locker and dressing spaces are provided. _____

65. The design of dressing, drying, and shower areas reduces foot traffic to a minimum and establishes clean, dry aisles for bare feet. _____

66. Teaching stations are properly related to service facilities. _____

67. Toilet facilities are adequate in number. They are located to serve all groups for which provisions are made. _____

68. Mail services, outgoing and incoming, are included in the plans. _____

69. Hallways, ramps, doorways, and elevators are designed to permit equipment to be moved easily and quickly. _____

70. A keying design suited to administrative and instructional needs is planned. _____
71. Toilets used by large groups have circulating (in and out) entrances and exits. _____

Climate Control
1. Provision is made throughout the building for climate control—heating, ventilating, and refrigerated cooling. _____
2. Special ventilation is provided for locker, dressing, shower, drying, and toilet rooms. _____
3. Heating plans permit both area and individual room control. _____
4. Research areas where small animals are kept and where chemicals are used have been provided with special ventilating equipment. _____
5. The heating and ventilating of the wrestling gymnasium have been given special attention. _____

Electrical
1. Shielded, vapor-proof lights are used in moisture prevalent areas. _____
2. Lights are strategic areas are key-controlled. _____
3. Lighting intensity conforms to approved standards. _____
4. An adequate number of electrical outlets are strategically placed. _____
5. Gymnasium and auditorium lights are controlled by dimmer units. _____
6. Locker room lights are mounted above the space between lockers. _____
7. Natural light is controlled properly for purposes of visual aids and avoidance of glare. _____
8. Electrical outlet plates are installed three feet above the floor unless special use dictates other locations. _____
9. Controls for light switches and projection equipment are suitably located and interrelated. _____
10. All lights are shielded. Special protection is provided in gymnasiums, court areas, and shower rooms. _____
11. Lights are placed to shine between rows of lockers. _____

Walls
1. Movable and folding partitions are power-operated and controlled by keyed switches. _____
2. Wall plates are located where needed and are firmly attached. _____
3. Hooks and rings for nets are placed (and recessed in walls) according to court locations and net heights. _____
4. Materials that clean easily and are impervious to moisture are used where moisture is prevalent. _____
5. Shower heads are placed at different heights—4 ft (elementary) to 7 ft (university) for each school level. _____
6. Protective matting is placed permanently on the walls in the wrestling room, at the ends of basketball courts, and in other areas where such protection is needed. _____
7. An adequate number of drinking fountains are provided. They are properly placed (recessed in wall). _____
8. One wall (at least) of the dance studio has full length mirrors. _____
9. All corners in locker rooms are rounded. _____

Ceilings
1. Overhead supported apparatus is secured to beams engineered to withstand stress. _____
2. The ceiling height is adequate for the activities to be housed. _____
3. Acoustical materials impervious to moisture are used in moisture-prevalent areas. _____
4. Skylights in gymnasiums, being impractical, are seldom used because of problems in waterproofing roofs and the controlling of sun rays. _____
5. All ceilings except those in storage areas are acoustically treated with sound-absorbent materials. _____

Floors
1. Floor plates are placed where needed and are flush-mounted. _____
2. Floor design and materials con-

form to recommended standards and specifications. _____

3. Lines and markings are painted on floors before sealing is completed (when synthetic tape is not used). _____

4. A coved base (around lockers and where wall and floor meet) of the same water-resistant material used on floors is found in all dressing and shower rooms. _____

5. Abrasive, nonskid, slip-resistant flooring that is impervious to moisture is provided in all areas where water is used—laundry, swimming pools, shower, dressing, and drying rooms. _____

6. Floor drains are properly located, and the slope of the floor is adequate for rapid drainage. _____

Appendix 4

Checklist for Planners of Swimming Pools[1]

General Considerations

1. A clear-cut statement has been prepared on the nature and scope of the design program and the special requirements for space, equipment, and facilities dictated by the activities to be conducted. _____

2. The swimming pool has been planned to meet the total requirements of the program to be conducted as well as any special needs of the clientele to be served. _____

3. There are other recreational facilities nearby for the convenience and enjoyment of swimmers. _____

4. An experienced pool consultant, architect, or engineer has been called in to advise on design and equipment. _____

5. The design of the pool incorporates the most knowledge and best experience available regarding swimming pools. _____

6. The plan has been considered from the standpoint of handicapped persons (e.g., there is a gate adjacent to the turnstiles). _____

7. All plans and specifications have been checked and approved by the local board of health. _____

8. The pool is the proper depth to accommodate the various age groups and types of activities it is intended to serve. _____

9. The bathhouse is properly located, with entrance to the pool leading to the shallow end. _____

10. The locker rooms are large enough and have been considered from the standpoint of supervision. _____

11. The pool layout provides the most efficient control of swimmers from showers and locker rooms to the pool. Toilet facilities are provided for wet swimmers separate from the dry area. _____

---

1. *Planning Facilities for Athletics, Physical Education and Recreation.* Rev. ed. (North Palm Beach, Fla.: Athletic Institute, and Reston, Va.: American Alliance for Health, Physical Education, Recreation, and Dance, 1979), pp. 94-97. Reprinted with permission.

12. Seating for swimmers is provided on the deck. _____

13. There is an area set aside for eating, apart from the pool deck. _____

14. The area for spectators has been separated from the pool area. _____

15. There is adequate deck space around the pool. More space has been provided than indicated by the minimum recommended deck/pool ratio. _____

16. The swimming instructor's office faces the pool. There is a window through which the instructor may view the entire pool area. There is a toilet-shower-dressing area next to the office for instructors. _____

17. The specifications for competitive swimming have been met (7-ft lanes; 12-in. black lines on the bottom; pool 1 in. longer than official measurement; depth and distance markings). _____

18. If the pool shell contains a concrete finish, the length of the pool has been increased by 3 in. over the "official" size in order to permit eventual tiling of the basin without making the pool too short _____

19. The width of the movable bulkhead has been considered in calculating total pool length. _____

20. Consideration has been given to the method of moving the bulkhead. _____

21. Provision has been made for the switch to metric distances. _____

22. There is adequate deep water for diving (minimum of 12 ft for 1 m, 13 ft for 3 m boards, and 17 ft for 10 m towers). _____

23. Adequate space has been provided between diving boards and between the diving boards and sidewalks. _____

24. Recessed steps or removable ladders are located on the walls so as not to interfere with competitive swimming turns. _____

25. There is adequate provision for life-saving equipment and pool cleaning equipment. _____

26. All diving standards and lifeguard chairs have been properly anchored. _____

27. Lifeguard stands are provided and properly located. _____

28. Separate storage spaces have been allocated for maintenance and instructional equipment. _____

29. There is a coping around the edge of the pool. _____

30. The deck is of nonslip material. _____

31. All metal fittings are of non-corrosive material. _____

32. A properly constructed overflow gutter extends around the pool perimeter. _____

33. The gutter waste water has been valved to return to the filters and also for direct waste. _____

34. Where skimmers are used, they have been properly located so that they are not on walls where competitive swimming is to be conducted. _____

35. The proper pitch to drains has been allowed in the pool, on the pool deck, in the overflow gutter, and on the floor of shower and dressing rooms. _____

36. Inlets and outlets are adequate in number and located to ensure effective circulation of water in the pool. _____

37. There is easy vertical access to the filter room for both people and material (with stairway if required). _____

38. The recirculation pump is located below the water level. _____

39. The recirculation-filtration system has been designed to meet the anticipated future pool load. _____

40. Underwater lights are the 12 volt type, and all metal in the pool area is grounded to a ground-fault interrupter. _____

41. Consideration has been given to underwater lights, underwater observation windows, and underwater speakers. _____

42. Underwater lights in end racing walls have been located deep enough and directly below surface lane anchors, and they are on a separate circuit. _____

43. Access from deck to underwater windows is direct and uncomplicated. _____

44. There is a tunnel around the outside of the pool or a trench on the deck permitting ready access to pipes. _____
45. The gas chlorinator (if used) has been placed in a separate room accessible from and vented to the outside. _____
46. A pool heater has been considered in northern climates. _____
47. Automatic controls for water chemistry have been considered. _____

Indoor Pools

1. There is proper ventilation. _____
2. There is adequate acoustic treatment of walls and ceilings. _____
3. There is adequate overhead clearance for diving (16 ft above 1 m and 3 m boards, 11 ft above 10 m platforms). _____
4. There is adequate lighting (60 to 100 ft candles at the water surface are recommended). _____
5. Reflection of light from the outside has been kept to the minimum by proper location of windows or skylights. (Windows on sidewalls are not desirable.) _____
6. All wall bases are coved to facilitate cleaning. _____
7. There is provision for proper temperature control in the pool room for both water and air. _____
8. The humidity of the pool room can be controlled. _____
9. The wall and ceiling insulation are adequate to prevent "sweating." _____
10. An adjacent area is suitable for movies and lectures. _____

Outdoor Pools

1. The site for the pool is in the best possible location (away from railroad tracks, heavy industry, trees, and dusty open fields). _____
2. Sand and grass have been kept the proper distance away from the pool to prevent them from being transmitted to the pool. _____
3. A fence has been placed around the pool to assure safety when not in use. _____
4. Proper subsurface drainage has been provided. _____
5. There is adequate deck surface for sunbathing. _____
6. The outdoor lights are placed far enough from the pool to prevent insects from dropping into the pool. _____
7. Diving boards or platforms face north or east. _____
8. Adequate parking space has been provided and properly located. _____
9. The pool is oriented correctly in relation to the sun. _____
10. Wind shields have been provided in situations where heavy winds prevail. _____

Index

STUDENT SURVEY

Neil J. Dougherty & Diane Bonanno

Management Principles in Sport and Leisure Services

Students, send us your ideas!

The authors and the publisher want to know how well this book served you and what can be done to improve it for those who will use it in the future. By completing and returning this questionnaire, you can help us develop better textbooks. We value your opinion and want to hear your comments. Thank you.

Your name (optional)＿＿＿＿＿＿＿＿＿＿＿＿＿＿ School ＿＿＿＿＿＿＿＿＿＿＿＿＿

Your mailing address ＿＿＿＿＿＿＿＿＿＿＿＿＿＿＿＿＿＿＿＿＿＿＿＿＿＿＿

City＿＿＿＿＿＿＿＿＿＿＿＿＿＿＿＿＿＿＿＿＿ State ＿＿＿＿＿ ZIP ＿＿＿＿＿

Instructor's name (optional)＿＿＿＿＿＿＿＿＿＿ Course title＿＿＿＿＿＿＿＿＿

1. How does this book compare with other texts you have used? (Check one)

   ☐ Superior   ☐ Better than most   ☐ Comparable   ☐ Not as good as most

2. Circle those chapters you especially liked:

   Chapters: 1   2   3   4   5   6   7   8   9   10   11   12

   Comments:

3. Circle those chapters you think could be improved:

   Chapters: 1   2   3   4   5   6   7   8   9   10   11   12

   Comments:

4. Please rate the following. (Check one for each line)

	Excellent	Good	Average	Poor
Readability of text material	( )	( )	( )	( )
Logical organization	( )	( )	( )	( )
General layout and design	( )	( )	( )	( )
Up-to-date treatment of subject	( )	( )	( )	( )
Match with instructor's course organization	( )	( )	( )	( )
Illustrations that clarify the text	( )	( )	( )	( )
Selection of topics	( )	( )	( )	( )
Explanation of difficult concepts	( )	( )	( )	( )

(Over, please)

5. List any chapters that your instructor did not assign. _____

_____

6. What additional topics did your instructor discuss that were not covered in the text?

_____

_____

7. Did you buy this book new or used?
   ☐ New   ☐ Used

   Do you plan to keep the book or sell it?
   ☐ Keep it   ☐ Sell it

   Do you think your instructor should continue to assign this book?
   ☐ Yes   ☐ No

8. After taking the course, are you interested in taking more courses in this field?
   ☐ Yes   ☐ No

   Did you take this course to fulfill a requirement, or as an elective?
   ☐ Required   ☐ Elective

9. What is your major? _____

   Your class rank? ☐ Freshman ☐ Sophomore ☐ Junior ☐ Senior ☐ Other, specify:

10. GENERAL COMMENTS:

May we quote you in our advertising?   ☐ Yes   ☐ No

Please remove this page and mail to: Mary L. Paulson
                                            Burgess Publishing Company
                                            7108 Ohms Lane
                                            Minneapolis, MN 55435

THANK YOU!